INTRODUCTION
TO
CLASSICAL
CHINESE
PHILOSOPHY

INTRODUCTION TO CLASSICAL CHINESE PHILOSOPHY

Bryan W. Van Norden

Hackett Publishing Company, Inc.
Indianapolis/Cambridge

Copyright © 2011 by Hackett Publishing Company, Inc.

Printed in the United States of America

15 14 13 12 11   1 2 3 4 5 6 7

For further information, please address
Hackett Publishing Company, Inc.
P.O. Box 44937
Indianapolis, Indiana 46244-0937

www.hackettpublishing.com

Cover design by Abigail Coyle
Text design by Mary Vasquez
Composition by Agnew's, Inc.
Printed at Sheridan Books, Inc.

Library of Congress Cataloging-in-Publication Data

Van Norden, Bryan W. (Bryan William)
    Introduction to classical Chinese philosophy / Bryan W. Van Norden.
      p. cm.
    Includes bibliographical references.
    ISBN 978-1-60384-468-0 (pbk.)—ISBN 978-1-60384-469-7 (cloth)
    1. Philosophy, Chinese—To 221 B.C. I. Title.
    B126.V28 2011
    181'.11—dc22   2010042112

The paper used in this publication meets the minimum requirements of American National Standard for Information Sciences—Permanence of paper for Printed Library Materials, ANSI Z39.48–1984.

∞

For Barbara
Lucy to my Ricky and Lois to my Peter

■ CONTENTS ■

Preface   XI
Map of China   XIII
Selected Translations   XIV
Selected Secondary Works   XVI

1. THE HISTORICAL CONTEXT
   I. Myth   2
   II. Early History   5
   III. The Period of the Philosophers   10
   IV. Timeline   13

2. KONGZI AND CONFUCIANISM
   I. Kongzi's Social Context and Life   18
   II. Five Themes of Confucianism   21
      1. Happiness in the Everyday World   21
      2. Revivalistic Traditionalism   22
      3. The Family and Differentiated Caring   24
      4. Ritual and Functionalism   25
      5. Ethical Cultivation   29

3. KONGZI AND VIRTUE ETHICS
   I. Three Normative Theories   34
   II. Confucianism as Virtue Ethics   38
      1. Living Well   38
      2. The Virtues   39
      3. Ethical Cultivation and Human Nature   43
   III. Limitations of Confucianism   44
   IV. Kongzi's Particularism   45

4. MOHIST CONSEQUENTIALISM
   I. The Fixed Standard of Consequentialism   51
   II. Criticisms of Confucianism   52

III. Political Philosophy   58
IV. Divine Command Theory   60
V. "Against Fatalism" and Dialectic   62
VI. "On Ghosts" and Truth   64
VII. Historical Significance   67

5. YANG ZHU AND EGOISM
   I. What Is Egoism?   70
      1. Psychological Egoism   70
      2. Ethical Egoism   74
   II. What Is the Nature of a Thing?   75
   III. Early Debates over Yang Zhu's Way   76
   IV. The Contemporary Debate   79

6. MENGZI AND HUMAN NATURE
   I. The Mohists, Profit, and Impartiality   87
   II. Yang Zhu and Human Nature   88
   III. The Virtues   91
   IV. Ethical Cultivation   92
   V. Cosmology   97
   VI. Historical Significance   98

7. LANGUAGE AND PARADOX IN THE "SCHOOL OF NAMES"
   I. Deng Xi and the Origins of the "School"   102
   II. Hui Shi   103
   III. Gongsun Long   108
   IV. The Later Mohists   111
      1. Resolving the Paradox of Deng Xi   112
      2. Resolving the Paradoxes of Hui Shi   112
      3. Resolving the White Horse Paradox   113
      4. The New Foundation of Mohist Ethics   114
      5. The Limits of Logic   116
   V. Historical Significance   118

8. THE *DAODEJING* AND MYSTICISM
   I. Myth and Reality   122
   II. Five Themes   125

  1. Social Ills and Their Solution   125
  2. Nonaction   126
  3. The Teaching That Is without Words   130
  4. The Way   131
  5. Mysticism   133
 III. Historical Significance   135

9. ZHUANGZI'S THERAPEUTIC SKEPTICISM
   AND RELATIVISM
   I. Zhuangzi's Context   142
   II. Skepticism   143
   III. Relativism   144
   IV. Detachment in Society, Not from Society   147
   V. Nonaction   150
   VI. Doctrine or Therapy?   152
   VII. Conventional or Radical?   155
  VIII. Historical Significance   159

10. XUNZI'S CONFUCIAN NATURALISM
    I. Xunzi's Context   164
    II. Naturalism and Ritual   164
    III. History and Objectivity   168
    IV. Human Nature and Psychology   171
    V. Ethical Cultivation   178
    VI. Historical Significance   180

11. HAN FEIZI
    I. Life and Context   186
    II. Critique of Confucianism   187
    III. The Five Elements of Han Feizi's Theory of Government   190
      1. The Power of Position   190
      2. Administrative Methods   191
      3. Laws   193
      4. The Two Handles of Government   194
      5. The Way of the Ruler   195
    IV. The Question of Amoralism   196
    V. Historical Significance   198

12. LATER CHINESE THOUGHT

I. Qin Dynasty   202
II. Han through Six Dynasties   203
III. Sui through the Ming   207
IV. Qing through Mao Zedong   211
V. China Today and Tomorrow   220

APPENDIX A: Hermeneutics, or How to Read a Text

I. Faith and Suspicion   224
II. "Our" Worldview and "Theirs"   228

APPENDIX B: The Chinese Language and Writing System

I. The Five Types of Chinese Characters   236
II. Spoken Chinese   242
III. Radicals and Dictionaries   243
IV. The Sapir-Whorf Hypothesis   244
V. For Further Reading   246

APPENDIX C: Kongzi as Systematic Philosopher

I. The "One Thread" of *Analects* 4.15   250
II. The "Rectification of Names" of *Analects* 13.3 252
III. The "Broadening of the Way" of *Analects* 15.29 254
IV. Conclusion

Sources for Facts and Myths   257
Illustration Credits   258
Endnotes   259

■ PREFACE ■

This book is an introduction, both philosophical and elementary, to ancient Chinese thought. Because my approach is philosophical, I devote a considerable amount of space to explaining the basic vocabulary of contemporary philosophy. My hope is that readers will be inspired to pursue Chinese thought in more depth but will also be able to cross over easily to the study of Western philosophy, should they wish to do so. There are, of course, alternative ways of studying Chinese thought and culture that are equally valuable, but I hope no scholars will begrudge me this methodology simply because it is not their own.

Because this is an elementary introduction, I have greatly simplified many aspects of both Chinese and Western history and culture. Understanding any tradition is daunting. As one Confucian put it, "The more I look up at it the higher it seems; the more I delve into it, the harder it becomes. Catching a glimpse of it before me, I then find it suddenly at my back" (*Analects* 9.11). Consequently, introducing too many nuances and scholarly controversies might overwhelm the beginner. By simplifying some points that are not central to my narrative, I hope to enable the reader to understand and grapple with other complex and profound issues. Cognoscenti should bear this in mind when they notice that I have typically not done justice to the multifaceted nature of the Western philosophers whom I cite as subjects of comparison nor to the complexities and controversies regarding Chinese history and philology.

In order to make this book as readable as possible, bibliographical information is exclusively in the endnotes (which are marked with Roman numerals). There is no need for the student to interrupt the flow of her reading by looking up an endnote unless she needs to know the source of a quotation. I have also tried to keep footnotes (which are marked with Arabic numerals) to a minimum, using them mainly for cross-references.

Translations are usually taken from Ivanhoe and Van Norden's *Readings in Classical Chinese Philosophy,* 2nd ed. An asterisk after a quotation indicates either that the passage is not found in *Readings* or that I have significantly modified the translation in that work. For passages from the *Analects* and *Mengzi* not found in *Readings,* I often quote Edward Slingerland's complete translation-with-commentary *Confucius: Analects with Selections from Traditional Commentaries* or my own *Mengzi: With Selections from Traditional Commentaries.* I do not note if I make a slight change from the translations given in one of these texts.

Following many contemporary academic works, years are identified as either BCE (before the Common Era) or CE (Common Era), meaning the era common to Christianity and the other great world religions. These designations are used in place of BC and AD, not to downplay or denigrate the significance of Christianity, but merely to provide a usage comfortable to those with other beliefs.

My thanks to Paul Goldin, Aaron Stalnaker, Justin Tiwald, and Brad Wilburn, all of whom offered helpful suggestions and advice on earlier versions of this work. I am also grateful to Deborah Wilkes, Senior Editor at Hackett Publishing Company, for her support throughout this project with everything from matters of style to hunting gargoyles; Mary Vasquez, Project Editor at Hackett, for tirelessly answering my queries; and Simone Payment, my copyeditor, for making me sound more articulate than I am. Special thanks to Scott Thomson of Positively Postal, who generously provided images of the Chinese stamps that grace some of our chapter headings. Most of all I wish to thank my students, whose endless enthusiasm for Chinese thought is an inspiration and a challenge.

For those who wish to continue their study of this fascinating topic, the translations and secondary works listed below are just a fraction of the best work available.

Bryan W. Van Norden

*Jin was divided into Three Kingdoms: Wei in the south, Han in the middle, and Zhao in the north (453 B.C.E.)

■ SELECTED TRANSLATIONS ■

- Cleary, Thomas, trans. *Sun-Tzu: The Art of War.* Boston: Shambhala, 2005. A readable, popular translation of the writings attributed to Sunzi, along with selections from classical commentaries.

- Csikszentmihalyi, Mark, trans. *Readings in Han Chinese Thought.* Indianapolis: Hackett Publishing, 2006. A well-chosen selection of translations on a variety of topics, with extremely helpful introductions and supporting material.

- Gardner, Daniel K., trans. *The Four Books: The Basic Teachings of the Later Confucian Tradition.* Indianapolis: Hackett Publishing, 2007. The *Analects* of Confucius, the *Mengzi,* and two shorter texts as interpreted by later Confucian orthodoxy.

- Graham, Angus C., trans. *Chuang-tzu: The Inner Chapters.* Reprint. Indianapolis: Hackett Publishing, 2001. A challenging interpretive translation of the *Zhuangzi.*

- Ivanhoe, Philip J., and Bryan W. Van Norden, eds. *Readings in Classical Chinese Philosophy,* 2nd ed. Indianapolis: Hackett Publishing, 2005. Includes selections from all the major ancient Chinese philosophers.

- Johnston, Ian, trans. *The Mozi: A Complete Translation.* New York: Columbia University Press, 2010. The only complete English translation of the diverse Mohist writings. Includes the Chinese text on facing pages.

- Lau, D.C., trans. *Tao Te Ching.* New York: Penguin Books, 1963. An elegant translation based on the traditional text of the *Daodejing.* Lau's revised translation is also available in the Everyman's Library series (Alfred A. Knopf, 1994).

- Legge, James, trans. *The Chinese Classics,* 5 vols. Reprint. Taibei: SMC Publishing, 1991. This is one of many reprints of James Legge's Victorian-era translation of the *Four Books* (the *Great Learning, Analects, Mengzi,* and *Mean*) and three of the *Five Classics* (the *Odes, History,* and *Spring and Autumn Annals* with the *Zuo Commentary*). Although Legge's language is often archaic, this work is still very useful because it includes the Chinese texts of all works and extensive notes.

- Lynn, Richard John, trans. *The Classic of the Way and Virtue: A New Translation of the* Tao-te ching *of Laozi as Interpreted by Wang Bi.* New York: Columbia University Press, 1999. This fine translation includes what is perhaps the most seminal commentary on the *Daodejing.*

- Mair, Victor M., trans. *Tao Te Ching.* New York: Bantam Books, 1990. A translation based on the Mawangdui versions of the *Daodejing.*

- Sawyer, Ralph D., trans. *Sun Tzu: Art of War.* Boulder: Westview Press, 1994. A fine translation of the *Art of War,* with an informative scholarly introduction.

- Slingerland, Edward, trans. *Confucius: Analects with Selections from Traditional Commentaries.* Indianapolis: Hackett Publishing, 2003. Invaluable for its fine translation combined with selections from classic commentaries on each passage. An abridged version is also available as *Confucius: The Essential Analects* (2006).

- Van Norden, Bryan W., trans. *Mengzi: With Selections from Traditional Commentaries.* Indianapolis: Hackett Publishing, 2008. This is a complete translation with an interlineal commentary. An abridged version with commentary separated from the translation is also available as *The Essential Mengzi* (2009).

- Watson, Burton, trans. *Chuang Tzu: Basic Writings.* New York: Columbia University Press, 1964. This translation of the *Zhuangzi* is beautiful for its directness and fluency.

- Watson, Burton, trans. *Han Fei Tzu: Basic Writings.* New York: Columbia University Press, 1964. Selections from the *Han Feizi.*

- Watson, Burton, trans. *Hsun Tzu: Basic Writings.* New York: Columbia University Press, 1963. Selections from the *Xunzi.*

- Watson, Burton, trans. *Mo Tzu: Basic Writings.* New York: Columbia University Press, 1963. Selections from the "synoptic chapters" of the *Mozi.*

■ SELECTED SECONDARY WORKS ■

- Csikszentmihalyi, Mark, and Philip J. Ivanhoe, eds. *Essays on Religious and Philosophical Aspects of the* Laozi. Albany: State University of New York Press, 1999. Anthology of essays on the work also known as the *Daodejing* (*Tao Te Ching*) by Laozi (Lao Tzu).

- Graham, Angus C. *Disputers of the Tao.* Chicago: Open Court Press, 1989. General history of ancient Chinese philosophy. Particularly helpful on the Mohists and the "School of Names."

- Ivanhoe, Philip J. *Confucian Moral Self Cultivation,* 2nd ed. Indianapolis: Hackett Publishing, 2000. Readable and reliable introduction to some of the major issues among Confucians over two millennia.

- Kjellberg, Paul, and Philip J. Ivanhoe, eds. *Essays on Skepticism, Relativism and Ethics in the* Zhuangzi. Albany: State University of New York Press, 1996.

- Kline, Thornton C., and Philip J. Ivanhoe, eds. *Virtue, Nature, and Moral Agency in the* Xunzi. Indianapolis: Hackett Publishing, 2000.

- Kupperman, Joel J. *Learning from Asian Philosophy.* New York: Oxford University Press, 1999. This thoughtful book illustrates how classic Chinese thought can contribute to contemporary philosophical discussions.

- Liu, Xiusheng, and Philip J. Ivanhoe, eds. *Essays on the Moral Philosophy of Mengzi.* Indianapolis: Hackett Publishing, 2002.

- Schwartz, Benjamin. *The World of Thought in Ancient China.* Cambridge: Harvard University Press, 1985. A broadly humanistic approach to the study of Chinese philosophy.

- Tanner, Harold M. *China: A History.* Indianapolis: Hackett Publishing, 2009. A handy one-volume overview. Also available in a two-volume version.

- Van Norden, Bryan W., ed. *Confucius and the* Analects: *New Essays.* New York: Oxford University Press, 2002. Essays from a variety of perspectives and methodologies, including philosophical, philological, comparative, and historical.

- Van Norden, Bryan W. *Virtue Ethics and Consequentialism in Early Chinese Philosophy.* New York: Cambridge University Press, 2007. A more detailed defense of my philosophical methodology, and my interpretations of Kongzi, the Mohists, Yang Zhu, and Mengzi.

- Yearley, Lee H. *Mencius and Aquinas: Theories of Virtue and Conceptions of Courage.* Albany: State University of New York Press, 1990. A seminal comparative study that launched the contemporary application of virtue ethics to Confucianism.

■ 1 ■

THE HISTORICAL CONTEXT

I am not of their age or time and so have not personally heard their voices or seen their faces, but I know this by what is written on bamboo and silk, etched on metal and stone, and inscribed on basins and bowls that have passed down to us through succeeding generations.
—Mozi, "Impartial Caring"

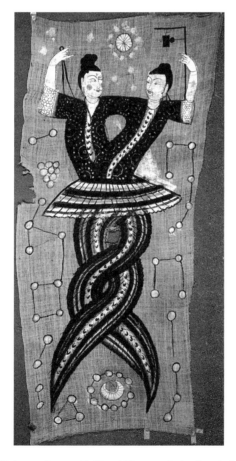

In this image, the sages Fu Xi and Nuwa are depicted symbolically as intertwined snakes.

In order to understand early Chinese philosophers, we must understand the context in which they lived. As with every culture, this context consists of historical reality as well as their myths. The distinction is not sharp: myths often contain an element of historical truth, and what passes for historical truth often has mythical elements. In addition, there are different versions of the myths in early Chinese texts. I will present only one account, but we shall see in it many figures and themes that are important in the self-understanding of Chinese culture.[i]

I. Myth

According to Chinese tradition, the earliest people had a precarious existence, living in fear of wild animals, subsisting day to day on whatever they could forage, and sleeping in tree houses or drafty caves. They had no technology, no rituals, and no culture. Human life gradually improved and civilization developed through the actions of a series of sages, the earliest of whom are referred to as the Three Sovereigns and the Five Emperors. The first and second sovereigns were Fu Xi and his wife, Nuwa. Fu Xi taught people to hunt, fish, and trap. He created the institution of marriage and also developed the earliest portions of the *Yijing*, a work of divination that would come to have great significance in later Chinese cosmology. (The *Yijing*, or *Classic of Changes*, had scant influence on philosophy, per se, in the period this book covers, so we will have little to say about it.) Legends say that Nuwa was responsible for even more amazing feats than was her husband, such as keeping the Heavens from collapsing by repairing them when they were damaged. Nuwa thus became a symbol, in later Chinese history, for the power and importance of women. For example, the classic Chinese novel, *Dream of the Red Chamber*, noted for its strong female characters, recounts the legend of Nuwa in its opening.

Nuwa was not only Fu Xi's wife, she was also his sister. This is intriguing, because the highest of the Greek gods, Zeus, was also married to his sister, Hera. Furthermore, in the Bible, God is said to have made Eve from Adam's rib, so she is, in a sense, his twin sister. Because these cultures developed independently, the similarity in their myths may reflect some deep need or tension that humans share. A Freudian, using a hermeneutic of suspicion, might suggest that the myths are a projection of subconscious, incestuous desires. In contrast, using a hermeneutic of faith we might interpret the myths as an expression of the legitimate human longing to find that masculinity and femininity are distinct (symbolized by the fact that Fu Xi and Nuwa are male and female) yet complementary (symbolized by their marriage) and fundamentally unified, rather than dualistic (symbolized by the fact that they have the same parents).[1]

The third sovereign was Shen Nong, whose name means "spiritual farmer." Shen Nong discovered how to plant crops and domesticate animals. He also was a pioneer of Chinese medicine. One day, when he wasn't looking, a leaf fell into his cup of water. Drinking it, he noticed that it tasted different. In this way, he discovered tea. Experimenting by using different leaves for tea, he discovered their medicinal effects; using himself as a test subject, he tried different herbs, and noted what effects they had on his body.

The first of the Five Emperors was the Yellow Emperor, or in Chinese Huang Di. During his era, criminals and invading barbarian tribes terrorized the Chinese people. Although he preferred peace, the Yellow Emperor saw that it was necessary to institute armies and judicial punishments to protect the people. Huang Di's practices led to a decisive military victory over his enemies, a victory that is often considered to be the founding of the Chinese as an ethnic group.

Others in Huang Di's circle also made lasting contributions. The Yellow Emperor's wife, after inspecting a caterpillar infestation in the emperor's mulberry orchard, discovered how to spin and weave silk. Thereafter, weaving silk became a characteristically female task. Another distinctive cultural innovation, Chinese written characters, was supposedly invented by one of the Yellow Emperor's officials, Cang Jie.

So Fu Xi taught the people how to hunt, while Shen Nong taught them to farm. Modern archaeology teaches us that the earliest humans moved from place to place, hunting animals and gathering wild plants. Then, with the agricultural revolution, humans learned to plant crops and domesticate animals. This led to settled human communities. These communities allowed for the development of more complex forms of technology and civilization (including writing), but also created the need to protect one's territory and control crime. Consequently, the stories of Fu Xi, Shen Nong, and the Yellow Emperor, although mythical in their details, may represent a dim memory of the human transition from nomadic hunter-gatherers to farmers, and then to city dwellers.

The next three important emperors were Yao, Shun, and Yu. Yao, in addition to being a humane and wise ruler, is associated with discovering the rudiments of astronomy and the regularity of the seasons, important knowledge for any agricultural civilization. Thus, Kongzi (Confucius) said of him, "It is

---

1. See Appendix A on the difference between a hermeneutic of suspicion and a hermeneutic of faith.

Heaven that is great, and it was Yao who modeled himself upon it" (*Analects* 8.19). As he approached the end of his life, Yao decided to find a virtuous successor to follow him as ruler. Searching his kingdom, Yao heard about Shun, a simple farmer who was known for his great filial piety.

Shun had what we would describe today as a dysfunctional family. His father, stepmother, and stepbrother repeatedly schemed to murder him and steal his wealth. According to one story, Shun's family asked him to dig a well. They planned to remove the ladder and cover over the well while Shun was still inside. Thinking that they had succeeded in their plot, Shun's brother told his parents that they could have Shun's livestock and his storehouses of grain. "But his spear and shield—mine! His zither—mine! His bow—mine! And his two wives shall service me in my bed!" However, Shun had survived the murder attempt. Despite their plots against him, Shun continued to love and care for his family, until eventually he won them over with his devotion. Impressed by stories of his character and achievements, Yao made Shun his prime minister. He was so successful in this position that when Yao passed away the people made Shun the new emperor.

As ruler, Shun was concerned with the problems of flood control and irrigation. These had long been issues in China. The Yellow River Valley is the heartland of Chinese civilization because of its fertile soil and because the river provides easy transportation and water for crops. However, the Yellow River often floods, leading to devastation. Consequently, some have referred to China as a "hydraulic civilization" because of how important organizing water control is to society. One speculation is that this encouraged a strongly centralized government, with the resources to organize massive irrigation, flood control, and canal-building projects.

It is not surprising that Shun felt the need to appoint an able minister, Yu, to supervise flood control. Yu worked tirelessly, dredging silt out of rivers and building canals. Yu eventually became Shun's prime minister and, in a parallel with the previous succession, his abilities led the people to treat him as the new emperor upon Shun's death.

Yu was a great ruler in his own right, and when he grew old he followed the pattern set by Yao and Shun of choosing the person he found most worthy as his successor. However, this time the people did not accept the emperor's choice. Instead, out of affection and respect for Yu, they treated Yu's son as the emperor. Because of this, Yu became (posthumously) the founder of the first Chinese dynasty, the Xia. It is significant that the people's preference for a ruler was taken to be of greater importance than even the great Yu's decision. Traditional Chinese culture was never democratic but always emphasized the well-being and happiness of the people as the ultimate arbiter of political legitimacy.

The traditional Chinese view is that dynasties follow a cyclic pattern: a saga-cious ruler founds a dynasty, bringing prosperity and order to society, but in a way that is noncoercive. The people willingly and joyfully follow him. Over the cen-turies there is a gradual decline in the quality of the rulers, with a corresponding increase in social disorder, dissatisfaction, and dis-affection. The decline is typically not linear: great kings will arise during a period of mediocrity to temporarily restore a dynasty to its greatness. However, eventually a dynasty will reach its nadir, and an evil last king will inspire full-fledged revolt against his atrocities, leading to the arrival of a sage who will found the next dynasty.

> **Myth:** *"The Chinese word for 'crisis' literally means 'danger + opportunity.'"*
>
> **Fact:** *The Chinese word for "crisis" means, well, crisis. It is composed of two words, which mean "danger" and "crucial point."*

So Yu was the sage who founded the Xia dy-nasty, which was brought to an end centuries later by the evil Tyrant Jie. The sage-king Tang overthrew Jie and went on to found the Shang dynasty. (The Shang dynasty is sometimes also called the Yin, after the name of the last capital city of the dynasty.)

II. Early History

At some point during the Shang dynasty, written records begin and we emerge from the enchanting mists of myth into the clearer light of actual history. The story of how the Shang dynasty moved from myth to history is intriguing. Near the end of the nineteenth century, "dragon bones" could be bought for their alleged medicinal properties. They were thought to be dragon bones because of their great age and because of the odd markings on them. However, a pair of Chinese scholars who examined the bones realized that the markings were ar-chaic forms of Chinese characters written on ancient "oracle bones." These bones (often the flat bottom shell of a tortoise) were used in a ceremony where-by the Shang king would divine the future and make inquiries of the spirits of his ancestors. A bone was heated until it cracked, while the king made a pair of ritual pronouncements, "Our attack on the barbarians will be successful. Our attack on the barbarians will perhaps not be successful." By interpreting the cracks, the king would divine which pronouncement was correct. What is per-haps most fascinating is that, *after* the ritual was completed, the questions asked were typically inscribed into the oracle bone. If we today are lucky, the answer divined was also inscribed into the bone. And if we are *really* lucky, the actual outcome was inscribed too. These brief and frequently difficult to interpret in-scriptions give us a narrow window into Shang civilization.

When the source of the "dragon bones" was excavated, archaeologists found tombs of the Shang kings who ruled in the city of Yin. Here was hard physical evidence for the historicity of the Shang dynasty. (We lack evidence like this for the Xia dynasty, which is why it is still considered mythical.) The earliest surviving oracle bones date from around 1200 BCE, and we may be confident that the dynasty existed at least as far back as the sixteenth century BCE. This was a Bronze Age culture, using the metal for weapons and for ceremonial vessels to make offerings of food and wine to the spirits of the ancestors. The staple crop was millet, a kind of wheat still grown in China today. (Rice doesn't grow well in comparatively dry northern China, so it is not until much later, when Chinese culture spread into the high-rainfall areas of the south, that rice became almost emblematic of China.)

The war chariot was the tank of the era: in it rode a driver, an archer, and a spearman. To see one approaching at full gallop must have been an intimidating sight. The size of a state was often expressed in terms of how many chariots its army could field (e.g., "a state of a thousand chariots"). But the Shang also used infantry, armed with spears, shields, and light body armor.

This Bronze Age culture was patriarchal, but some women held high status through some combination of noble birth and personal excellence. Most notably, Fu Hao was a noblewoman who commanded armies. After her death, ritual sacrifices were made to her, just as to noble male ancestors, and her burial tomb included goods almost equal in grandeur to that of a king.

The traditional view of history requires that the last king of the dynasty be evil: the (supposedly) evil last king of the Shang was Tyrant Zhou. The name of the dynasty that succeeded the Shang is also romanized as "Zhou." In Chinese, you would never confuse the two, because they are written with different characters and pronounced with different tones: *Zhòu* 紂 is the tyrant and *Zhōu* 周 is the dynasty. To keep them straight in English, "Zhou" without qualification will mean the dynasty and "*Tyrant* Zhou" will always be the last ruler of the Shang.

Tyrant Zhou was clever, fearless, and physically powerful. However, he was also ruthless, cruel, and dissolute. The ancient historian Sima Qian reports that "by a pool filled with wine, through meat hanging like a forest, he made naked men and women chase one another and engage in drinking long into the night."[ii] Tyrant Zhou had a loyal minister in his uncle, Bi Gan, who warned him that his actions would eventually turn his subjects against him. Tyrant Zhou replied that sages supposedly have larger hearts than others, and since Bi Gan spoke like a sage, he wished to see whether Bi Gan also had the heart of a sage. With that, he ordered his guards to cut the heart out of Bi Gan's chest.

Tyrant Zhou was overthrown, and a new dynasty was begun by the Zhou people. The Zhou justified their conquest through the theory of dynastic cycles. I will let them speak for themselves, in documents that date back some three thousand years:

> Examining the men of antiquity, there was the founder of the Xia dynasty [King Yu]. He guided his mind, allowing his descendants to succeed him and protecting them. He acquainted himself with Heaven and was obedient. But in the process of time the mandate in his favor fell to the ground. So also when we examine the case of Shang. Heaven guided its founder [King Tang], so that he corrected their errors and so it protected his descendants. He too acquainted himself with Heaven and was obedient. But now the mandate in favor of him has fallen to the ground.[iii]

> When Heaven rejected and made an end of the mandate in favor of the great state of Shang, there were many of the former intelligent kings of Shang in Heaven. However, the king who had succeeded them [Tyrant Zhou], the last of their line, from the time of his entering into their appointment, proceeded in such a way as at last to keep the wise in obscurity and the vicious in office. The poor people in such a case, carrying their children and leading their wives, made their moan to Heaven. They even fled away, but were apprehended again. Oh, Heaven had compassion on the people of the four quarters. Its favoring mandate lighted on our earnest founders. Let our king feverishly revere Virtue![iv]

> King Wen [of the Zhou people] was able to make bright his Virtue and be careful in the use of punishments. He did not dare to show any contempt to the widower and widows. He appointed those worthy of appointment and revered those worthy of reverence. He was terrible to those who needed to be awed, so getting distinction among the people. It was thus he laid the first beginnings of the sway of our small portion of the empire, and one or two neighboring countries were brought under his improving influence, until throughout our western regions all placed in him their reliance. His fame ascended up to the High Ancestor, who approved of him. Heaven then gave a great charge to King Wen to exterminate the great dynasty of Shang and receive its great mandate, so that the various states belonging to it and their peoples were brought to an orderly condition.[v]

These passages don't just lay out a cyclic view of history, they specify a *philosophy of history* that explains those cycles. The founder of a dynasty is given a mandate (*mìng* 命) to rule by Heaven (*tiān* 天). Because of this intimate relationship between Heaven and the king, the ruler is often referred to as the "Son of Heaven." "Heaven" can refer to the sky or the place where the spirits of the ancestors dwell, but in the period this book covers it most typically refers to a higher power that is thought of more or less anthropomorphically. The Mohists, a movement we shall examine in Chapter 4, conceived of Heaven as very much like a personal God, while the Confucians increasingly thought of Heaven as a more abstract higher power. Heaven bestows the mandate to rule based on a person's Virtue (*dé* 德). Virtue, here, is a sort of ethical charisma a person has because they possess attributes such as kindness, wisdom, and reverence for Heaven. If this notion of Virtue or ethical charisma seems naive to a modern reader, consider the extent to which the successful leadership of people such as Mahatma Gandhi and Reverend Martin Luther King, Jr., depended upon their perceived virtues. The mandate bestowed based on Virtue is transmitted to one's descendants, but it will be revoked for viciousness and given to someone more worthy. Even in modern Chinese, the word for "revolution" (as in "Cultural Revolution") is *gémìng* 革命, which is literally "stripping of the mandate."

It is easy to apply a hermeneutic of suspicion to the doctrine of the mandate of Heaven. The Zhou people wanted to rationalize their conquest of the Shang and their story that they had a Heaven-given mandate to rule sounds as suspect as Western notions like manifest destiny or the divine right of kings. As the saying goes, "the winners get to write history," and it is possible that Tyrant Zhou was a good ruler who simply had the bad luck to be defeated by ambitious invaders. In general, the doctrine of the mandate of Heaven conveniently justifies the rule of the victors: if they won, it proves they had the mandate, which means that they are ethically superior to those they defeated.

A hermeneutic of faith reveals another side to the doctrine: it implies that a ruler is legitimate only as long as the people are happy. The king may have to use force against the occasional obdurate rebel or bandit, but by and large the people must acquiesce in being ruled. Thus, the king reminds a duke that "Heaven's mandate is not constant." He further warns him, "When you show a great discrimination, subduing men's hearts"—as opposed to coercing them with force—"the people will admonish one another, and strive to be obedient. Deal with evil as if it were a sickness in your person." In other words, do not be harsh in a way that causes unnecessary suffering and harm "and the people will entirely put away their faults. Deal with them like caring for a baby, and the people will be tranquil and orderly."[vi] We now understand what another duke means when he states, "Our king has received the mandate.

Unbounded is the happiness connected with it, but unbounded is the anxiety. Oh, how can he be other than reverent?"[vii]

So the suffering people of Tyrant Zhou "made their moan to Heaven," which stripped him of the mandate and gave the mandate to King Wen, leader of the Zhou people, because he "was able to make bright his Virtue." However, out of loyalty, deference, and love of peace, King Wen restrained himself from rebelling against Tyrant Zhou. It was King Wen's son, King Wu, who finally led the conquest of the Shang. Wen (whose name means "cultured") is praised for his gentle forbearance, while Wu (whose name means "martial") is praised for his righteous use of force. They might be said to reflect two sides of Chinese culture.

King Wu's victory was quick and decisive because Tyrant Zhou's own soldiers turned against him. Tyrant Zhou retreated to his palace and, fearless and haughty to the last, set it afire and immolated himself in the palace rather than allowing himself to be captured.

When did the Zhou conquest of the Shang take place? The traditional date listed in many reference works is 1122 BCE, but current scholars believe this is wrong. We do know that in 1059 BCE there was a conjunction of all five of the planets visible with the unaided eye. As did the people of many ancient civilizations, the Chinese studied the Heavens carefully and believed that unusual celestial events provided portents of the future. Consequently, this conjunction would have led people to expect that a major change was about to take place, and this belief might have emboldened those anxious to rebel against Tyrant Zhou. In fact, the conjunction is mentioned in one ancient Chinese historical text, which states that the founding of the Zhou dynasty occurred twenty years later. This would seem to give us an exact date for the conquest. However, the dates given in this particular text seem to be off due to errors introduced by later scribes. Correcting these dates is a matter of guesswork, but many scholars think that King Wu defeated the Shang and established the Zhou dynasty around 1040 BCE.

King Wu's rule was short-lived; he died of natural causes a few years after the conquest. His son, King Cheng, succeeded him on the throne, but Cheng was only a child. To have a minor on the throne immediately after the founding of a new dynasty, with potentially rebellious subjects to govern, was a precarious situation. King Cheng's regent was his uncle, the Duke of Zhou. It must have been tempting for the Duke of Zhou to seize the throne. He could certainly have made a plausible claim to it: he was the brother of recently deceased King Wu and a son of King Wen. However, the Duke of Zhou supported King Cheng with loyalty and wisdom throughout his life. Because of this, he became a paragon of Virtue among later Confucians.

The strategy the Zhou used to control their newly expanded territory was to divide it into states of various sizes. A noble, typically a duke, governed each state. Many of these dukes were relatives of the Zhou royal family. Each duke had his own army and was responsible for maintaining order and collecting taxes in his state. He answered to the king, and upon a duke's death the king would approve his successor. This system worked well for centuries. However, the dynasty gradually decayed as weak kings lost the respect of the dukes. Perhaps this was inevitable. Imagine that you and your ancestors have ruled a state for generations. Within your state, you levy and collect taxes, make and enforce laws, and command your own personal army. Obeying the so-called king might seem unnecessary and, if the other dukes were ignoring the king, positively foolish.

The dynasty reached a low point under King You. King You's legitimate son by his queen was heir apparent. However, You fell in love with a seductive concubine, who bore him a second son. He decided to replace the legitimate queen and heir with his concubine and his second son. Given that his former queen had powerful relatives, this was immensely imprudent. The former queen's relatives raised an army to depose King You and put his elder son on the throne. While this army was secretly assembling, King You had taken to entertaining his new queen by lighting the beacon fires used to summon the armies of the dukes in case of emergency. Having been fooled by this prank more than once, the dukes decided not to answer the king's next signal. As a result, when the army of the deposed queen and heir attacked and King You lit the beacon fires to summon help, no one came. King You, his concubine-turned-queen, and his second son were all killed. His elder son was installed as king in a new capital city, further to the east. This marks the transition between the Western Zhou dynasty (c.1040–771 BCE) and the Eastern Zhou dynasty (770–221 BCE).

III. The Period of the Philosophers

The philosophers we study in this book all lived during the Eastern Zhou dynasty, and it is especially important to understand the context in which they lived, argued, and wrote. The new, eastern capital was deeper in Chinese territory and hence easier to defend against barbarian raids. However, the events surrounding the deposing of King You demonstrated the weakness of the Zhou royal house and its dependence upon the power and support of lesser nobles. This crippled the Zhou dynasty, and the Zhou kings were mere figureheads from this point on. Real power lay in the hands of the dukes and other nobles who ran the various states into which China was divided. In the absence of centralized authority, the states schemed against one another, formed alliances, broke those alliances, and frequently engaged in interstate warfare. The common people suffered horribly: they were robbed and assaulted by brigands the governments could not control, they were taxed to exhaustion by rulers who wanted to supply their armies and feed their own greed, and the planting and harvesting of their crops was interrupted by invading armies or by forced government labor. In the bitter words of the *Daodejing* (53):

> The court is resplendent,
> Yet the fields are overgrown.
> The granaries are empty,
> Yet some wear elegant clothes.
> Fine swords dangle at their sides;
> They are stuffed with food and drink,
> And possess wealth in gross abundance.
> This is known as taking pride in robbery.
> Far is this from the Way!

As is often the case, a chaotic and desperate situation stimulated philosophical thought as thinkers struggled to find a solution to the problems their society faced.

What these Chinese thinkers were looking for was the *dào* 道, which we render "Way." This crucial philosophical term has five related senses. "*Dao*" can mean a path or road (as in the modern Chinese compound "*dàolù* 道路," roadway). In both Chinese and English, there is a natural metaphorical extension from "way" in the sense of a literal *path* to "way" in the sense of *a way to do something*. Closely related to this is "Way" as *the linguistic account of a way* of doing something. From these senses, "Way" came to refer to *the right way to live one's life and organize society*. Eventually the term also came to mean *the ultimate metaphysical entity* that was responsible for the way the world is and the way that it ought to be (see Chapter 8). Although it can have any of these five senses, the primary meaning of *dao* (for most Eastern Zhou thinkers) is the right way to live and organize society.

Two important eras within the Eastern Zhou are the Spring and Autumn Period (722–481 BCE) and the Warring States Period (403–221 BCE). The former is named after the *Spring and Autumn Annals*, a cryptically terse historical chronicle of the years in question, written from the perspective of Kongzi's home state, Lu.[2] The *Zuo zhuan* is a commentary on the *Spring and*

---

2. According to tradition, Kongzi himself wrote the *Spring and Autumn Annals* and subtly encoded in its statements his judgments about the events described. However, most scholars today doubt this.

Autumn Annals that provides considerably more narrative detail about the period. Scholars disagree over how reliable it is as a historical account, but we shall have occasion to cite it at several points.

One of the opening stories in the *Zuo zhuan* gives a feel for what the Spring and Autumn Period was like. The ruler of a certain state had two sons. The mother disliked the older son, supposedly because she had a difficult labor with him, and favored the younger son. She asked the duke to declare the younger son his heir and pass over the older son, but the duke refused. When the father died and the older son became the new duke, his mother asked him to give his younger brother command over an important city. Eventually, the duke acceded to his mother's requests. Using the city as his new power base, the younger brother proceeded to usurp the prerogatives of the duke and prepare his soldiers for war. The duke refrained from taking action against his younger brother for as long as he could, despite the entreaties of his advisors. However, when the duke discovered that his mother had agreed to open the gate to his capital for his brother's invading army, the duke sent a force of two hundred war chariots against his brother. Support for the rebellious younger brother crumbled quickly, and he was forced to flee. The duke thereupon put his mother under permanent house arrest, vowing to not see her again "until we meet underground" (i.e., after death). After some time, the duke missed his mother, but felt that he could not break his vow. His dilemma was resolved when a clever servant suggested that the duke have a tunnel dug; there he could meet his mother underground. Thus, the duke and his mother were reconciled.

This inventive solution to the duke's quandary is typical of much Chinese ethical thought. In addition, this story illustrates the complex interrelationship between family and politics in this era. We can see why Confucians might stress the importance of loving and respecting members of one's own family, but we can also see why others (like the Mohists) would seek to minimize the role of familial relations in government.

In the power vacuum created by the impotence of the Zhou king, the institute of the Hegemon developed. The Hegemon (sometimes also called "Lord Protector") was a leader of one of the states who was able, through his individual military strength and judicious alliances, to become de facto ruler of China. The institution of the Hegemon officially existed to "support the king and repel the barbarians" that were raiding the Chinese states. However, the Hegemon actually ruled in the place of the king. The institution was intrinsically unstable, though, because the Hegemon was only one among several powerful rulers, alliances were fluid under even the best of circumstances, and any ruler who was too successful would incite the fear and envy of the others. Perhaps the most famous of the Hegemons were Duke Huan of the state of Qi and Duke Wen of Jin. Duke Huan's success was due in part to his brilliant minister, Guan Zhong. Many rulers and ministers wished to emulate Duke Huan and Guan Zhong, but Confucians typically condemned them for usurping the authority of the Zhou king and ruling by force and guile rather than by Virtue. Nowadays, when the People's Republic of China condemns U.S. hegemony (*bàquán* 霸權) they are using a word derived from the ancient title "Hegemon" (*bà* 霸).

The Warring States is a period of even more intense inter- and intrastate conflict. During this period, rulers of some of the more powerful states were declaring themselves king, usurping the title that was still supposedly the sole prerogative of the Zhou dynasty. In addition, the most wealthy and powerful families in a state were sometimes usurping the power of the hereditary rulers, so that some dukes became mere figureheads, just like the Zhou king.

At the very beginning the Eastern Zhou period, one noble had been particularly distinguished in defending the surviving members of the royal family against attack by barbarian raiders, thereby ensuring the survival of the dynasty. As a reward, the new king made him ruler of a semi-barbarian territory in northwestern China. This became the state of Qin. Ironically, it was a descendant of this same noble who led Qin when, in 256 BCE, it accepted the surrender of the last Zhou king. A few years later, in 221 BCE, Qin succeeded in conquering all the other states and unifying China. This event brings the Warring States Period and the Zhou dynasty to a close. The ruler of Qin thereupon bestowed upon himself the title "First Emperor." The grandiose title "emperor" (*huángdì* 皇帝) was constructed from the titles of the Three Sovereigns ("huang") and the Five Emperors ("di"). The Qin ruler obviously had no lack of confidence in his own abilities, and he predicted that he would be the First Emperor of ten thousand in his dynasty. What actually happened after his death . . . well, to tell you would be getting ahead of our story. For now we are finally ready to consider the first great philosopher of the Chinese tradition, Kongzi.

IV. Timeline

- Yao becomes emperor, and chooses Shun as his prime minister.
- Yao dies. The people choose Shun as the new emperor. Shun puts Yu in charge of flood control. Yu's success in this leads Shun to choose him as his prime minister.
- Shun dies. The people choose Yu as the new emperor.
- Yu dies. The people choose his son as the new emperor, thereby creating the first Chinese dynasty: the Xia.

- Over many generations, the Virtue of the Xia kings declines, culminating in the vicious rule of Tyrant Jie.

- Tyrant Jie is overthrown by the sage Tang, who becomes king of the second Chinese dynasty: the Shang.

- Over many generations, the Virtue of the Shang kings declines, culminating in the vicious rule of Tyrant Zhou.

- King Wen patiently endures Tyrant Zhou, but his Virtue increasingly draws the support of the people and other nobles.

- Circa 1040–771 BCE: Western Zhou dynasty.

  - King Wen's son, King Wu, leads the rebellion that overthrows Tyrant Zhou and founds the third Chinese dynasty: the Zhou.

  - A few years after the conquest, King Wu dies of natural causes, leaving his young son, King Cheng, on the throne. King Cheng's regent is his uncle, the Duke of Zhou, who loyally advises and defends King Cheng, solidifying Zhou rule.

  - Over many generations, the Virtue of the Zhou kings declines.

  - 771 BCE: A group of disaffected nobles and "barbarians" attacks and murders King You.

- 770–221 BCE: Eastern Zhou dynasty.

  - A surviving member of the Zhou royal family is established as king in a new capital to the east, deeper in the Zhou territory.

  - 722–481 BCE: Spring and Autumn Period.

    - 680 BCE: Duke Huan of Qi, with the assistance of his Prime Minister Guan Zhong, becomes the first Hegemon.

    - 551–479 BCE: Lifetime of Kongzi (Confucius).

  - Fifth century BCE: Lifetime of Mozi, anti-Confucian philosopher who advocated "impartial caring."

  - 403–221 BCE: Warring States Period.

    - Fourth century BCE:

      - Birth of Yang Zhu, egoist philosopher.

      - Birth of Mengzi (Mencius), Confucian who argued "human nature is good."

      - Birth of Hui Shi, key figure in the "School of Names."

      - Birth of Zhuangzi, Daoist philosopher who advocated emptying rather than cultivating one's heart.

      - Birth of Xunzi, Confucian who argued "human nature is bad."

- Third century BCE:
  - Possible date of composition of the *Daodejing*, attributed to Laozi.
  - Birth of Han Feizi, Legalist philosopher.
- 221–207 BCE: The Qin dynasty, founded by the self-proclaimed "First Emperor," unifies China, bringing the Warring States Period to a close.

Review Questions

1. According to the traditional Chinese philosophy of history, what cycle does each dynasty go through? Explain the role of Heaven, the mandate, and Virtue in this philosophy.

2. The figures in this chapter who will be referred to most frequently are Yao, Shun, Yu, Jie, Tang, Tyrant Zhou, Wen, Wu, and the Duke of Zhou. Give at least one sentence identifying something distinctive about each of these individuals.

3. Give the names of the Three Dynasties in the historical order in which they occurred. Name the first ruler of each dynasty and the last ruler of the first and second dynasties.

4. The last of the Three Dynasties is divided into two periods. What are these two periods called, and what event marks this historical division? The second half of this dynasty is divided into what two subperiods?

5. Briefly describe the governmental structure of the last of the Three Dynasties. In particular, what were the responsibilities of the dukes and the king?

6. In what century was the last of the Three Dynasties founded? What year is conventionally taken as the end of this dynasty?

7. What are the five senses of *dao,* "Way"?

KONGZI AND CONFUCIANISM

How could I dare to lay claim to either sageliness or Goodness?
What can be said about me is no more than this: I work at it
without growing tired and encourage others without growing weary.
—Kongzi, *Analects* 7.34

All of later Chinese thought reacts in one way or another to Kongzi.

I. Kongzi's Social Context and Life

According to the philosophy of history that the Zhou used to justify their conquest of the Shang, political power can only be obtained and maintained by Virtue, which accrues to a person who is respectful of his ancestors, kind to the people, and wise in his judgments. However, this view had come to seem increasingly quaint and irrelevant to many rulers and ministers during the Spring and Autumn Period. The Zhou king, who supposedly had the mandate from Heaven to rule, was now a mere figurehead. The rulers of the various states vied for supremacy through warfare and intrigue, each hoping to become Hegemon, de facto ruler of all China. For example, in 529 BCE, when the state of Jin was dominant and the state of Lu attempted to resist its authority, a leading minister of Jin ominously informed a representative of the state of Lu:

> Our ruler has here 4,000 chariots of war. Even if he acts contrary to the Way, it is still necessary to fear him; if he, beyond that, is acting in accordance with the Way, who can prove his opponent? If even a small ox were to attack a pig, would you not fear the pig would die? . . . If we lead on the multitudes of Jin, using also the forces of the other states . . . if we come thus to punish Lu for its offenses . . . what can we seek that we shall not get?[i]

Consequently, many rulers and ministers preferred power politics and sneered, "Of what use is culture?" (*Analects* 12.8*). The *Art of War* by Sunzi is traditionally dated to this era. While it may actually be a later text, the view of warfare that it espouses would have been endorsed by many Spring and Autumn rulers. It begins, "Warfare is the greatest affair of the state, the basis of life and death, the Way to survival or extinction. It must be thoroughly pondered and analyzed."[ii] Thus, for Sunzi, the Way is no longer the Way of Virtue; it is the Way of warfare. And with this Way comes a particular set of values. Sunzi tells us to master the art of deception, to motivate our soldiers with anger toward the enemy and the promise of spoils if they win.

Kongzi (551–479 BCE; better known in the West as Confucius) lived during this era. His attitude toward the reigning philosophy of militarism is captured by the story of his brief visit to the state of Wei. The duke of Wei asked Kongzi for advice about the arrangement of military formations. Kongzi icily replied, "I know something about the *arrangement* of ceremonial stands and dishes for ritual offerings, but I have never learned about the *arrangement* of battalions and divisions." Kongzi left the very next day (*Analects* 15.1). Instead of looking for a military solution to the problems of society, Kongzi called for putting into government people who were benevolent, wise, and reverent. Kongzi believed that such people would rule skillfully; in addition, the ethical example they set would inspire others to follow them willingly, without the need for force. When an influential official in Kongzi's home state asked him what he thought about capital punishment, Kongzi replied, "In your governing, Sir, what need is there for executions? If you desire goodness, then the common people will be good. The Virtue of a gentleman is like the wind, and the Virtue of a petty person is like the grass—when the wind moves over the grass, the grass is sure to bend" (12.19).

We should, of course, try to understand Kongzi in his own historical context. But, to think of him in today's terms, consider this: The kind of person who wants to "get tough on crime" and prefers government spending on defense to spending on domestic programs would probably have sided with Sunzi. People who think that a well-fed and well-educated population will also be more law abiding and who believe that war should only be a last resort would probably align themselves with Kongzi.

Kongzi's family had noble ancestors, but his father died when Kongzi was young, so he and his mother fell on hard times and he had to take many menial jobs in order to survive (9.6). He nonetheless managed to become very well educated and sought to enter government service. However, the times were unreceptive to his message. The duke of Lu, the state in which Kongzi was born, was a mere figurehead. Real power rested with the Three Families—wealthy, powerful clans whose members became the prime ministers of Lu. Kongzi complained that the Three Families taxed the people to pay for warfare and personal luxuries (11.17) and usurped prerogatives and government authority that they were not entitled to (3.1).

The Ji family did appoint Kongzi to office, but they apparently ignored his criticisms. Eventually, the state of Qi sent a group of "dancing girls" to the head of the Ji family, who enjoyed their services in private and did not show up to court for three days, ignoring his official duties. This was the last straw, and Kongzi resigned and left Lu, trying to find a ruler who would put his proposals into effect (18.4*). In light of this, we can perhaps understand the frustration that led Kongzi to sigh, "I have yet to meet a man who loves Virtue as much as he loves sex" (9.18).

For the next few years, Kongzi wandered from state to state, giving advice to rulers and seeking office. His life was difficult. He was almost murdered more than once (7.23, 9.5) and nearly starved to death on another occasion. This led his disciple Zilu to bitterly complain, "Does even the gentleman encounter hardship?" Kongzi replied, "Of course the gentleman encounters hardship. The difference is that the petty man, encountering hardship, is overwhelmed by it" (15.2).

In order to understand this exchange, we must fully grasp what a "gentleman" is. The term we render "gentleman" is "jūnzǐ 君子," which literally means "son of a ruler." As such, it has aristocratic connotations (as does "gentleman" in British English). In this sense, it is opposed to the "petty man" (literally, "small person"), meaning those of lower social class. However, Kongzi claimed that being a gentleman is not about social class but about being a good person. In Kongzi's view, a person of high social class might actually be a "petty man," because he is cruel, foolish, and arrogant, while a person born into poverty and obscurity might be a real gentleman, because he is benevolent, wise, and reverent. Consequently, when Zilu asked Kongzi if "even the gentleman" must go without food, he was whining, Why should an upper-class person like myself have to go hungry? Kongzi's reply means, If you are truly a gentleman, you will have the perseverance to endure suffering; if you cannot, then you are a petty man, regardless of how aristocratic your background.

Myth: "Confucius said, 'A journey of a thousand miles begins with one step.'"

Fact: No, he didn't. This saying is actually from the Daodejing *(a work discussed in Chapter 8). It is common to see inspiring quotations falsely attributed to Confucius. If he were alive today, Confucius might agree with baseball legend Yogi Berra: "I didn't say most of the things I said."*

Kongzi never found the opportunity that he sought to take office under a ruler who wished to govern with benevolence and wisdom, and he eventually returned to Lu. For the rest of his life he focused on training disciples. Given his own impoverished upbringing, it is not surprising that Kongzi did not discriminate in accepting disciples based on their wealth or social status. He remarked that all he demanded as tuition was a symbolic gift of "as little as a bundle of silk or bit of cured meat" (7.7; cf 15.39). He hoped that his disciples would take part in public affairs and change the world for the better, and some of them were quite successful. But he did not think of himself as founding a movement, much less one named for him. In fact, the term we render "Confucian" in English is "rú 儒," which is etymologically unrelated to the name "Kǒngzǐ 孔子." Nonetheless, his personal ethical charisma (his Virtue) and the profundity of his teachings (his Way) formed the basis of a multifaceted social and intellectual movement that has inspired both fervent admiration and intense criticism. It remains one of the most challenging and important of the major philosophical and religious traditions in the world today.

So what was the Way of Kongzi? This has been hotly debated over two millennia. Even a complete book could not begin to do justice to the complexities of the discussion. Part of the difficulty is that Kongzi left behind no writings of his own. Traditionally, the authorship of certain works has been attributed to him, but most contemporary scholars would say we are in the same evidential position in regard to Kongzi as we are with Jesus, Socrates, and the Buddha. We know each of these world-historical individuals only through what their followers and critics have said about them. Our primary source of the sayings of Kongzi is the *Analects*, a text divided into twenty "books" (closer to the size of chapters), each of which is subdivided into "chapters" (which range in length from one sentence to a few paragraphs in length). The *Analects* is traditionally said to have been recorded by the disciples of Kongzi soon after his death. However, among contemporary scholars there is considerable debate about how soon after the death of Kongzi each book in the *Analects* was composed, and hence how reliable each is as a guide to Kongzi's own thought. Based on linguistic evidence, Books 16–20 seem to have been written much later than the time of Kongzi, and some scholars believe there is stylistic evidence that Books 3–9 were written the earliest. However one dates individual passages, five themes are clearly central to the thought of Kongzi, and to everything that might plausibly be labeled "Confucianism" over the next twenty-five hundred years: the everyday world, tradition, the family, ritual, and ethical cultivation. In this chapter, we shall explore each of these themes in more detail.

II. Five Themes of Confucianism

1. Happiness in the Everyday World

While Kongzi did not deny that there is an afterlife, he thought that our primary ethical obligations relate to finding happiness for ourselves and others in this world. Thus, when Kongzi's disciple Zilu asked about how to serve ghosts and spirits, Kongzi replied, "You are not yet able to serve people—how could you be able to serve ghosts and spirits?" Zilu persisted, asking about death, but Kongzi just answered, "You do not yet understand life—how could you possibly understand death?" (11.12; cf 6.22) The significance of this emphasis becomes clearer if we contrast it with one major strain of Western thought. According to Plato, there is another world beyond the material realm. This other world is more perfect, more real, and more valuable than this world. It is inhabited by the gods and by the souls of the virtuous. Our actions in this life have value through their relationship to the other world. Thus, Plato says, the true philosopher makes dying his profession. Plato's ideas have influenced many in the West, including Christians such as Simone Weil. She expressed this perspective when she wrote, "There is a reality outside the world, that is to say, outside space and time, outside man's mental universe. . . . That reality is the unique source of all the good that can exist in this world: that is to say, all beauty, all truth, all justice, all legitimacy, all order, and all human behaviour that is mindful of obligations."[iii]

As Weil's reference to our obligations makes clear, her Platonistic version of Christianity requires that we act virtuously in this life. But our ultimate goal should be to transcend our bodily desires, as much as we can, so that our souls will be purified and ready to ascend to the higher realm after death. In contrast, for Kongzi and later Confucians, the goal of human existence is to do good in this world and to live well in this world. Thus, when he is asked what his aspirations are, Kongzi mentions values manifested among humans in this world: "To bring comfort to the aged, to inspire trust in my friends, and be cherished by the youth" (5.26; cf 6.30).

2. Revivalistic Traditionalism

The Confucian emphasis on tradition is also related to how it differs from Platonism. Because Plato believed that we have intellectual access to a higher world beyond this one, he was willing to radically question the beliefs and morality of his society. For example, in the *Republic,* Plato describes a utopian society in which the members of the ruling class will have no families, never even knowing who their own fathers and mothers are. But for Kongzi there is no higher standard of judgment than human civilization at its best. Thus he said of himself, "I transmit rather than innovate. I trust in and love the ancient ways" (7.1). It is possible within a Confucian framework to modify or reject elements of one's tradition, but this must be done by appealing to other values, beliefs, and practices within that same tradition. For example, when people switched from using linen ceremonial caps to cheaper ones made of silk, Kongzi approved of the change, because it was more frugal, yet maintained the spirit of the ritual (9.3).

Many modern readers will object to this idea, arguing that we must think for ourselves rather than let tradition think for us. There is an irony here, though, in that we are following a tradition (that of the Enlightenment) when we assume that thinking for ourselves and thinking through our tradition are inevitably opposed. A popular bumper sticker says "Question Authority," but in commanding us to do this, the bumper sticker has itself assumed the role of an authority. This irony reveals a deep philosophical point. Every time we think for ourselves, we must (whether we like it or not) begin from the concepts, beliefs, practices, and values that have been handed down to us from tradition. One must argue that any change is, in reality, a deeper and more consistent expression of the tradition. It is tempting to say that natural science gives us a technique for getting at the truth ahistorically. Although it would be far beyond the scope of this book to illustrate the case in detail, suffice it to say that almost all contemporary philosophers of science would acknowledge that science is a communal and historical enterprise in which progress can only occur via each generation of scientists learning the tradition before they extend it. For example, Einstein revolutionized our understanding of space, time, mass, and energy, but he could only do this by starting from within the Newtonian scientific tradition he learned in school. Similarly, Galileo overturned the medieval physics that preceded him, but this was only possible because of the puzzles identified and discussed within the Aristotelian tradition by the "impetus" theorists of the Middle Ages.

We might say that Kongzi is advocating not traditionalism or conservatism but rather revivalism. Revivalism is a movement to effect positive social change in the present by rediscovering the deep meaning of the texts, practices, and values of the past. Many of the great progressive social movements of history have been revivalistic, including the American civil rights movement. Reverend Martin Luther King, Jr. called on Americans to actually live up to the principles of freedom, equality, and human dignity central to the Christian tradition and to Western democratic thought rather than merely pay lip service to them:

> When the architects of our republic wrote the magnificent words of the Constitution and the Declaration of Independence, they were signing a promissory note to which every American was to fall heir. . . . Now is the time to make real the promises of democracy. . . . [E]ven though we must face the difficulties of today and tomorrow, I still have a dream. It is a dream deeply rooted in the American dream that one day this nation will rise up and live out the true meaning of its creed—we hold these truths to be self-evident, that all men are created equal.[iv]

King realized that the implications of reviving and living up to the deep meaning of tradition would be not conservative but radical. The same was true of Kongzi. He sought to awaken people to the highest values implicit in their own tradition in order to give them alternative ideals to force, violence, and greed. Just as King was motivated by a dream, so Kongzi said that he dreamed of the Duke of Zhou (7.5), whose loyal, wise, and humane government Kongzi admired and wished to restore. Therefore, we should not be quick to dismiss Kongzi's emphasis on tradition. His approach is actually consistent with some of the most sophisticated trends in contemporary philosophy, and it grows out of his desire to effect positive social change through revivalism.

3. The Family and Differentiated Caring

It is not surprising that a philosopher who emphasized the everyday world and tradition would also emphasize the family. The family is important in Confucianism in two related ways. First, it is as part of a family that one initially learns to be a good person. A disciple of Kongzi made this point when he said, "The gentleman applies himself to the roots. 'Once the roots are firmly established, the Way will grow.' Might we not say that filial piety and respect for elders constitute the root of Goodness?" (1.2). To put it in very modern terms, it is by loving and being loved by one's family members that one learns to be kind to others, and it is by respecting the boundaries of others in one's family and having one's own boundaries respected that one develops integrity. This is an insight to which modern Western developmental psychologists are only beginning to catch up.

The second way in which the family is important in Confucianism is "differentiated caring" (also called "graded love"). Differentiated caring is the doctrine that one has stronger moral obligations toward, and should have stronger emotional attachment to, those who are bound to oneself by community, friendship, and especially kinship. For example, the duke of one state bragged to Kongzi that his people were "upright," explaining that one son had turned in his own father for stealing a sheep. Kongzi replied, "Among my people, those whom we consider 'upright' are different from this: fathers cover up for their sons, and sons cover up for their fathers. 'Uprightness' is to be found in this" (13.18). The Confucian view on this topic has been criticized for encouraging nepotism and favoritism. In China, the Mohists (whom we shall study in Chapter 4) were particularly harsh critics of Confucianism on this topic. Many Westerners (and modernizers in China) have argued in favor of a morality based on respect for another person simply as a human being, regardless of personal relationships. However, other thinkers, notably feminists who advocate an ethics of care, hold a position similar to that of Confucians on this point.

Confucians would make several points in their own defense. First, we need an ethics that is practical for humans as they actually are rather than one that makes unrealistically impartial demands on us.[1] Second, differentiated caring

---

1. See the discussion of *Mengzi* 3A5 in Chapter 6.

means greater concern for certain people; it does not entail indifference, much less hostility, toward strangers. One of Kongzi's disciples spoke for millennia of Confucians when he said, "Everyone within the Four Seas is one's brother" (12.5). Third, in ancient China the king and the nobles of individual states were hereditary rulers; therefore government was intertwined with familial relations. Confucians did not see any way this government system could work unless people developed the love and respect that would inhibit political rivalry among family members.

4. Ritual and Functionalism

So far I have been emphasizing themes that are readily understood from our contemporary Western perspective, even if we may disagree with the stance Confucians take on these themes. However, one of the themes most important in Confucianism is much more difficult for many of us to understand and appreciate today: rituals or rites (*lǐ* 禮). The rituals encompass what we would classify today as belonging to fundamentally different kinds of activities. In the most basic sense, rituals are religious activities, such as offering food and ale to the spirits of one's ancestors, using the oracle bones for divination, and performing a funeral. Some rituals were very lively, involving elaborate dances accompanied by music. However, ritual also includes matters of what we would describe as etiquette, such as how to greet or say farewell to a guest, and the appropriate manner in which to address a subordinate ("pleasant and affable"), a superior ("formal and proper"; 10.2), or a person in mourning ("respectful"; 10.25). Finally, Kongzi sometimes speaks as if ritual refers to all of ethics (12.1).

The *Analects* notes, in what is generally taken to be a description of Kongzi acting in accordance with ritual, "He would not sit unless his mat was straight" (10.12). This line has been used for two thousand years to parody Kongzi and Confucians as obsessively observant of the minutiae of etiquette, perhaps to the point of absurdity. But how could Confucianism have captured so many of China's greatest minds, generation after generation, if it were really as shallow as that?

One simpleminded way of thinking about ritual is as a kind of primitive technology. For example, the king becomes ill. One performs a divination to determine what restless ancestral spirit is afflicting him, then offers a sacrifice to appease that ancestor, hoping to make the illness go away. Certainly, rituals have sometimes been used in this way in China (and in the West). However, philosophical Confucianism at its best has always had a much more sophisticated conception of ritual, one that is broadly functionalist.

Functionalism is a doctrine associated with the great sociologist Émile Durkheim. According to functionalism, the question to ask about a ritual is what social or psychological needs or goals it satisfies. Functionalists see rituals as expressing and reinforcing emotions and dispositions that are necessary for the maintenance of communities. To understand how a ritual could perform such functions, consider the example of a marriage ceremony. Ideally, getting married is an expression of love and commitment to another person. Of course, simply saying "I love you" performs a similar function, but most people would agree that a wedding allows for a fuller and more intense expression of these feelings. In addition, participating in the ceremony typically makes the participants feel more invested in the relationship, thereby strengthening it. Of course wonderful relationships can exist without weddings, and marriage ceremonies sometimes fail to have good effects, but as the existence of commitment ceremonies attests, it is not only the legal benefits of marriage that leads gays and lesbians to seek the legal right to participate fully in this social institution.

The importance of ritual can be seen even in everyday matters of etiquette. Try to imagine navigating your social life without any rituals. Do you ever shake a person's hand? This is a ritual action. Or are you the sort of person who greets others with a hug? This, too, is a ritual. If you maintain that hugging is just an expression of how you feel, you would be correct. But it is a *ritual* expression of how you feel. If you doubt that this is the case, try hugging someone in a culture without this ritual and see what reaction you get.

It seems to be precisely a functionalist view of ritual that the later Confucian Xunzi is expressing when he writes,

> One performs the rain sacrifice and it rains. Why? I say: There is no special reason why. It is the same as when one does not perform the rain sacrifice and it rains anyway. When the sun and moon suffer eclipse, one tries to save them. When Heaven sends drought, one performs the rain sacrifice. One performs divination and only then decides on important affairs. But this is not for the sake of getting what one seeks, but rather to give things proper form. Thus, the gentleman looks upon this as proper form, but the common people look upon it as connecting with spirits. (*Xunzi* 17; *Readings,* p. 272)

In another passage, Xunzi makes clear that "proper form" is connected with the expression and reinforcement of one's emotions and dispositions: "In every case, ritual begins in that which must be released, reaches full development in giving it proper form, and finishes in providing it satisfaction. And so when ritual is at its most perfect, the requirements of inner dispositions and proper form are both completely fulfilled" (*Xunzi* 19; *Readings,* p. 276).

Although our society and Kongzi's China are different in countless ways, they do have some things in common. Both now and then, many people feel alienated from one another and see no point to anything other than satisfying their own immediate needs. At their best, rituals remind us of how we are connected with and dependent upon other humans. Consequently, rituals can help humans form and maintain genuine communities, in which people care for and respect one another.

Ritual includes a range of activities from elaborate religious ceremonies to matters of everyday etiquette to how to live well in general. What do these activities, which our society categorizes separately, have in common? Kongzi believed that the proper underlying attitude in a religious ceremony is reverence or awe. Because they see not only religious ceremonies but also many other spheres of human life as ritual, Confucians invite us to do everything with the same serious attentiveness. Whether putting flowers on a relative's grave or studying for a test, giving a speech before Congress or working in the checkout line, Confucians would urge you to focus on what you are doing, take it seriously, and do it to the best of your ability. This does not mean that your life should be somber and joyless. Far from it! Kongzi had a good sense of humor himself, one that was charmingly dry and droll.[2] The point is that whether you laugh, cry, love, or compete, invest everything you do with importance by doing it with the same intensity that a believer gives to a religious ceremony. Thus, Kongzi's comment that "If I am not fully present at the sacrifice, it is as if I did not sacrifice at all" (3.12) has wider application than it seems at first glance. Be "fully present" in everything that you do—even if it is simply straightening your mat before you sit down on it.

Some of the most famous, and controversial, of the Confucian rituals have to do with funerals and mourning. In the Eastern Zhou, a Confucian funeral was often elaborate, with inner and outer coffins, special garments for the corpse, and other goods buried in the grave. After the funeral, there was a ritual period of mourning, the length of which depended upon how close the relation was. Mourning the death of one of your parents was the longest, and lasted three years (this meant just into the third year, or twenty-five months). During this time, the mourner was to wear plain clothes, eat simple food, maintain a somber demeanor, and curtail practical activities as much as possible. The Mohists, among others, criticized these practices as wasteful. It is interesting to note, though, that Kongzi himself emphasized appropriate feelings over ostentatious display. "When it comes to ritual, it is better to be spare

2. See 5.7*, 9.2, 14.29, 17.4*.

than extravagant. When it comes to mourning, it is better to be excessively sorrowful than fastidious" (3.4). This fits a functionalist interpretation, according to which the real point of the rituals is not the amount one spends or getting every minor detail right.

In another passage, Kongzi's disciple Zai Wo complains that the mourning period for parents is too long and wasteful, and proposes a one-year period. Kongzi asks, "Would you feel comfortable then eating your sweet rice and wearing your brocade gowns?" When the disciple replies that he would, Kongzi states, "Well, if you would feel comfortable doing so, then by all means you should do it." However, after the disciple leaves the room, Kongzi sighs, "This shows how lacking in Goodness this Zai Wo is! A child is completely dependent upon the care of his parents for the first three years of his life—this is why the three-year mourning period is the common practice throughout the world. Did Zai Wo not receive three years of care from his parents?" (17.21). We see again in this passage that Kongzi emphasized inner feeling over outward form in the rites. But we also see that Kongzi thought there were certain emotions a person ought to have, and that someone could be praised or blamed not only for their actions, and not just for their intentions in acting, but also for how they *feel*.

Immanuel Kant had a very different view. Kant held that while emotions may be conducive to, or an impediment to, moral conduct they are never morally right or wrong in themselves. The reason that we cannot be praised or blamed for our emotions is that we have no control over them. I cannot help whether I hate, love, or am indifferent to you, Kant says. But even if I hate Jane, I am morally responsible for treating her with respect because she is a human being. And my kindness toward John has no *moral* value unless it is given because he is a human being and not because he is my friend.

Kant is a paradigmatic modern thinker, so it would not be surprising to be sympathetic to his view. However, consider someone who hates people based on their race but who manages to force herself to treat everyone the same. Or imagine a man who holds women in contempt but who acts as if he does not, because he thinks that he is morally required to treat them as equals. Can we say that there is *nothing* ethically wrong with racism and misogyny as long as people keep it to themselves? This takes us back to the question of whether it is possible to change our emotions. The Western Stoics thought that emotions and beliefs were always perfectly consistent. If you believe the snake you see is poisonous, then you will be afraid of it. If you recognize that it is a harmless insectivore, you will not be afraid of it. However, this seems inadequate. I might have a phobia of all snakes, even ones that I firmly believe are not dangerous to humans.

5. Ethical Cultivation

The question of how emotions can change leads to the last of our five themes: ethical cultivation. Kongzi hoped to improve society by putting virtuous people into positions of authority, but he was well aware of how rare true Virtue is. Consequently, he pioneered educational techniques for making people not just more skillful or more knowledgeable, but more benevolent, wise, and reverent.[3] Kongzi's general philosophy of education is summed up in a pithy quotation: "If you learn without thinking about what you have learned, you will be lost. If you think without learning, however, you will fall into danger" (2.15). Much of the lively debate among Confucians over the twenty-five hundred years after Kongzi's death concerned the comparative emphasis one should give to "thinking" and "learning" in ethical cultivation, and what human nature must be like to justify this emphasis.[v]

"Learning," broadly speaking, is internalizing the actions, thoughts, and feelings of those who are virtuous, especially sages. If we are fortunate, these can be people we have actually encountered, but they can also be people we learn about through classic texts. The *Odes* seems to have been the primary classic text for Kongzi. This anthology of poetry was already quite old by Kongzi's time and is diverse in content, including poems about love, war, farming, major dynastic events, religious ceremonies, and lamentations. We begin to understand its role in ethical cultivation if we consider the very first ode. It is about an impending marriage, and Kongzi praised it on the grounds that it "expresses joy without becoming licentious, and expresses sorrow without falling into excessive pathos" (3.20). When we read the ode, we are drawn into the perspective of the poem and led to see (and to feel about) marriage a certain way. We see it as something happy and sensual but not frivolous or purely sexual. We sympathize with the natural longing of the lovers but not in a way that is self-indulgently lugubrious.

Other odes are more political in nature, such as that of the peasants who complain of overtaxation by singing of their ruler, "Big rat, big rat, / Do not gobble our millet! / Three years we have slaved for you, / Yet you take no notice of us."[vi] As someone who was raised in poverty, Kongzi no doubt wanted his students to learn to sympathize with the plight of farmers whose produce was the ultimate source of their salaries.

Kongzi summarized his approach to the *Odes* by saying that they "number several hundred, and yet can be judged with a single phrase: 'Oh, they will

---

3. See Appendix A for a comparison between Kongzi's virtue-centered view of education and the Platonistic and Baconian positions that are best known in the West.

not lead you astray'" (2.2). In other words, the *Odes* ultimately are a guide to not swerving from the Way. This passage also illustrates Kongzi's fondness for seeing multiple layers of meaning in a poem. The phrase "Oh, they will not lead you astray" is a quotation from the *Odes*, and in its original context it refers to a team of stout, reliable horses that will not go off the path. However, Kongzi used it as an ethical metaphor (cf 1.15 and 3.8). Some scholars think this shows that Kongzi did not care about the meaning of the *Odes* themselves, that they were simply a pretext for expressing his own views. However, many ethical traditions believe that the metaphorical sense of the classics is part of their meaning. Augustine, for example, gave an elaborate metaphorical reading of the creation story in Genesis and saw it as part of God's meaning.

Literature can also teach us to perceive and think about ethical matters in a more profound way. As Iris Murdoch said, "By opening our eyes we do not necessarily see what confronts us. We are anxiety-ridden animals. Our minds are continually active, fabricating an anxious, usually self-preoccupied, often falsifying *veil,* which partially conceals the world. . . . It is a *task* to come to see the world as it is."[vii] Trained as a philosopher, Murdoch became a novelist because she felt that imaginative literature often does a better job of helping us with this "task." The later Confucian Mengzi illustrates such a use of literature when one of his disciples cites an ode that says one must inform one's parents when getting married, and then asks why Sage-King Shun did not follow this injunction (*Mengzi* 5A2). Mengzi explains why Shun's abusive parents made his failure to inform them of his marriage a legitimate exception to the rule. This simple case shows how the *Odes* and the stories of the sages can help us to think more deeply about complex ethical situations. Examples abound in other traditions as well, including the fervent discussions in the Indian tradition of whether, in the *Ramayana,* King Rama treated Queen Sita fairly in banishing her. This kind of learning is possible because great literature consists not just of entertaining stories, but of narratives about complex people wrestling with difficult issues central to human life. To grapple with these issues is to grapple with our own existence.

Of course, Kongzi was also aware of the practical value of a good education for people who want to take part in public life. Being well read, eloquent in expression, and a careful reader are skills that are immensely useful and highly sought after in every literate society. Confucian learning was, therefore, something like a liberal arts education. It did not train one for any one particular task: as Kongzi put it, "The gentleman is not a vessel," meaning he is not a specialist good at only one thing (2.12; cf 9.6, 13.4, and 19.7). Rather, the gentleman has general skills that can be applied to a variety of activities. However, in Kongzi's society, as in our own, some were critical of the value of such a literary education, because it requires a great investment of time without providing training in any particular craft. So we can understand why Kongzi said, "It is not easy to find someone who is able to learn for even the space of three years without a thought given to official salary" (8.12; cf 9.2, 12.8).

We have been examining Kongzi's view of learning, but *thinking* is necessary for every aspect of learning. Kongzi himself never encouraged rote memorization or mindless repetition. If one learns in this way, one will be "lost" (2.15), knowing only a jumble of confused and undigested bits of trivia. As the later Confucian Xunzi put it, "The learning of the petty person enters through his ears and passes out his mouth. From mouth to ears is only four inches—how could it be enough to improve a whole body much larger than that?" (*Xunzi* 1; *Readings*, p. 259). Kongzi was therefore very demanding of his students:

> I will not open the door for a mind that is not already striving to understand, nor will I provide words to a tongue that is not already struggling to speak. If I hold up one corner of a problem, and the student cannot come back to me with the other three, I will not attempt to instruct him again. (7.8)

At the same time, Kongzi believed that unless thinking works upon what one has already internalized via learning, one will "fall into danger" (2.15). Why? This relates to a point we discussed earlier: Kongzi's emphasis upon tradition. If our thinking has any content to begin with, it frames that content in terms of the language, concepts, values, and paradigms that we have inherited from our culture. If our understanding of that cultural tradition is shallow, then our thinking will also be shallow. Thus, from an authentic Confucian perspective, the thoughtless conservative and the unrealistic radical are really just the flip sides of the same coin: someone who mouths slogans he does not understand, and rejects positions he does not fully appreciate. The true Confucian gentleman learns deeply, always thinking about what he has learned, and applies it in his life and in trying to change the world for the better.

What are some of the other characteristics of the Confucian gentleman? And how does the emphasis upon producing a morally exemplary person make Confucianism a form of virtue ethics? To these questions we turn in the next chapter.

Review Questions

1. What is the name of the Chinese historical era in which Kongzi lived? Kongzi lived around which of the following years BCE: 1040? 770? 722?

500? 403? 221? (Bonus points if you remember from last chapter what eras the other years begin.)

2. What is the most fundamental difference between the Way of Sunzi and the Way of Kongzi?

3. What was Kongzi's family situation when he was growing up?

4. Why did Kongzi leave his home state of Lu and visit other states?

5. Why is it ironic that we use the terms "Confucian" and "Confucianism" in English to describe the movement associated with Confucius?

6. What is the *Analects* and how was it composed?

7. What are Kongzi's two senses of "gentleman"? What are his two senses of "petty man"?

8. Explain the difference for Kongzi between emphasizing the "everyday world" and being "otherworldly."

9. Why might it be more accurate to describe Kongzi as "revivalistic" than as "conservative"?

10. What are the two aspects of the Confucian emphasis on the family?

11. According to functionalism, how should we understand ritual?

12. What are the two major aspects of Confucian ethical cultivation?

13. What are the *Odes,* and what roles did Kongzi think they played in ethical cultivation?

14. Explain how each of the following passages relates to one of the five themes of Confucianism: 11.12, 7.1, 1.2, 13.18, 3.4, and 2.15. (You will have a solid basic understanding of Confucianism if you can remember these passages.)

■ 3 ■

KONGZI AND VIRTUE ETHICS

*The gentleman has no biases for or against anything in the world.
He simply seeks to be on the side of the right.*
                                        —Kongzi, *Analects* 4.10

This time-lapse photograph illustrates Kongzi's saying in *Analects* 2.1 that "one who rules through the power of Virtue is analogous to the Pole Star: it simply remains in its place and receives the homage of the myriad lesser stars."

In terms of the categories of Western normative ethics, Confucianism is a form of virtue ethics. In order to understand what is distinctive about virtue ethics, it is easiest to begin by explaining its alternatives: consequentialism and deontology. Most simply, consequentialism and deontology emphasize what kinds of actions one ought to *do,* while virtue ethics is about what kind of person one ought to *be.*

I. Three Normative Theories

Consequentialism is one of the most intuitive normative theories. Nineteenth-century philosopher Jeremy Bentham, a seminal Western consequentialist, argued that what makes an action right is that it produces the "greatest happiness for the greatest number of people." For example, in considering whether capital punishment is morally right, a consequentialist would ask whether executing criminals produces more happiness, on balance, than other alternatives, such as life imprisonment. In most cases an execution will make the prisoner and his family unhappy, but it will make the victim's family and friends happy. Bentham would also consider the long-term consequences of execution. Does the example set by execution deter crime and thereby increase happiness, or not? Does life imprisonment consume tax dollars that would produce more happiness if redirected to hospitals, schools, and public parks? Taking everything into account, if executing a prisoner produces more happiness than alternatives such as life imprisonment, then executing him is the right thing to do.

The form of consequentialism derived from Bentham and his later followers (such as John Stuart Mill and contemporary philosopher Peter Singer) is called "utilitarianism." Utilitarians generally identify the good with some positive mental state, like pleasure, happiness, or, more technically, "preference satisfaction." Act-consequentialists, like Bentham, say we should judge each individual action by how much impartial good it produces. Rule-consequentialists, like Mill, argue that we should act according to rules that, if we follow them, produce the most impartial good. For example, Mill would admit that particular instances of free speech may have bad consequences overall, such as a speech given by a Nazi. However, Mill thinks it will produce the best consequences if society follows a general rule permitting free speech, rather than tries to make a case-by-case judgment about when free speech should be allowed. (We'll see in Chapter 4 that the Chinese Mohists were consequentialists.)

Some objections commonly raised against consequentialism are facile and easily refuted. For example, some people object that we can't know every consequence of any one action. This is true, but we are only responsible for choosing the action most likely to have the best consequences. And our uncertainty about the future doesn't stop us from making all kinds of other choices based on probable outcomes, from choosing whether to try a new flavor of ice cream, to picking an elective course in college, to deciding where to invest our retirement funds.[i]

A deeper objection is whether good consequences are quantifiable in a way that allows us to add them up and determine the best possible outcome. How can I compare arithmetically the pleasure you get as a result of selling me candy, the pain I get from developing a cavity, and the pleasure the dentist gets from charging me to fix my cavity? Even within my own perspective, does the pleasure I get from reading a good book differ only in amount from the pleasure I get from eating ice cream, or are they different in kind? Utilitarian John Stuart Mill agreed that these pleasures are different in kind, but once one admits that, one can no longer simply add up pleasure as if it were a homogenous good.

The second deep objection to consequentialism concerns whether it is always right to do what has the best consequences. Consider the use of the atomic bomb on Hiroshima and Nagasaki in World War II. There is continuing debate about whether these bombings were justified. Consequentialists debate whether, for example, it was possible for the United States to demonstrate the power of the bomb by dropping it on an uninhabited region of Japan and thereby convince Japan to surrender without having to obliterate a city. But if invading Japan had been necessary, it would have cost many casualties on both sides. Estimates of potential U.S. casualties alone range up to one hundred thousand. Suppose using the A-bomb on a city really would cost fewer lives than invading Japan. In that case, wouldn't everyone agree with the consequentialist that bombing Hiroshima was the morally right decision?

No. Philosopher Elizabeth Anscombe argued forcefully that the bombings of Hiroshima and Nagasaki were intrinsically immoral and unjustifiable, regardless of whether on balance they saved lives by ending the war more quickly. Why? Anscombe states that it is justifiable to target soldiers in wartime, because doing so is an extension of one's general right to self-defense. However, she says that it is never justifiable to intentionally kill civilians, since they are not a direct threat. To put her point in terms with contemporary relevance, targeting civilians is *terrorism,* not an act of war. Now, one of the main reasons that Hiroshima and Nagasaki were "good targets" for the A-bomb was that they were largely intact, even after four years of war: they had not been targeted for prior aerial bombardment because they were of minimal military importance. In other words, Hiroshima and Nagasaki were *civilian* targets, not *military* targets. Consequently, according to Anscombe, bombing them was intrinsically morally wrong.[ii]

Anscombe was a deontologist. Broadly speaking, a deontologist claims that sometimes the right action is not the one that produces the most "good" (pleasure, happiness, and so on) overall. Ask yourself if the ends justify the means. If you think that the end does justify the means (as long as the end is good from an impartial perspective), then you are a consequentialist. If you think that the end does not always justify the means (because some means are simply wrong), then you are a deontologist. Many deontologists are (like Anscombe) rule-deontologists. Rule-deontologists claim that we can do what we like as long as we do not violate certain moral imperatives, such as "Do not murder," "Do not steal," "Do not lie," and "Do not assault others." At the other extreme, act-deontologists think that imperatives like those above are, at best, useful rules of thumb to which there will always be exceptions. For example, as a general rule, one should not steal, but what if one steals a loaf of bread from a well-stocked supermarket to feed one's starving family?

So far I have explained some standard technical terms in philosophy and used them in well-established senses. However, it is useful at this point to mark a less-common distinction. Imagine a horizontal line representing a spectrum of views. At the left end is extreme generalism while at the right end is extreme particularism. Extreme generalism is the view that one substantive rule captures all moral evaluations. Extreme particularism is the view that there are no substantive, useful moral rules: all moral evaluation is completely context sensitive. Bentham's utilitarianism is at the extreme generalist end of the spectrum while act-deontology is at the extreme particularist end. Most ethical views fall somewhere in between these two extremes, but they can be described as closer to the generalist or the particularist end of the spectrum. For example, some rule-deontologists think that there are several substantive, highly general, inviolable moral rules, such as "Do not lie" and "Do not murder." Aristotle was a bit more of a particularist: he thought that moral rules provide guidance but they require substantial interpretation to be correctly applied in concrete situations.

As different as they are, consequentialism and rule-deontology both emphasize what a person ought to *do*. Virtue ethics is an alternative position that emphasizes what a person ought to *be*. To put it another way, consequentialism and rule-deontology are theories about *right action,* while virtue ethics is a theory about *good character.* There are different forms of virtue ethics, but all of them address four questions: (1) What is it to live well? (2) What traits of character (virtues) does one need to live well? (3) What is human nature like (such that one can live well and have the virtues)? (4) How can one cultivate the virtues (given what human nature is like)?

Virtue ethics can simply be a complement to a consequentialist or rule-deontological position. For example, a consequentialist like Bentham might answer the four questions of virtue ethics in the following way. (1) What is it to live well? Living well is being happy, including taking pleasure in the happiness of others. (2) What virtues does one need to live well? One needs to be intelligent and benevolent. Intelligence is the ability to figure out the best means to achieve happiness, and benevolence is enjoying the happiness of others. (3) What is human nature like? Human nature is not fixed but is shaped by social conditioning. (4) How can one cultivate the virtues? Through good childhood education, enlightened laws, and social conditioning, humans can be taught to take happiness in helping others, and their intelligence can be maximized. So consequentialism tells us what we ought to *do,* and a "moderate virtue ethics" complements it by specifying what kind of person to *be* in order to do the right actions. Similarly, we could construct a moderate virtue ethics to accompany a rule-deontological position.

In moderate virtue ethics, claims about what kind of person one ought to be are logically dependent upon what one ought to do. However, according to "radical virtue ethics," what one ought to do is derived from what kind of person one ought to be. How would this work? One possibility is that ethics is derived from human nature. Perhaps we must first determine what the potential and limitations of human nature are, and only then can we determine our ethical obligations. For example, a radical virtue ethicist might object to Bentham's view, saying that before we know whether we ought to aim at the happiness of others, we must determine whether human nature allows us to do this. Suppose human nature makes it impossible for us to care about everyone equally. (This was the objection of some Confucians to the impartial consequentialism of the Mohists.) Or suppose human nature is purely self-interested, so that it is unnatural to care for anyone but oneself. (We'll see in a later chapter that this was the objection of Yang Zhu to both Mohist consequentialism and Confucianism.)

Many advocates of radical virtue ethics are highly particularistic. In response to the question, "What should I do?" the particularistic virtue ethicist answers, "You should do what a virtuous person would do in your particular situation." There is little to be said at a highly general level beyond this, because no simple rule captures what a virtuous person will do in every situation. She will, however, notice and appropriately respond to all kinds of aspects of situations that most of us will ignore or misinterpret. This is because the virtuous person has more wisdom than most of us. Wisdom is importantly different from intelligence. Intelligence comes in different forms, but we have ways to measure it, including IQ tests, standardized exams like SATs, and tests of skill at activities like mathematics. Wisdom is harder to quantify, but it is an important trait that we recognize and value in others. Think of someone who typically gives good advice about personal predicaments. Consider a person who is good at running meetings or solving practical problems. Imagine people who are generally happy and relaxed, but who also pay their bills, meet their deadlines, and are successful overall. All of these people are wise. One can just as easily imagine people who are extremely intelligent, but who fail miserably at all of these things, because they are not wise.

Many years ago, I was giving a guest lecture on Confucianism, and during the discussion session a young woman asked me, "What would Kongzi say if your parents didn't approve of the guy you were dating?" I could tell by the tone of her voice and the look on her face that this was not a purely hypothetical question. I began by explaining that Kongzi lived in a very patriarchal and sexist society, so he assumed that women should just marry the men their parents picked for them. However, I went on to say, we don't live in Kongzi's society, so we should focus on how contemporary Confucians would address this issue. They would probably say that it depends on the details of the situation. Do the parents dislike the guy because of his race or religion? If so, one should not follow their advice. Or do the parents dislike the guy because he treats their daughter disrespectfully? Do the young woman's friends agree with her parents' assessment? If her friends disagree among themselves, ask the friend who seems to be the best judge of people's characters. These are the kinds of questions and concerns that a wise person would begin by raising.

II. Confucianism as Virtue Ethics

It is a stereotype that Confucianism is monolithic and unchanging. In fact, Confucianism takes a variety of forms, which have evolved historically. However, Confucians disagree over the details of how to answer the four topics of virtue ethics.

1. Living Well

In the previous chapter, we saw that the Confucian conception of living well includes finding happiness and benefiting others in the everyday world, enjoying life with one's family and friends, a revivalistic use of tradition, participation in ritual, and educational activities aimed at making one a better person. A charming and moving passage that nicely illustrates the Confucian view of a good life is *Analects* 11.26:

> Zilu, Zengxi, Ran Qiu, and Zihua were seated in attendance. The
> Master said to them, "I am older than any of you, but do not feel

reluctant to speak your minds on that account. You are all in the habit of complaining, 'No one appreciates me.' Well, if someone were to appreciate you, what would you do?"

Zilu spoke up immediately. "If I were given charge of a state of a thousand chariots—even one hemmed in between powerful states, suffering from armed invasions and afflicted by famine—before three years were up I could infuse its people with courage and a sense of what is right."

The Master smiled at him.

Ran Qiu and Zihua (who noticed that Kongzi smirked at Zilu because of his overconfident answer) then tried to outdo each other in giving increasingly humble descriptions of their own political aspirations. Finally, Kongzi turned to Zengxi:

Zengxi stopped strumming his zither, and as the last notes faded away he set the instrument aside and rose to his feet. "I would choose to do something quite different from any of the other three."

"What harm is there in that?" the Master said. "We are all just talking about our aspirations."

Zengxi then said, "In the third month of Spring, once the Spring garments have been completed, I should like to assemble a company of five or six young men and six or seven boys to go and bathe in the Yi River and enjoy the breeze upon the Rain Dance Altar, and then return singing to the Master's house."

The Master sighed deeply, saying, "I am with Zengxi!"

Zilu, Ran Qiu and Zihua all aspire to help others via participation in government. This is a central aspect of the Confucian vision. However, Kongzi sighs in agreement with Zengxi, because his aspiration expresses the fact that political activity is merely a means to something that is even more important in Confucianism: enjoying simple everyday pleasures like a walk down to the river, going for a swim, singing, and hanging out with your friends and family.

2. The Virtues

So which virtues does Kongzi think one needs to live such a life? Kongzi's primary virtue term is *rén* 仁, which several fine translations render "Goodness." This reflects the fact that *ren* is, in a way, the highest human excellence for Kongzi. I slightly prefer to translate *ren* as "humaneness," for several reasons. First, "humaneness" suggests that one of the most important aspects of *ren* is "caring for others" (12.22). Indeed, for later Confucians this is its primary sense. Second, just as the word "humaneness" has the word "human" in it, so does the character *rén* 仁 have *rén* 人, "person," in it. (The other part of *rén* 仁 is 二, "two," suggesting that this is a virtue manifested in relationships between people.) Ultimately, though, it doesn't make much difference whether one says "Goodness," "humaneness," or something else, as long as one remembers that *ren* is the most important virtue for Kongzi, and it is manifested primarily in caring for others.[1]

Almost as important as Goodness, for Kongzi, is wisdom. The relationship between the two virtues is illustrated when a disciple, Fan Chi, "asked about Goodness":

> The Master replied, "Care for others."
> He then asked about wisdom.
> The Master replied, "Know others."
> Fan Chi still did not understand, so the Master elaborated: "Raise up the straight and apply them to the crooked, and the crooked will be made straight." (12.22; cf 2.19)

"Straight" and "crooked" are metaphors for moral rectitude and corruption, so to "raise up the straight" refers to Kongzi's strategy for reforming government by putting people with good character into positions of authority. Kongzi is implying that two traits are necessary to carry out this policy. One must be Good, which entails caring about the well-being of others, but caring is not enough. One must also be wise, which involves being able to recognize who is upright and who is corrupt. Without Goodness, one lacks the proper motivation; without wisdom, one lacks the skill to achieve one's goal.[2]

An important part of wisdom is being able to judge the character of others. Indeed, much of Book 5 of the *Analects* is taken up with Kongzi's appraisals of other people. For contemporary Western readers, Kongzi's emphasis on judging others may seem off-putting because we live in a society that frowns on people who are judgmental. But there is great irony in this, because to condemn others for being judgmental is to judge them yourself. This is more than an amusing paradox. The fact is, it is impossible to live without sometimes evaluating others. We all condemn certain kinds of people, such as the racist, the misogynist, and the child molester. And if

---

1. Some of the many passages in the *Analects* that discuss Goodness include 1.2, 1.3, 3.3, 4.1–6, 5.8, 5.19, 6.30, 7.30, 9.1*, 12.1–2, 14.1, 14.4, 15.9, 15.36, 17.6*, and 17.21.
2. Other passages that discuss Goodness and wisdom together include 4.1, 4.2, 6.22, 6.23, 9.29, 15.33*, and 17.8.

we are to be fair to our friends, we need to *evaluate* whether, for example, they are being honest for our own good, blunt but a bit tactless, or simply hurtful when they tell us a truth we do not want to hear. If being judgmental is a vice, it cannot mean simply having opinions about others, because we cannot help having opinions. Rather, to be judgmental is really to make judgments about others in a manner that is not informed and not thoughtful. A person cannot begin to be informed and thoughtful in her opinions as long as she keeps telling herself that she (unlike everyone else in the world) does not make any judgments.

The virtue of humility is required in order to avoid being judgmental, so Kongzi encourages us to "not delay in reforming if you make a mistake" (1.8*). He does not think he is above this advice: he admits that he is sometimes wrong in his judgments about others (2.9, 5.10), and he frequently notes his own failings (7.3, 7.33, 7.34, 9.8*) and praises the excellences of others (5.9). Kongzi sums up the importance of thoughtful evaluation when he says, "When walking with two other people, I will always find a teacher among them. I focus on those who are good and seek to emulate them, and focus on those who are bad in order to be reminded of what needs to be changed in myself" (7.22).

Appreciating the good and bad points of others is an important part of wisdom, but not the only one. Wisdom is also a metavirtue, in the sense that it requires understanding and being committed to other virtues. Thus, Kongzi asks, "How could someone who does not choose to dwell in Goodness be considered wise?" (4.1). General intelligence seems to be a third part of wisdom for Kongzi (5.9), as manifested in such things as interpreting the *Odes* with insight (1.15, 3.8, 3.11).[3]

Those who are familiar with Western ethics might wonder how Confucian wisdom differs from *phronēsis,* or "practical wisdom," in Aristotelian thought. There are some striking similarities. For both Kongzi and Aristotle, wisdom is something very different from theoretical intelligence, and it cannot be fully captured in any set of rules. Whereas some philosophers (such as the Mohists and Western utilitarians) think of ethics as being almost like mathematics, Confucians and Aristotelians conceive of wisdom as more like the learnable but uncodifiable skill of a master craftsperson. Furthermore, for both Confucians and Aristotelians, wisdom requires understanding and being committed to the other virtues. However, there are important differences between the two views as well. For Aristotle, *phronēsis* is the master virtue that subsumes

---

3. Other passages about wisdom (sometimes also translated as "knowledge" or "understanding") include 2.17*, 5.18*, 7.20, 7.28, 8.9, 11.12, 15.4*, 15.8*, 15.34*, 16.8, 16.9, 17.3*, 17.24*, 19.25*, and 20.3*.

all the others. In contrast, Goodness is the overarching virtue in the thought of Kongzi.

Righteousness, dutifulness, trustworthiness, and courage are four virtues that are important for Kongzi but much more narrow than Goodness. The Good person will possess these lesser virtues, but none of them, by itself, is sufficient to render a person Good. Righteousness is the integrity of a person who will not do what is wrong, even when confronted with strong temptations. The same Chinese term is used to describe the rightness of the actions the righteous person performs. In fact, many interpreters of the *Analects* consistently translate it "rightness" because they think that (for Kongzi at least) it is primarily a quality of actions rather than the name of a virtue. Insofar as it may be considered a virtue, it is clear that a righteous person does what is right even in the face of danger or the lure of wealth: "The gentleman understands rightness, whereas the petty person understands profit" (4.16).[4]

Myth: "Chinese characters are all pictures."

Fact: Fewer than 3 percent of Chinese characters were originally pictograms or ideograms. So what are they? Read Appendix B to find out.

Dutifulness and trustworthiness are virtues that Kongzi frequently mentions together (1.4, 1.8*, 5.28, 7.25*, 12.10*, 15.6*). Dutifulness is a sort of devotion or loyalty, especially when that commitment conflicts with one's own self-interest (5.19). However, Kongzi stresses that dutifulness is never blind loyalty: "If you care for someone, can you fail to encourage him? If you are dutiful to someone, can you fail to instruct him?" (14.7*).

As the structure of the character suggests, to be trustworthy (*xìn* 信) is to be a person (*rén* 人) who stands by his words (*yán* 言): to be honest and sincere. This is important for Kongzi, because he sees a key difference between genuine Goodness and the superficial semblance of Goodness that is provided by being "glib" (15.11) or having a "clever tongue" (1.3). A true gentleman is reticent (12.3*) and does not promise more than he can deliver (14.27).

Kongzi distinguishes being courageous from being rash. Thus, when the always headstrong Zilu expresses a willingness to rush into a dangerous situation, Kongzi dryly remarks, "Zilu's fondness for courage exceeds my own" (5.7*). A person does not lack courage because she is unwilling to expose herself to needless danger. Rather, "to see what is right yet not do it is to lack courage" (2.24*). This is similar to the view of most Western virtue ethicists. However, Aristotle and Plato considered courage an extremely important vir-

---

4. Other passages that discuss rightness/righteousness include 1.13*, 2.24*, 4.10, 5.16*, 6.22*, 7.3, 7.16, 12.10*, 12.20*, 13.4, 14.12, 14.13, 15.17*, 15.18, 16.10*, and 16.11*.

tue, whereas Kongzi seldom mentions it, and he seems to spend more time discouraging excessive courage than he does encouraging genuine courage (8.2, 8.10*, 14.4, 14.12, 17.8, 17.23, and 17.24*; but contrast 9.29). This may have something to do with the fact that a paradigm of courage (in both China and the West) is bravery in battle; however, Kongzi wanted to discourage his contemporaries from thinking in militaristic terms as much as possible.

A number of other virtues are named in the *Analects,* but the preceding are the most important.

3. Ethical Cultivation and Human Nature

It is not surprising that a philosopher's conception of human nature and her theory of ethical cultivation are typically closely related: how we should cultivate the human potential to be virtuous depends upon what that potential is. We saw in the previous chapter that Kongzi stresses both thinking and learning in ethical cultivation (2.15). But Kongzi was vague about the relative importance of these two factors and how they relate to human nature. Consequently, this was the subject of intense debate in the later Confucian tradition. Here I shall present an interpretation of Kongzi that is close to that of Xunzi. However, be aware that for the last millennium, most Confucians have believed that Mengzi's position best elaborates what is implicit in Kongzi's thought.[5]

One of the disciples closest to Kongzi remarked that one could not hear him talk about human nature (5.13). Indeed, his only explicit statement on the topic is that "By nature people are similar; they diverge as the result of practice" (17.2). But this is so vague that it is consistent with almost any view; human nature could be good, bad, or morally neutral. Kongzi does seem to have an implicit view of human nature, though. He praises a disciple who compares ethical cultivation to the laborious process of grinding and polishing jade (1.15). Furthermore, in what has been called Kongzi's "spiritual autobiography," he describes how he committed himself to learning at the age of fifteen and only fifty-five years later, at the age of seventy, could he "follow [his] heart's desires without overstepping the bounds of propriety" (2.4). And in a pronouncement to his most talented disciple, Kongzi characterizes Goodness as "restraining yourself and turning to the rites" (12.1). Taken together, these comments suggest that humans are not innately disposed toward the virtues and that human nature is actually very resistant to ethical cultivation.

---

5. For Xunzi, see Chapter 10; for Mengzi's view, see Chapter 6; for later Confucian views of Kongzi, see Chapter 12.

Becoming ethical is a process of re-forming a nature with desires and dispositions that are actively opposed to virtue (such as arrogance, combativeness, inflexibility, greed, and lust). Although thinking is certainly important, what is really crucial in becoming a better person is to reshape oneself through studying classic texts, participating in communal rituals, and modeling oneself on sages and worthies.

It might not be clear at first why the issue of human nature is important, but consider some of the alternatives to Kongzi's view, which we shall explore in later chapters. The Mohists held that human nature is morally neutral and highly malleable, so that humans can easily be led to care for everyone impartially. Yang Zhu claimed that human nature is self-interested, so that trying to force humans to act for the benefit of others is impractical. Mengzi argued that human nature is good, so we innately have compassion for others, but this care is naturally stronger for our relatives and friends than for strangers. Finally, Xunzi stated explicitly that human nature is bad, in the sense that our innate desires are opposed to the Way, so we must arduously cultivate virtues that we do not have at birth.

III. Limitations of Confucianism

Now that we understand (at least at a basic level) what Kongzi's Way is, we are ready to discuss some common objections to it. We have seen that Kongzi is committed to a thoughtful and revivalistic appropriation of culture rather than blind traditionalism. Nonetheless, Kongzi does state, "I transmit rather than creating" (7.1), and many later Confucians have emphasized the conservative aspects of his teachings. The Mohists raise a sensible objection to this kind of traditionalism:

> Confucians say, "A gentleman conforms to the old rather than creating." We answer them: In antiquity Yi created the bow, Zhu created armor, Xi Zhong created vehicles, and Qiao Chui created boats. Would they say that the tanners, armorers, and carpenters of today are all gentleman, whereas Yi, Yu, Xi Zhong, and Qiao Chui were all petty people? Moreover, some of those whom the Confucians follow must have been creators. So (according to their own teaching) what they conform to is the Way of petty people.[iii]

If the Confucians acknowledge that the sages of the past created new things (like Fu Xi teaching people to hunt, Shen Nong inventing farming, and the Yellow Emperor's wife discovering the secret to silk making), how can they deny that people of the present and future will continue to innovate and create worthwhile texts, institutions, inventions, and ideas?

A second limitation of Confucianism is that it does not have a pluralistic conception of living well. The traditional Chinese social hierarchy was, from top to bottom, scholars-farmers-craftsmen-merchants. Ideally, people recognized that each class was necessary for the proper functioning of society and that membership in a class should be determined by talent rather than birth (so Shun, born a farmer, became Emperor Shun). However, being a scholar is simply a better life than being a farmer, which is a better life than being a merchant. In contrast, according to pluralism, there is more than one way to live a good life. The pluralist says that a senator, a kindergarten teacher, a corporate CEO, an auto mechanic, and a jazz musician all have the potential to lead equally worthwhile lives.[6]

In summary, traditional Confucianism has two major limitations: (1) it assumes all worthwhile cultural, social, and ethical innovation has already occurred; and (2) it does not recognize the plurality of worthwhile ways of life. Contemporary advocates of Confucianism as a philosophy acknowledge that these are weaknesses. However, they argue that the fundamental insights and values of Confucianism can be made consistent with recognition of social evolution and pluralism. For example, contemporary Confucians agree that democracy is a much better form of government than the paternalistic monarchy that Kongzi himself envisioned. However, they will add that even democracies need government officials who have virtues like Goodness, wisdom, and dutifulness. Similarly, present-day Confucians acknowledge that many different kinds of wedding and funeral ceremonies can perform the same functions as did the rituals of Kongzi's era.

There continues to be much debate about the extent to which Confucianism can be made consistent with modern life and whether a modernized Confucianism would be a quaint anachronism or a valuable contribution to contemporary thought. In this respect, Confucianism is in the same boat with other great traditional systems of thought, including Buddhism, Christianity, Hinduism, Islam, and Judaism.

IV. Kongzi's Particularism

We noted that moderate virtue ethics is logically subordinate to consequentialism or rule-deontology, while radical virtue ethics takes good character to

---

6. See Appendix A for a discussion of pluralism and an explanation of how it differs from relativism.

be more fundamental. Kongzi's Way seems to be a sort of radical virtue ethics. For Kongzi, the Way does not simply aim to produce the best consequences overall. Indeed, Kongzi suggests that aiming at benefit is characteristic of a petty person rather than a true gentleman. Kongzi certainly did take very seriously ethical rules, such as those provided by the rituals. However, there is something more fundamental than the rituals, since Kongzi allows for ritual change or even violations of ritual in some cases.

Consider the immense variation in the answers Kongzi gives to the same question. When he is asked about Goodness, he gives five different answers to five different disciples (6.22, 12.1, 12.2, 12.3*, and 17.6*). He is asked how to govern a state on six occasions, and on each he gives a different answer (12.7, 12.11, 12.14*, 12.17, 13.1*, and 13.16). Kongzi's variability apparently puzzled even some of his own disciples. On one occasion, Kongzi's disciple Zilu asked whether one should immediately put into practice a moral teaching one has learned. Kongzi responded in the negative, telling Zilu that one must first seek the advice of one's elders before acting. Later, Ran Qiu asked the very same question: should one immediately put into practice a moral teaching one has heard? Kongzi replied that one should indeed act immediately. A third disciple heard both exchanges, and asked Kongzi why he gave different answers to the same question. Kongzi replied simply, "Ran Qiu is overly cautious, so I wished to urge him on. Zilu, on the other hand, is too impetuous, and so I sought to hold him back" (11.22).

Kongzi hoped to produce gentlemen, people who had genuine Virtue (regardless of their original social class). These gentlemen would have compassion for the suffering of others and the wisdom to know how to respond to the complex and fluid political and social situations they faced. They would take seriously and generally uphold the moral rules, rituals, and laws handed down by tradition, but their virtues would enable them to go beyond any rules or formulations if required by the details of a particular situation.

Don't we need more specific guidance about following the Way than this? Some philosophers long for a clearer and more direct standard for ethics. We turn to such a thinker in the next chapter.

Review Questions

1. How does consequentialism differ from deontology?
2. How is rule-consequentialism different from act-consequentialism?
3. How is rule-deontology different from act-deontology?
4. Explain the generalism-particularism spectrum.
5. What are the four questions virtue ethics addresses?

6. What is the difference between moderate and radical virtue ethics?
7. What is Goodness for Kongzi?
8. What are the different aspects of wisdom for Kongzi?
9. Explain the four other major virtues that Kongzi discusses.
10. How does Kongzi's implicit view of human nature seem to require him to emphasize learning to a somewhat greater extent than thinking?

■ 4 ■

MOHIST CONSEQUENTIALISM

When one advances claims, one must first establish a standard of assessment. To make claims in the absence of such a standard is like trying to establish on the surface of a spinning potter's wheel where the sun will rise and set. Without a fixed standard, one cannot clearly ascertain what is right and wrong or what is beneficial and harmful.

—*Mozi,* "A Condemnation of Fatalism"

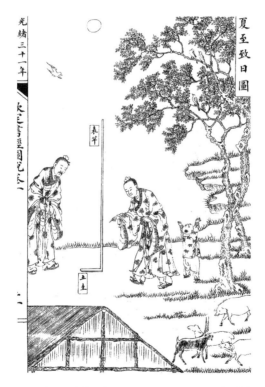

According to a myth recorded in the *History,* Sage-King Yao ordered the Xi and He brothers to determine the times of the solstices and equinoxes. Above is an illustration of one of the Xi brothers using a gnomon to perform this task.

I have offered a sympathetic portrayal of Confucianism, but not everyone in ancient China had a positive view of Kongzi or Confucians in general. The first major alternative philosophical and social movement was Mohism, which said that a typical Confucian

> is indolent and arrogant. Self-indulgent in drinking and eating and too lazy to work, he often suffers from hunger and cold and is in danger of freezing and starvation, but lacks the ability to avert them. He behaves like a beggar, grasps food like a hamster, stares blankly like a he-goat, and rises up like a pig. When the gentlemen all laugh at him, he becomes angry and exclaims, "What do undisciplined men know about a good Confucian like me?" In spring and summer he begs for grain. After the five grains are gathered, he resorts to conducting funerals. . . . When a death takes place in a rich family he will rejoice greatly, for it is his opportunity for clothing and food.[i]

In the same passage, the Mohists accused Kongzi of everything from hypocrisy to encouraging a war merely because of a personal grudge he had against a ruler.

The founder of this movement, Mozi, lived during the fifth century BCE. We don't know much about his life, but one intriguing anecdote is that Mozi heard the state of Chu was planning to attack the state of Song and immediately visited the ruler of Chu to try to dissuade him. The ruler was unconvinced by Mozi's arguments that the attack would be both unrighteous and disadvantageous to Chu, so Mozi took off his belt and put it on the floor in the shape of a city wall. He invited Chu's top general to explain how he would breach the wall. The general proposed nine strategies, and Mozi explained how Song could defeat each of them. Frustrated, the general said, "I know how to defeat you, but I will not say it." Mozi cagily replied, "And I know how you can defeat me, but I will not say it." The ruler of Chu insisted that Mozi say what he thought the general's secret strategy was, and Mozi explained that the general planned to have him murdered so that he could not tell the people of Song how to repulse Chu's attacks. However, Mozi added, I already have three hundred disciples on the walls of the capital city of Song. Even if you kill me, they will use my techniques against you. The ruler of Chu thereupon gave up his plan to attack Song, and let Mozi go.[ii]

As this anecdote suggests, the Mohists were opposed to aggressive warfare aimed at obtaining wealth or power. In this respect, they did not disagree with the Confucians. Where the Mohists did differ from the Confucians was in promoting defensive warfare by inventing new defensive military technologies, which they freely taught. The Mohists believed that if every state could mount a strong defense, everyone would come to recognize the futility of warfare, thereby bringing about peace. For example, a common offensive strategy in both China and the West was to tunnel under a defensive wall to either collapse the wall or sneak troops inside the city. One Mohist innovation was to dig a tunnel on the inside of a city wall and put a large drum at the bottom, which would resonate with and amplify the sound of enemy miners so they could be detected. More than two thousand years later, the television show *Mythbusters* recreated the Mohist technique and verified that it works as well as or better than contemporary electronic amplifiers!^{liii}

I. The Fixed Standard of Consequentialism

The Mohist emphasis on defensive military technology was not their most fundamental difference from Confucianism, though. As the quotation that heads this chapter suggests, the Way of Mozi is based on the search for a fixed standard. Contrast this with the particularism that was central to the Way of Kongzi. He said, "With regard to the world, the gentleman has no predispositions for or against anything. He merely seeks to be on the side of what is right" (4.10). The Mohists would ask how it is possible to determine what is right without first establishing a "standard of assessment" (*Readings*, p. 111).

The Mohists found their fixed standard in the perspective of Heaven. "I hold to the will of Heaven as a wheelwright holds to his compass and a carpenter his square," Mozi said. This provides "the clearest standard in all the world" (94). Of course, Confucians also appealed to Heaven as a justification for their Way. But for the Mohists what is most distinctive about the perspective of Heaven is that it is perfectly impartial: Heaven "sheds light upon all impartially" and "lays claim to all impartially" (93). Consequently, the obligation "of a benevolent person is to promote what is beneficial to the world and eliminate what is harmful" (68) without any partiality toward one's own state, city, family, or friends. Mozi had high hopes that such impartiality would be a panacea for the ills of his era:

> If people regarded other people's states in the same way that they regard their own, who then would incite their own state to attack that of another? For one would do for others as one would do for oneself. . . . If people regarded other people's families in the same way that they regard their own, who then would incite their own family to attack that of another? For one would do for others as one would do for oneself. (*Mozi* 16; *Readings*, pp. 68–69)

Mozi evaluates actions or rules in terms of their benefits for people in general, which makes Mohism a form of consequentialism. Any consequentialist ethics needs a conception of what counts as benefits as opposed to what counts as harms. Jeremy Bentham's utilitarianism identified pleasure as what is good or beneficial, and pain as what is bad or harmful. The Mohists give a more objective characterization of benefit as wealth, populousness, and social order, and of harm as poverty, depopulation, and social chaos (e.g., *Readings*, pp. 61, 80, 110).

The Mohists' conception of benefits require some explanation. It may seem surprising that any Chinese philosopher advocated populousness as a goal in itself. However, China's overpopulation problem is a recent phenomenon. Ancient China had the opposite concern. So many lives were lost due to war, disease, and famine that states competed to attract immigrants to farm their lands and man their armies. Wealth might seem more obvious as a goal. However, it is important to understand that by "wealth" the Mohists meant material goods that meet basic human needs. They felt that luxury goods waste resources better spent on other things:

> What is the purpose of clothes? It is to protect us from the cold of winter and the heat of summer. The proper way to make clothes is such that they keep one warm in winter and cool in summer and that is all. Whatever does not contribute to these ends should be eliminated. What is the purpose of houses? It is to protect us from the wind and cold of winter, the heat and rain of summer, and to keep out robbers and thieves. Once these ends are secured that is all. Whatever does not contribute to these ends should be eliminated. (*Mozi* 20; *Readings*, p. 78)

Order may seem like a vague goal, but the Mohists simply meant by "order" a society in which violence, thievery, and civil war are lessened as much as possible (and ideally eliminated).

II. Criticisms of Confucianism

On the basis of their consequentialist values, the Mohists rejected several aspects of Confucian ritual practices. Confucian funerals waste wealth, the Mohists argued, because they require such things as inner and outer coffins, special garments for the deceased, and ritual utensils that are left in the grave. They decrease population because they encourage mourning to the extent that it endangers health and discourages procreation. Finally, because those mourning their relatives are prohibited from working, social order will decay as those in government abandon their official posts and farmers abandon their fields. The Mohists did not want to completely eliminate burial, of course. They merely advocated "moderation in funerals," so that they would be less expensive. As for mourning, they said, "there should be crying as one sees the departed off and as one comes back from the grave. But as soon as people have returned to their homes, they should resume their individual livelihoods" (89).

Many other Confucian rituals involved elaborate musical performances and ritual dances. Consequently, when Mozi repeatedly announced "Musical performances are wrong!" he was criticizing Confucianism. The Mohist position on music is easy to misunderstand. They were not against all music and certainly would not ban simple singing and dancing. What the Mohists opposed were elaborate orchestral performances by professional musicians and dancers. The Mohists argued that such performances waste resources in at least three ways. First, the people must be taxed in order to make the instruments and the ritual accoutrements of the dancers. Then skilled men and women must be diverted from productive occupations to play the instruments and perform the dances. Finally, the audiences who attend the performances will be taking time away from their own jobs.[1]

Myth: "A traditional Chinese curse is 'May you live in interesting times.'"

Fact: No Chinese source has ever been found for this quaint quotation.

Perhaps the most significant challenge to Confucianism stems from the impartiality of Mohist ethics. Recall that Confucians advocated differentiated caring, the doctrine that one should care more for and have stronger moral obligations toward friends and relatives than strangers. (*Analects* 13.18, in which Kongzi condemns a son who turns in his father for stealing, is a classic expression of this position.) The Mohists strongly rejected this doctrine, stating that "it is those who are partial in their dealings with others who are the real cause of all the great harms in the world. This is why our teacher Mozi says, 'I condemn partiality'" (68). However, the Mohists recognized that differentiated caring was the common sense view of most people in their society (as well as in our own). Consequently, the Mohists had to *argue* for this conclusion.

An argument is different from either an assertion or a quarrel. An *assertion* is a statement that one has not yet substantiated. A *quarrel* is a mutual expression of disagreement, typically one that involves some animosity. So if Susan says simply, "Capital punishment is murder," she is making an assertion. If

---

1. See *Mozi* 32; *Readings,* pp. 105–10.

John and Susan are standing outside a prison and John chants, "Make the guilty pay for their crimes!" while Susan, on the other side of the barricade, shouts, "Capital punishment is murder!" they are having a quarrel. In contrast to both an assertion and a quarrel, an *argument* attempts to provide good justification for accepting a particular conclusion. Different cultures and different historical eras have different conceptions of what counts as a good argument. However, in every culture that has been studied, humans engage in argumentation and distinguish between good and bad arguments in one way or another. Therefore, in order to understand another culture, we have to take their arguments seriously as arguments. In other words, we have to evaluate whether their arguments really do provide good justifications for their conclusions. To try to understand the arguments of another culture without judging whether they are persuasive is like trying to learn French without ever using it to say or do anything.

There are some arguments in the *Analects*. However, one of the reasons that the Mohists are so important is that they pioneered the extensive use of explicit argumentation in Chinese philosophy. One argumentative technique the Mohists developed is the "thought experiment" (also known by its German name, "Gedankenexperiment"). In a thought experiment, you imagine what would happen in a hypothetical situation, as a way of discovering facts or values that you did not previously realize were consequences of your current beliefs and commitments. That's a bit abstract, so let's look at how the Mohists use a thought experiment to argue in favor of impartial caring:

> Suppose there were two people: one who maintains partiality and one who maintains impartiality. . . . And so when his friends are hungry, the partial person does not feed them. When his friends are cold, he does not clothe them. When his friends are ill, he does not nurture them. [However,] when the impartial person's friends are hungry, he feeds them. When his friends are cold, he clothes them. When his friends are ill, he nurtures them. . . . Suppose one must put on one's armor and helmet and go to war in a vast and open wilderness where life and death are uncertain; or suppose one was sent by one's ruler or high minister to the distant states of Ba, Yue, Qi, or Jing and could not be sure of either reaching them or ever returning from one's mission. Under such conditions of uncertainty, to whom would one entrust the well-being of one's parents, wife, and children? Would one prefer that they be in the care of an impartial person or would one prefer that they be in the care of a partial person? I believe that under such circumstances, there are no fools in all

the world. Even though one may not advocate impartiality, one would certainly want to entrust one's family to the person who is impartial. But this is to condemn impartiality in word but prefer it in deed, with the result that one's actions do not accord with what one says. And so I don't see what reason any person in the world who has heard about impartiality can give for condemning it. (*Mozi* 16; *Readings*, pp. 69–70)

This is sometimes referred to as the Caretaker Argument. When you encounter an argument in a text, you should first try to paraphrase the argument in your own words, making clear what conclusion the argument is trying to establish. Next, you should evaluate the argument, deciding why you think it does or does not provide a good justification for its conclusion.

There is more than one right way to paraphrase and evaluate an argument, but this is how I interpret the Caretaker Argument. The Mohists invite us to imagine a situation in which we are sent on a dangerous mission from which we may not return. In such a situation, should we entrust the care of our spouse, children, and elderly parents to a partial person or an impartial person? The impartial person (who follows Mohist teachings) would care for our relatives as if they were his own relatives. In contrast, the partial person would not care for our relatives at all. The Mohists conclude that anyone would prefer to leave their relatives in the care of the impartial person. They think this demonstrates that we are all committed to supporting impartiality, whether we recognize it or not.

Now let's evaluate the Mohist argument. First, is it true that we would prefer an impartial caretaker to a partial caretaker? Given how the Mohists have characterized our two options, it seems clear that we would in fact prefer the impartial person as the caretaker, because the partial person would not care for our relatives at all. However, there is a significant problem with the Mohist argument, because it is presenting us with what is technically called a "false dichotomy." In a false dichotomy, someone says that we must choose either P or Q, but in actuality there are other options open to us. The Mohists suggest that we must pick either a caretaker who cares for everyone impartially or a caretaker who is so selfish that he doesn't care for anyone other than himself. But there is obviously a third option here: a Confucian, who cares for everyone to some extent but cares more for his friends than for strangers. So the real question is this: would you entrust your family to (1) someone who is completely selfish and does *not* care for your family at all, (2) a Mohist, who cares for your family *as much as* he cares for everyone else, or (3) a Confucian, who cares *more* for your family than he does for strangers because he is your friend? There is good reason to believe that a Confucian who is your friend would often do a better job of taking care of your family than a Mohist. Perhaps there are some special circumstances in which an impartialist would take better care of your family than a Confucian, but because their argument offers a false dichotomy, the Mohists have not shown that we are all implicitly committed to impartiality.

The Mohists not only argue in favor of impartial caring, they also respond to some objections against it, including the suggestion that it is impractical because it demands a level of impartiality that is inconsistent with human nature. The Mohist Practicability Argument cites several examples of rulers who achieved striking modifications of seemingly natural human behavior among their subjects:

> In the past, King Ling of the state of Chu was fond of slender waists. During his reign the people of Chu ate no more than one meal a day and became so weak that they could not raise themselves up without the support of a cane nor could they walk without leaning against a wall. Curtailing one's food is something very difficult to do, but masses of people did it in order to please King Ling. Within a single generation the people changed because they wanted to accord with the wishes of their superior. (*Mozi* 16; *Readings,* p. 75)

The Mohists also give the examples of a ruler who was so fond of bravery that his soldiers would march onto burning ships at his command and a ruler whose subjects wore coarse, uncomfortable clothing to please him. On this basis, they conclude,

> If only there were superiors who delighted in them, who encouraged their practice through rewards and praise, and threatened those who violate them with penalties and punishments . . . the people would take to impartially caring for and benefiting one another just as naturally as fire rises up and water flows down. (*Mozi* 16; *Readings,* p. 76)

People often object at this point that the Mohists are being inconsistent, because forcing one's subjects to starve themselves, or march onto burning ships, or wear uncomfortable clothing is a *violation* of impartial caring rather than an example of it. This objection misses the Mohists' point, though. They are not advocating the specific policies of the preceding rulers. They simply cited them to illustrate the general point that human motivations and dispositions are almost infinitely malleable. In other words, the Mohists deny that there is a fixed human nature that puts practical and ethical constraints on our behavior. Rather, humans are shaped by the rewards and punishments in their environment. So humans can be led to act in accordance with impartial caring (or anything else, for that matter).

So how should we evaluate the Practicability Argument? The prevalence of eating disorders and unrealistic expectations about weight and body image in our own society lends great poignancy to the example of King Ling of Chu. However, the Mohists made a universal claim about the plasticity of human motivations based only on a few specific examples. This is a weakness of any anecdotal argument. In order to properly evaluate the Mohist claim, we would need to consider much more evidence about the extent to which human behavior varies in different cultural settings. Modern anthropology has undertaken just this sort of investigation. But the findings are complex and the conclusions of anthropologists are varied.

Western anthropology developed against the background of Enlightenment thinkers who tended to assume that human nature is fixed and universal. When other cultures failed to manifest what was regarded as normal human behavior, they were dismissed as primitive or inferior to Western culture. However, twentieth-century anthropology, especially under the influence of Franz Boas and his students Margaret Mead and Ruth Benedict, embraced the diversity of cultural practices. Indeed, some went so far as to suggest that humans are almost purely a *tabula rasa,* a blank slate, on which experience and social conditioning write. In other words, they came close to the Mohist position.

Recently, some anthropologists have argued for a more moderate position, which perhaps does the most justice to the actual evidence. Human cultures do share certain general features: all cultures make jokes, have rituals of some kind for mourning the dead, compose verse and distinguish it from prose, recognize the same facial expressions for seven basic emotions (anger, happiness, fear, surprise, disgust, sadness, and contempt), have a taboo against at least some kinds of incest, mark the distinction between male and female in some way, and so on. However, the specific manner in which these features are manifested varies from culture to culture. To pick an obvious example, all cultures have language, but the languages they speak vary.[iv]

How does this apply to the issue of impartial caring? There certainly are some people who achieve impartial caring. For example, Buddhist monks like the Dalai Lama and Catholic nuns like the late Mother Teresa seem to have achieved such universal compassion; in pursuit of this goal, they have taken vows of celibacy to discourage attachments that might hinder impartiality. However, we admire such individuals in part because they are so unusual.

The particular forms that differentiated caring takes vary greatly. In traditional Chinese culture, one has strong obligations even to very distant relations in one's extended family. In contrast, in the contemporary United States some people have only sporadic—or no—communication with extended family members. Nonetheless, the vast majority of people in every culture studied practice some version of differentiated caring. For example, I am not at all unusual in the fact that, although I hope all children are happy, I do care more for my own children than for my neighbor's children and I feel that I have a greater ethical obligation toward my own children. So the evidence suggests that converting people to impartial caring cannot be done as easily "as fire rises up and water flows down" (76).

III. Political Philosophy

A brilliant Mohist innovation was the use of a state-of-nature argument. A state-of-nature argument begins with a hypothesis about what life was like for humans prior to the institution of government and social structure. It then attempts to draw conclusions about why these conditions justify the institution of government and society. In the West, a number of philosophers, including Thomas Hobbes and John Locke, have used forms of this argument. But the Mohist version is original, distinctive, and intriguing:

> In ancient times, when people first came into being and before there were governments or laws, each person followed their own norm for deciding what was right and wrong. And so where there was one person there was one norm, where there were two people there were two norms, where there were ten people there were ten different norms. As many people as there were, that was how many norms were recognized. In this way people came to approve their own norms for what is right and wrong and thereby condemn the norms of others. . . . Throughout the world, people used water, fire, and poison to harm and injure one another, to the point where if they had strength to spare, they would not use it to help each other, if they had excess goods, they would leave them to rot away rather than distribute them to one another, and if they had helpful teachings, they would hide them away rather than teach them to one another. The chaos that ruled in the world was like what one finds among the birds and beasts. It is clear that what made the world chaotic was a lack of rulers. Hence, the most worthy and capable in the world was selected and established as the Son of Heaven. (*Mozi* 11; *Readings,* p. 65)

This argument begins with the hypothesis that without government or social-ization there would be almost unlimited variety in human values or norms. This is consistent with the Mohist view that there is no fixed human nature. If there were a human nature, we would expect humans to agree about at least some norms even in the state of nature. But if the Mohists are right that human moti-vations are the products of their environments, then the lack of a common social structure should lead humans in a dizzying diversity of directions.

The Mohists argue that this diversity of norms will lead to violence and chaos. Perhaps John believes in a strong right to private property while Jim thinks that property should be held in common. Susan thinks adultery should be a criminal offense, but Sally advocates free love. Then Jim takes something that John thinks belongs to him, so John sets fire to Jim's crops in retaliation. Susan finds out that her husband has been cheating on her with Sally, so she poisons Sally's drinking water. As long as there is no agreement over norms and no common military or police authority to enforce compliance with them, such disputes and violence will continue endlessly. The Mohists be-lieved that this chaos was what first led to an extremely benevolent and intel-ligent person being selected to be Son of Heaven (that is, the ruler of the world). The Son of Heaven decided for everyone else what was right and wrong, and appointed worthy people as ministers to assist him in carrying out these norms. He then told the people, "Whenever your superior approves of something as right you too must approve of it. Whenever your superior condemns something as wrong you too must condemn it" (66). The Mohists concluded, "If we look into how good order was maintained in the world, what do we find? Was it not simply because the Son of Heaven was able to unify the norms followed within the world that he was able to maintain good order in it?" (67).

According to the Mohist doctrine, the rule of the first Son of Heaven was successful because of the proper application of punishments and rewards. Those who violated the norms of their superiors were punished. Those who followed them and did their jobs well were given what we might call the three Ps: praise, prosperity, and promotions. The Mohists were admirably meritocratic: they stressed that these rewards should be based on actual talent and achievement, not on whether someone had aristocratic ancestors or was a relative of the king (62–63). Rulers should follow the ancient sage-kings in "honoring the worthy," the policy that even "someone who worked as a farm-er, artisan, or merchant, if they had talent they were promoted, given high rank and a handsome salary, entrusted with responsibility, and empowered to have their orders obeyed" (63).

The Mohist doctrine of the malleability of human motivations plays a role again here. They believed that proper rewards and punishments would result in not only behavioral compliance with standardized social norms, but would actually get everyone to personally accept those norms (just like the soldiers of the King of Yue who became so committed to bravery that they would burn or drown themselves at his command [75–76]).

From our contemporary perspective, the Mohist position may seem highly authoritarian. But it is important to keep in mind that neither the Mohists nor the Confucians—nor anyone else in ancient China—even considered democracy as a political system. Given that China in that era was a massive state with a population composed largely of illiterate peasants and lacking in easy means of transportation or communication, democracy would not have been practical anyway. Furthermore, the Mohists did recognize some role for criticism of the government: "Should a superior commit any transgression, one must offer proper remonstrance" (66). Of course, this criticism would have to be in line with the official norms.

A final limitation on the authoritarianism of the Mohist political philosophy is that the norms and actions of the Son of Heaven are not arbitrary: "The Son of Heaven does not make up his own standard. There is Heaven to govern him" (91). And what standard does Heaven use? "Heaven desires [the world] to have life and dislikes death, desires to have wealth and dislikes poverty, desires to have good order and dislikes disorder" (91). In other words, the Son of Heaven is answerable to Heaven, and Heaven commands that the ruler impartially benefit the people by maximizing their wealth, populousness, and social order.

IV. Divine Command Theory

We must now confront a question we have skirted up to this point. Mozi says he follows the "will of Heaven" because it is "the clearest standard in all the world" (94). But he also says that the "business of a benevolent person is to promote what is beneficial to the world and eliminate what is harmful" (68). He obviously thinks that these two standards coincide: the will of Heaven is that we be benevolent. But which standard is more fundamental to Mozi's thought? In other words, does Heaven command us to be benevolent because it is right to be benevolent, or is benevolence right only because Heaven dictates that it is right? Suppose Heaven ceased to dictate benevolence and instead commanded us to wage aggressive wars of conquest: would Mozi then say that aggressive wars are now right (because Heaven commands them), or would he say that aggressive war is still wrong (because benevolence is right, independently of Heaven's will)?

This issue has been much discussed in the West since it was raised in Plato's *Euthyphro*. In that dialogue, Socrates asks whether an action is pious because the gods approve of it or whether the gods approve of it because it is pious. Socrates argues that the gods approve of actions because they have the quality of being pious, independently of the gods' wills. Centuries later, a brilliant medieval Christian philosopher, William of Ockham, argued for the opposite conclusion. He said that what makes an action morally right is simply that God wills that it be right. Ockham's position came to be known as Divine Command Theory.

Defenders of the Platonic position point out that if Divine Command Theory were true, then there is no reason why God chose "love thy neighbor" over "wantonly slaughter the innocent" as a moral requirement. If God had willed the latter, it would then be a moral requirement. However, this seems absurd. On the other hand, defenders of Divine Command Theory ask how it is possible for any standard to constrain a supreme being. The Mohists seem to be making this point when they note that

> a standard is not given by subordinates to govern their superiors but rather must come from superiors to govern subordinates. . . . The gentlemen of the world clearly understand that the Son of Heaven governs the three high counselors and feudal lords, the ministers and officials of the people. But that Heaven governs the Son of Heaven is something that people do not yet clearly understand. (*Mozi* 26; *Readings,* p. 91)

I don't think Mozi ever confronted this issue directly, so we can't definitively determine his opinion. However, there is historical evidence and a theoretical consideration that suggest Mozi would probably reject Divine Command Theory. The historical evidence is that the Later Mohists apparently dropped all reference to "Heaven" in formulating their position.[2] They would have been unlikely to do so if the will of Heaven were a foundational notion in Mozi's ethics. What motivates philosophers like Ockham is the belief that God is radically different from the world that He created. Because God is so different, He cannot be limited by anything other than His own will, and we (as finite creatures) cannot rationally understand Him. Heaven does have some characteristics similar to those of God as conceived of in the Jewish, Christian, and Islamic traditions. However, in early Chinese thought, Heaven, Earth, and Humans are typically thought of as forming an interdependent whole, with hierarchy but without metaphysical transcendence. So the under-

---

2. We will examine the Later Mohists in Chapter 7.

lying metaphysical assumptions that motivate Divine Command Theory are simply absent in ancient China.

V. "Against Fatalism" and Dialectic

Although the Mohists believe in Heaven, they are strongly opposed to a belief in what they call fatalism. Fatalism, as the Mohists use the term, is the doctrine that "[i]f one is fated to live a long time, then one will live a long time; if one is fated to die young, then one will die young. If something is fated to occur, then no matter how hard one tries to change this, what good will it do?" (110–11). In arguing against fatalism, the Mohists developed an intriguing theory of the forms of argumentation (called "dialectic" or "rhetoric" in the West):

> When one advances claims, one must first establish a standard of assessment. To make claims in the absence of such a standard is like trying to establish on the surface of a spinning potter's wheel where the sun will rise and set. . . . And so, in assessing claims, one must use the three gauges. (*Mozi* 35; *Readings,* p. 111)

The word rendered "gauge" here is literally "gnomon." Although gnomons are no longer part of our everyday lives, civilization as we know it would never have developed without them. At its simplest, a gnomon is a straight rod perpendicular to the ground. Though very basic, it is an extremely informative astronomical tool. If you are in the northern hemisphere, when the shadow cast by the gnomon is shortest, it points due north. Gnomons can also tell the time of day (as part of a sundial) and determine when the solstices and equinoxes occur. So we can see why the Mohists would invoke the gnomon as a metaphor for evidential standards in general.

The Mohists say that the three gnomons (or gauges, as we'll call them) are precedent, evidence, and application:

- "One looks up for precedents among the affairs and actions of the ancient sage-kings."
- "One looks down to examine evidence of what the people have heard and seen."
- "One implements it as state policy and sees whether or not it produces benefit for the state, families, and people." (*Mozi* 35; *Readings,* p. 111)

The Mohists apply the gauge of precedent to the existence of fate by asking rhetorically, "Did any of the laws of the early kings ever say, 'Blessings cannot be invoked and disaster cannot be avoided; reverence will not do any good and cruelty will not do any harm'?"[v] They also cite texts in which ancient sages criticized Tyrant Jie and Tyrant Zhou for their beliefs that their reigns were fated (and hence they need not worry about governing benevolently).[vi] But why should we care what the ancient sage-kings did or said? The sage-kings are regarded as reliable authorities because they ruled well and successfully due to their benevolence and intelligence. Consequently, their actions are good models for how we should act, and their pronouncements are reliable guides to truth. Put in modern terms, we might think of them as providing expert testimony on the issues. Just as I have good reason for believing what Bill Gates says about how to build up and run a business, so do I have reason to have confidence in what is said by successful rulers like the sage-kings Shun or Wu. Does this mean that they are always right? Of course not. Expert testimony can be mistaken (just like a gnomon can fail to work on a cloudy day). Nonetheless, it is one useful indicator of truth.

The gauge of evidence is confirmation gained from our senses of sight, hearing, touch, smell, and taste. Since we frequently appeal to empirical evidence in our own culture, this may seem like a familiar and unproblematic indicator of truth. However, the Mohists use empirical evidence in a very narrow way to judge whether or not a particular entity exists. So the Mohists argue against the existence of fate by simply asking,

> From antiquity to the present, since the beginning of humans, has anyone seen such a thing as fate, or heard the sound of fate? Of course not. If you consider the common people stupid and their senses of hearing and sight unreliable, then why not inquire into the recorded statements of the feudal lords? But from antiquity to the present, since the beginning of humans, has any of them heard the sound of fate or seen such a thing as fate? Of course not.[vii]

The gauge of application is a pragmatic test: are the consequences of acting in accordance with a doctrine beneficial or harmful? Of course, it might be beneficial to believe a doctrine even though it is false. For example, positive thinking can make us better at a variety of activities, even if it gives us a slightly overoptimistic view of the situation. On the whole, though, we share the Mohist intuition that true beliefs work, while false beliefs fail. Mohists argue that the consequence of fatalism is to make people lazy and complacent:

> In ancient times, the miserable people indulged in drinking and eating and were lazy in their work. Thereupon their food and clothing became insufficient, and the danger of hunger and cold was approaching.

They did not acknowledge, "I was stupid and insolent and was not diligent at work." Instead, they would say, "It is but my fate to be poor."[viii]

The Mohists accuse the Confucians of advocating fatalism.[ix] However, this seems to be a misinterpretation. Kongzi encouraged his students to always strive to improve themselves and make the world a better place. He also believed that in the long run Heaven would reestablish the Way in the world. However, Kongzi knew that sometimes bad things happen to good people and our best efforts may fail, so he thought people would be happier and less bitter if they learned to *psychologically* accept bad luck when it befell them, while still *striving* to do the best they could. For example, when one of Kongzi's disciples expressed sadness that he had to go into exile as a result of a political setback, another disciple encouraged him by saying:

> I have heard it said, "Life and death are governed by fate, wealth and honor are determined by Heaven." A gentleman is respectful and free of errors. He is reverent and ritually proper in his dealings with others. In this way, everyone within the Four Seas is his brother. (*Analects* 12.5)

This is not encouraging the sad disciple to give up. On the contrary, the point is that he must keep doing the best he can, even while he psychologically accepts the way things are.[3]

Even if the Mohists had a clearer understanding of the Confucian view of fate, I think they would still have disagreed with it. Kongzi believed there is no guarantee that right action will be rewarded or that wrongdoing will be punished. In contrast, a key aspect of Mohist thought was that the virtuous will succeed and flourish while the evil will fail and suffer. This leads to one of the most controversial aspects of the Mohist Way.

VI. *"On Ghosts" and Truth*

Their consequentialism, interest in technology, and skillful use of argumentation make the Mohists seem akin to many modern Western secular philosophers. Consequently, their essay "On Ghosts" frequently surprises readers with its firm insistence that ghosts and spirits exist and that they intervene in human affairs to reward the virtuous and punish the wicked:

---

3. See also *Analects* 6.10, 9.5, 11.9, and 14.36 and *Mengzi* 2B13.

King Xuan of Zhou killed his minister Du Bo even though he was completely innocent. Before he died Du Bo said, "My lord is killing me even though I am completely innocent. If the dead are indeed unconscious, then that will be the end of it. But if the dead are conscious, within three years' time my lord shall know of this!" Three years later King Xuan and various feudal lords were off hunting in the wilds. There were several hundred chariots and several thousand men on foot; the hunting party filled the entire field. At high noon, Du Bo appeared in a plain chariot pulled by white horses. He was wearing vermillion clothes and a hat, holding a vermillion bow, and clasping vermillion arrows under his arm. He pursued King Xuan of Zhou and shot him as he rode in his chariot; the arrow pierced the king's heart and splintered his spine. King Xuan collapsed in his chariot and, draped over his own bow case, he died. None of the men from Zhou who were there at the time failed to witness this and none even in remote places failed to hear about it. The event was recorded in the court chronicle of Zhou. (*Mozi* 31; *Readings,* p. 96)

Although most of us find stories like this incredible, the Mohists appeal to each of the three gauges to defend the existence of ghosts and spirits. Regarding precedent, they note that "from the average person to nobles alike, all say that the sage-kings of the three dynasties are adequate models of conduct" (99). These sage-kings paid careful attention to performing ritual sacrifices and made official announcements to ghosts and spirits at the ancestral shrine and the altar of soil. This shows that "[i]n ancient times, sage-kings always showed their devotion to the ghosts and spirits in these ways and their devotion was generous and substantial" (101).

Turning to the gauge of evidence, the Mohists declare that "[i]f there really are people who have heard and seen something, then you must accept that such things exist. If no one has heard of seen anything, then you must accept that such things do not exist" (95). But there are, the Mohists claim, numerous cases of people who have heard and seen ghosts and spirits. The case of the ghost of Du Bo taking vengeance on King Xuan is a prime example. The Mohists obviously selected it carefully to answer the objections they anticipated. Perhaps King Xuan merely imagined that he saw something. No, the ghost was seen clearly by "several thousand" people at "high noon." Perhaps they did see *something,* but maybe it was just fog or an animal and King Xuan died from fright or overexertion. No, the ghost left concrete physical evidence of its actions: King Xuan's heart was pierced and his spine was splintered.

Finally, the Mohists argue that belief in ghosts and spirits satisfies the gauge of application, because "[i]f the ability of ghosts and spirits to reward the worthy and punish the wicked could be firmly established as fact throughout the empire and among the common people, it would surely bring order to the state and great benefit to the people" (104). This is because people who do not believe in ghosts and spirits mistakenly think that they can get away with wrongdoing. In reality, though, "[e]ven in the deepest valleys or vast forests, in those hidden places where no one lives, you must always act properly. For the ghosts and spirits will see what you do!" (99).

"On Ghosts" has struck some readers as so incongruous with the rational tone of the rest of the Mohist Way that they have argued the Mohists did not really believe in the existence or actions of ghosts and spirits. This suspicion gains some support from the following passage:

> If it were the case that ghosts and spirits do not really exist, then in offering sacrifices, all we would be doing is expending resources of wine and millet. But though we would be expending these resources, we would not simply be pouring the wine into a ditch or gully or throwing the millet away. Primary clan members and people living out in the villages and towns all have a chance to drink the sacrificial wine and partake of the offerings. And so even if the ghosts and spirits did not exist, these offerings would still be a means for welcoming and bringing together close family and gathering together and increasing fellowship among people living out in the villages and towns. (*Mozi* 31; *Readings,* p. 104)

So perhaps the Mohists do not really believe in ghosts and spirits but merely want to encourage "the people" to believe in them in order to promote social order. Communal rituals are simply a technique for "increasing fellowship." In addition, "if we could just persuade the people of the world to *believe* that ghosts and spirits can reward the worthy and punish the wicked, then how could the world ever become disordered?" (95; emphasis mine).

Further support for this hypothesis comes from the discomfort some readers feel with the three gauges as indicators of truth. Isn't precedence really a fallacious appeal to authority? Empirical evidence might seem like a test of truth, but perhaps it is really just an indicator of what seems plausible to the people. Finally, isn't the question of the truth of a doctrine completely distinct from the issue of whether believing it would have good consequences?

In reply to the above arguments, we note first that many brilliant people have believed in supernatural entities, including the philosophers Augustine and Thomas Aquinas. So it is narrow-minded to suggest that the Mohists could not really have believed in ghosts and spirits just because they were smart. In addition, although the Mohist application of the three gauges may be unfamiliar to us, these standards are actually in use in current society:

• Precedent: The Surgeon General has determined that smoking is hazardous to your health.

• Evidence: The coelacanth is a fish that was thought to be extinct, but samples have recently been found in fishing nets.

• Application: The herbal remedy echinacea does not help the body fight infection, because people get sick and remain sick just as long whether they take it or not.

Finally, the Mohists repeatedly and unequivocally state that ghosts and spirits really do exist. Mozi himself is quoted as stating, "The ghosts of the past and of the present are not different. There are Heavenly ghosts, there are ghosts and spirits of the mountains and waters, and there are also people who die and become ghosts."[x] In "On Ghosts" they ask in frustration six times, "How can we doubt that ghosts and spirits exist?" The Mohists even warn people that if sacrifices to the spirits are ever stopped,

> the Lord on High, ghosts, and spirits would discuss this among themselves up above, saying, "Which is better? To have or to not have such people? I suppose there is no difference to us whether they exist or not!" Then were the Lord on High, ghosts, and spirits to send down calamities and punishments and abandon such a people, would this not merely be fitting? (*Mozi* 25; *Readings,* p. 85)

The Mohists' use of this argument would be fallacious and sophistical if they did not really believe in ghosts and spirits.[xi]

VII. Historical Significance

Mohism is an original and powerful philosophical system. In its effort to find a clear, quantifiable standard for ethical evaluation in the consequences of actions, it has some similarities to Western utilitarianism. However, in its reverence for Heaven and confidence in the agency of ghosts and spirits, it is reminiscent of theology. Its well-argued challenges to lavish funerals, prolonged mourning, elaborate musical performances, and differentiated caring must have raised serious doubts about Confucianism.

Mohism died out as an independent philosophical movement at the end of the Warring States Period, but it deeply enriched Chinese philosophy with its pioneering use of techniques such as thought experiments and state-of-nature arguments. Later Confucians like Mengzi (Chapter 6) and Xunzi (Chapter 10), did not just react against Mohism, they absorbed some of its concepts and argumentative techniques. In addition, Mohism was much appreciated by many twentieth-century Chinese philosophers, particularly in the New Culture Movement (Chapter 12), who sought an alternative to Confucianism.

Although Mohism and Confucianism might seem to be polar opposites, another philosophical position arose that challenged both of them in a very fundamental way. To this philosophy we now turn.

Review Questions

1. What type of normative ethical theory is Mohism? What type is Confucianism?
2. What three benefits does Mohism seek to maximize?
3. Why did the Mohists research military technology?
4. Why did the Mohists oppose Confucian funeral and mourning practices?
5. What kind of music did the Mohists object to, and why?
6. How is an argument different from an assertion or a dispute?
7. What is a thought experiment? What is the German name for it?
8. Explain the Caretaker Argument for impartial caring.
9. What is a false dichotomy?
10. What is a state-of-nature argument? Explain the Mohist version of it.
11. What is the Mohist position on human nature? If true, how does it support their views on impartial caring and the state of nature?
12. What is Divine Command Theory? What are some arguments for and against it? What are some arguments for and against attributing such a theory to the Mohists?
13. What do the Mohists mean by "fatalism"? What was the Confucian view about fate?
14. What is a gnomon?
15. What are the three gauges? How do the Mohists apply them to fatalism and to the existence of ghosts and spirits? What are some arguments for and against the hypothesis that the Mohists did not really believe in ghosts and spirits?
16. How might Kongzi or other Confucians respond to some of the objections that the Mohists raise?

■ 5 ■

YANG ZHU AND EGOISM

Yang Zhu favored being "for ourselves." If plucking out one hair from his body would have benefited the whole world, he would not do it.

—Mengzi 7A26

A bonsai tree is a plant whose nature has been artificially warped.

Yang Zhu argued that we should act in accordance with human nature, and it is human nature to be self-interested or, as he put it, "for ourselves." Consequently, the Mohist and the Confucian Ways are both contrary to human nature, because each demands that we be willing to sacrifice ourselves for the well-being of others. This line of argument has some plausibility, especially in its original context. The Mohists and Confucians both claimed to be following the will of Heaven. But human nature is implanted in us by Heaven and what seems more natural for any human than to do what benefits him- or herself?

The preceding paragraph presents an outline of Yang Zhu's view, but we face two problems in understanding him in more detail. One is textual and one is conceptual. The textual difficulty is that there are no surviving writings by Yang Zhu. All we know about Yang Zhu is what other people said about him. In this chapter, I'll present one possible reconstruction of the Way of Yang Zhu, based on texts that may reflect his influence. But keep in mind that many scholars would disagree with my account.

The conceptual difficulty is in understanding exactly what egoism and human nature are. So before we turn to the specifics of Yang Zhu's formulation, we need to get clear about (1) the distinction between psychological egoism and ethical egoism, and (2) the notion of the nature of a thing.

I. What Is Egoism?

Psychological egoism and ethical egoism are often confused with one another, but they are actually very different doctrines. In order to understand Yang Zhu's argument, we need to clear up this confusion. Consequently, I will explain these doctrines before turning to Yang Zhu himself.

Loosely and intuitively, psychological egoism says that everyone *does* only care about him- or herself, while ethical egoism says that everyone *ought* to only care about him- or herself. More precisely and technically, psychological egoism is the doctrine that the only object of anyone's motivations is self-interest. Psychological egoism is thus a descriptive claim; it claims that something is the case. Ethical egoism is the doctrine that the only good reason anyone has for doing something is self-interest. Ethical egoism is thus a prescriptive claim; it claims that people ought to act a certain way.

1. Psychological Egoism

My experience has been that many nonphilosophers find psychological egoism plausible. They are therefore surprised to learn that almost all serious philosophers regard psychological egoism as obviously and demonstrably false. Indeed, only one major philosopher has advocated psychological egoism: Thomas Hobbes. Philosophers continue to find Hobbes interesting despite, not because of, his commitment to psychological egoism. So why are philosophers so confident that psychological egoism is mistaken?

Here are two simple, intuitive examples, each of which falsifies psychological egoism:

• Benevolence: My children saw a commercial about hungry, impoverished children in another country. They agreed to give up part of their weekly allowances to sponsor a child in that country, helping to provide her with food, medicine, and education. In other words, my children were bothered by the suffering of other children, and this motivated them to forgo some goods that they could have used to benefit themselves. Therefore, my children have at least some motivations that are not purely self-interested. So psychological egoism is false.

• Self-destruction: I have a friend who keeps trying to quit smoking for health reasons. However, she has repeatedly failed in her efforts because of her craving for nicotine. In other words, my friend gives in to her desire to smoke, even though in her own judgment it is not in her best interests to smoke. Therefore, my friend has at least one motivation that is not purely self-interested. So psychological egoism is false.

Let's examine these examples a bit more carefully. When we discuss human motivations and feelings, we can distinguish between the subject of a feeling and the object of the feeling. In other words, we can ask, *Who has this feeling?* but also *What is this feeling about?* For example, suppose we ask if Brad Pitt loves Jennifer Aniston or Angelina Jolie. We understand the question because although there is only one subject of the feeling (Brad is the one who feels love), there are two potential objects of the feelings (he loves either Jennifer or Angelina—or both). Of course, there are special cases in which the subject and the object of the feeling are the same. Why do I take vitamins? Because I don't always eat right and I want to make sure I get all the nutrients I need. So I am the subject of this motivation (the one who desires to take vitamins) but I am also the object of the motivation (I take the vitamins to benefit myself).

In the benevolence example, my children are the subjects of the feeling, and the object of their feeling is the suffering of another child. In the self-destructive example, my friend is the subject of the motivation, and the object is to satisfy her craving for nicotine (which leads her to act against her self-interest). Notice that in neither example is the object of the feeling or motivation self-interest.

There are a couple of ways that people try to evade these facts. One of the most common is to argue that the only motivations anyone really has are to maximize their pleasure and minimize their pain. In the benevolence case, my children were unhappy because of the suffering of another child, and their actions were really just a way of relieving their own suffering, which is purely self-interested. Likewise, in the self-destructive case, my friend was in pain because of nicotine withdrawal, and she smoked just as a way of relieving her own suffering, which is purely self-interested. However, these counterarguments are both fallacious. Let's see how.

In the benevolence case, the advocate of psychological egoism would concede that my children feel pain. But what is the object of their pain? What is their pain about? The only answer available is this: my children are pained about the suffering of another child. But if you say that, you have admitted that my children care about something other than themselves. Yes, my children do not like the pain they feel, and this pain is part of the explanation for their actions, but we do not have a complete explanation for why my children donate part of their allowances unless we take into account the person (external to themselves) whose suffering pains them. Unless they were concerned about the suffering child, they would feel no pain to alleviate.

The same kind of response cannot be given in the self-destructive case. My friend desires to smoke in order to relieve her own suffering, so she is both the subject and the object of her pleasure and suffering. Isn't this then a case of acting out of self-interest? No. Recall that, in the example, my friend judges that it is not in her own self-interest to smoke. She believes that the pleasure gained from smoking is outweighed by the cost to her health. When my friend gives in to the temptation to smoke, she is doing something that gives her pleasure (and so it does give her *some* benefit). However, even according to her own judgment, the pleasure she gets from smoking is not worth the damage to her health. Consequently, her smoking is not in her best interest overall. Hence, her motivation to smoke is not purely self-interested.

A second way people try to evade the counterexamples is to attribute to people hidden beliefs or motivations that are purely self-interested. Perhaps my children actually donate money to help another child because they want other people to help them if they ever need it. Perhaps the pleasure from smoking is actually worth the damage to my friend's health. Now, I would certainly agree that sometimes people act in what appears to be a benevolent manner or what looks like a self-destructive manner but really is not. The problem with this line of argument is that it requires that we systematically attribute duplicitous or subconscious motivations to people in literally billions of cases. In the vast majority of these cases there is no evidence for attributing these motivations other than the desire to insulate psychological egoism against falsification. There is no evidence that my children suffer from the concern that they might be born (reborn?) into crushing poverty in a nation with little infrastructure that has been devastated by a tsunami. There is no reason to attribute to them the belief that giving money to someone on the other side of the world is a better safety net for their own well-being than saving it for themselves. Similarly, what do we say when my friend asserts that smoking is not in her own self-interest? Is she lying? Does she somehow subconsciously think that smoking is in her best interests? A much simpler explanation is that people's motivations are usually about what they seem to be about.

Myth: *"Fortune cookies are a traditional Chinese dessert."*

Fact: *Although they are a staple of Chinese restaurants in the United States, most people in China have never even seen a fortune cookie. Because they are so popular in the United States, some entrepreneurs in China have imported fortune cookies, but they have never caught on.*

Finally, a good insight about self-interest that, ironically, is often misinterpreted as support for psychological egoism, is that it is frequently in a person's self-interest to care about things other than herself. A person who only cares about himself is likely to have a life that is empty and uninteresting. In contrast, a person with a number of strong interests in other people, activities, and causes has a better chance of having a full and exciting life. This is sometimes called the paradox of egoism. But this does not support egoism (of any form). What it does entail is that if you care about yourself, you should try to also care about other things, too. Here is an illustration. Because I care about the issues raised by philosophy, I enjoy reading, writing, and teaching about philosophy. It is certainly in my self-interest to feel enjoyment, but I can't feel this particular kind of enjoyment unless I really do care about philosophy. So it is in my self-interest to care not only about myself, but also about philosophy.

The *South Park* character Cartman illustrates what a genuine psychological egoist would be like. When Butters is mistakenly arrested for a crime that Cartman, Kyle, and Stan committed, Cartman is elated:

Cartman: You see guys, it all worked itself out.
Kyle: I still feel bad, Cartman.
Cartman: What? How can you feel bad? Somebody else is gonna pay for our crime.
Kyle: Yeah. That makes it even worse.
Cartman: But, Kyle, you don't seem to understand. We're not gonna get punished for this. Ever.
Kyle: I know.

Cartman: So then, how can you feel bad?
Stan: He feels guilty for doing it and for letting someone else pay for it.
Cartman: But he's not gonna get in trouble.
Stan: It doesn't matter if you get in trouble of not, you can still feel bad. [*To Kyle:*] I think you're right, Kyle. Maybe we should confess.
Cartman: What? Hey you guys! There's nothing to feel bad about! We're off scot-free!
Kyle: We feel bad for other people.
Cartman: For other—? Is it that you think you might get in trouble *later?*[i]

Kyle and Stan have normal human feelings. They care about other people (they are benevolent) and also have a sense of fair play (they are righteous), so it bothers them that Butters will be punished for something they did. In contrast, Cartman genuinely has no concern for anyone other than himself. Consequently, he does not care at all that Butters will suffer. In fact, he even has trouble understanding what could possibly be motivating Kyle and Stan.

The exchange between Cartman and his friends is not only amusing, it also illustrates the insurmountable flaw of psychological egoism. There *are* some people like Cartman in the world and, when we encounter them, it is sad or even frightening rather than funny. But most people are more like Kyle and Stan. Most importantly: *psychological egoism leaves us with absolutely no way of explaining the difference between people like Cartman and people like Kyle and Stan.* If psychological egoism were true, everyone in the history of the human species would be exactly like Cartman. But they are not. Therefore, psychological egoism fails as an explanatory hypothesis for human behavior.

2. Ethical Egoism

Although psychological egoism is dead, ethical egoism is still a serious position that could be true. Once again, psychological egoism is a descriptive claim (albeit a false one), while ethical egoism is a prescriptive claim. Ethical egoism is the doctrine that the only good reason anyone has for doing something is that it is in his or her self-interest. If an action is not in a person's overall self-interest, he has no good reason for doing it. The ethical egoist can happily admit that there exist many cases like the benevolence and self-destructive examples above, but the ethical egoist will assert that not only is my friend foolish to smoke, so are my children foolish to donate part of their allowance. The ethical egoist will admit that most people are *not* like Cartman— but they ought to be.

What is a person's "true self" or "human essence"? Robber Zhi explains that "[t]he eyes want to see colors. The ears want to hear sounds. The mouth wants to taste flavors. And the emotions want fulfillment. . . . If you're not gratifying your wishes and cherishing your days, then you do not understand the Way" (374). The earliest humans did understand this Way:

> In Shen Nong's time they lay down dead tired and got up wide awake. They knew their mothers but not their fathers, and lived together with the deer. They farmed their own food and wove their own clothes and had no idea of hurting each other. *This* was the high point Virtue achieved! (372)

Notice that this is another example of a state-of-nature argument. In the earlier Mohist use of this argument, the precivilized human condition is one of endless conflict and suffering. It is only the establishment of government authority, including the use of punishments, that rescues humans from this predicament by unifying human norms. However, in "Robber Zhi," the precivilized state of nature is a utopia, in which humans easily satisfy their basic desires for things like food and sex, without the need for violence, competition, or pointless greed. Far from being our salvation, the development of government institutions ruins this Edenic state. For example, among the supposed sages whom the Mohists and Confucians venerate, the Yellow Emperor waged war "until the blood flowed a hundred leagues" and "Tang exiled his lord, Wu killed Tyrant Zhou, and ever since the strong oppress the weak and the many tyrannize the few." Why did this happen? Because these people (like Kongzi) "all forcefully went against their essence and nature because profit confused them about their true self" (373). In other words, people fight to gain political power, to achieve a reputation for Virtue, and to amass more wealth than they can spend. The result is that they suffer, cause others to suffer, and even die. Robber Zhi notes that Bi Gan was supposedly a loyal minister, but he ended up getting his heart cut out of his chest.[1] Even Kongzi's own disciple Zilu died a violent death as a result of trying to follow his Master's teachings.

Someone sympathetic to Yang Zhu's teachings probably wrote this dialogue, so it ends with Kongzi dazed by Robber Zhi's arguments—and perhaps even convinced by them. However, another text presents Mozi getting the last word in a dialogue with a certain Wu Mazi, who seems to be influenced by Yang Zhu's ideas. Wu Mazi states,

---

1. For Shen Nong, the Yellow Emperor, Bi Gan, and the other figures mentioned in this paragraph, see Chapter 1.

"When I am beaten I feel pain. When others are beaten the pain does not extend to me. Why should I resist what does not give me pain and not resist what gives me pain? Therefore I would rather have them killed to benefit me than have me killed to benefit them."

Mozi replied, "Is this view of yours to be kept secret or to be told to others?"

Wu Mazi replied, "Why should I keep my opinion to myself? Of course I shall tell it to others."

Mozi said, "Then if one person is pleased with your doctrine, there will be one person who will desire to kill you in order to benefit himself. If ten persons are pleased with your doctrine, there will be ten persons who will desire to kill you to benefit themselves. . . . On the other hand, if one person is not pleased with your doctrine there will be one person who will desire to kill you as the propagator of an evil doctrine. If ten persons are not pleased with you there will be ten persons who will desire to kill you as the propagator of an evil doctrine. . . . So where, after all, does the benefit of your doctrine lie?"[iv]

Mozi here provides one of the classic arguments against ethical egoism: it seems that it is not in the self-interest of the ethical egoist for other people to accept ethical egoism. The best situation, from the perspective of a committed egoist, is one in which she is the only ethical egoist in a society of altruistic people. The altruists will benefit her, while she can take advantage of them. However, this is likely to be most successful only if the altruists do not know that the ethical egoist is not one of them. Some philosophers see this as a refutation of ethical egoism. However, ethical egoists respond that there is nothing logically or practically inconsistent with them wanting other people to not believe the truth.

A third text provides a dialogue between Yang Zhu, Meng Sunyang (a follower of his), and Qin Guli (a Mohist):

Qin Guli asked Yang Zhu, "If you could help the whole world by the loss of a hair off your body, would you do it?"

Yang Zhu replied, "The world would surely not be helped by a single hair."

"Supposing it did help, would you not do it?"

Yang Zhu did not answer him. Meng Sunyang said, "You have not fathomed what is in my Master's heart. Let me say it. Suppose for a bit of your skin you could get a thousand in gold, would you give it?"

"I would."

"Suppose that by cutting off a limb at the joint you could win a state, would you do it?"

Qin Guli was silent for a while.

Meng Sunyang continued, "That one hair matters less than skin and skin less than a limb is plain enough. However, go on adding to the one hair and it amounts to as much as skin, go on adding more skin and it amounts to as much as one limb. A single hair is certainly one thing among the myriad parts of the body, how can one treat it lightly?"[v]

Qin Guli's challenge to Yang Zhu is that it is absurd to be unwilling to sacrifice something as worthless as a single hair from his head if it would benefit the whole world. In response, Meng Sunyang gets Qin Guli to admit that he would give up a bit of skin for a thousand pieces of gold but would not give up an entire limb even to control an entire state. Meng Sunyang concludes with a rhetorical question. If we convert that question into a statement, it seems to mean this: One cannot treat even a single hair lightly, because it is certainly one among the myriad parts of the body. But how is this a response to Qin Guli's objection to Yang Zhu?

Perhaps Meng Sunyang attributes to Qin Guli the following argument: Because a single hair is absolutely worthless, it is absurd to be unwilling to sacrifice it to benefit others. Meng Sunyang's response is that if any part of the body, no matter how small, were absolutely worthless, then larger parts of the body composed of those parts would also be worthless. But large parts of one's body like limbs certainly are not worthless. Therefore, even an individual hair has some value, although it is very small. Because a hair has some value, it is not absurd to be unwilling to sacrifice it for the benefit of others.

How might Qin Guli respond to this? In particular, does Qin Guli assume that a hair is absolutely worthless or merely that its value is extremely small? Also consider a more general point: should Yang Zhu be reluctant to admit that he would not sacrifice a hair to benefit the world?

IV. The Contemporary Debate

Many traditional thinkers, in both the East and the West, have appealed to a view of human nature as a basis for their arguments. Among contemporary philosophers and scientists, some would say that the notion of the nature of a thing should be consigned to the dustbin of history, while others defend the appeal to human nature.

Some of those who reject the notion of human nature claim that it is simply implausible to believe in either a Heaven or God that endows humans with a nature. Others point out that the appeal to human nature has been used to justify various kinds of oppression, by classifying some groups of people as somehow less than fully human. Finally, many anthropologists claim that the great variety in flourishing human cultures shows that there is no single, universal human nature.

In reply, some biologists argue that evolution explains why humans would develop a common nature, whether or not there is any higher power. Charles Darwin himself believed that because humans are social animals who rely on their "pack" to survive, benevolence is a trait selected for by evolution. In addition, some philosophers suggest that progressive social movements also appeal to conceptions of human nature. The argument that all humans share a common nature was the philosophical basis for defending the equal rights of women, opposing discrimination against gays and lesbians, and criticizing slavery. It is also common for contemporary proponents of human nature to give a pluralistic rather than monistic conception of it. In other words, there is one human nature, which limits what ways of life are practical and worthwhile for humans. However, there is more than one way to instantiate this nature.

The debate over human nature is obviously of continuing relevance but our primary interest here is to see how it played out in early Chinese thought. Therefore, in the next chapter we shall consider a Confucian philosopher who appealed to his own conception of human nature to argue against both Yang Zhu and the Mohists.

Review Questions

1. Explain the difference between psychological egoism and ethical egoism.
2. Explain the difference between the subject and the object of a feeling or desire.
3. Use the distinction between the subject and the object of a desire to explain the different attitudes of Cartman and Kyle toward the arrest of Butters for their crime.
4. Explain the paradox of egoism.
5. What would an ethical egoist say about my friend who fails to quit smoking? What would she say about Mother Teresa devoting her life to helping the needy?
6. Explain how Heaven, the Way, and human nature are related to one another.

7. Explain the two senses of the nature of a thing.

8. What did those who followed Yang Zhu say was wrong with both Confucianism and Mohism?

9. According to those who followed Yang Zhu, why do some people mistakenly follow Confucianism or Mohism?

10. Explain the difference between the Mohist and Yangist uses of a state-of-nature argument.

11. Imagine an extremely ascetic philosophy that discouraged its adherents from enjoying music, good food, and sex, and encouraged them to sleep on wooden boards and take cold showers. How could one use the notion of "human nature" to criticize such a philosophy?

■ 6 ■

MENGZI AND HUMAN NATURE

*The doctrines of Yang Zhu and Mozi fill the world. If a doctrine
does not lean toward Yang, then it leans toward Mo.*
                                                    —*Mengzi* 3B9

Mengzi is sometimes called the Second Sage (second only to Kongzi) because of his
immense influence on Confucianism.

: year 319 BCE. We are in Liang, capital city of the state of Wei. King f Liang has invited the wisest scholars from all of China to come and :ir advice on how to govern. The royal court is a raised hall, looking ᴜᴏᴡᴠ ᴜnto a courtyard. The architecture is intimidating: those going to see the king must cross the courtyard and then ascend the steps under his august gaze. Even the most distinguished dignitary could be forgiven feeling some trepidation.

Today, the Confucian Mengzi has been favored with a royal audience. He ritually bows to the king before ascending the steps to enter the hall. The king addresses Mengzi with the utmost respect as he says, "Venerable sir, you have not regarded hundreds of leagues too far to come, so you must have a means to profit my state."

Immediately, Mengzi shoots back, "Why must Your Majesty speak of profit?! Let there simply be benevolence and righteousness!"

Everyone is shocked, reeling from Mengzi's audacity in rebuking the king. Before they can catch their breath, Mengzi explains,

> If Your Majesty says, "How can I profit my state?" the Chief Counselors will say, "How can I profit my clan?" and the nobles and commoners will say, "How can I profit my self?" Superiors and subordinates will seize profit from each other and the state will be endangered. When the ruler in a state that can field ten thousand chariots is assassinated, it will invariably be by a clan that can field a thousand chariots. When the ruler in a state that can field a thousand chariots is assassinated, it will invariably be by a clan that can field a hundred chariots. A thousand out of ten thousand or a hundred out of a thousand is certainly not a small amount. But if one merely puts righteousness last and profit first, no one will be satisfied without stealing more. Never have the benevolent left their parents behind. Never have the righteous put their ruler last. Let Your Majesty speak only of benevolence and righteousness. Why must one speak of "profit"? (*Mengzi* 1A1)

Mengzi's courageous reply puts the king on notice that, unlike so many other people in the royal court, he is not a sycophantic toady who will tell the king only what he wants to hear. Mengzi's response is also a brilliant philosophical argument. He might seem to be objecting to profit itself. But on what grounds does Mengzi instruct King Hui to avoid emphasizing profit? Emphasizing profit is itself unprofitable. A later Confucian summed up Mengzi's point concisely: "A gentleman never fails to desire profit, but if one is singlemindedly focused on profit, then it leads to harm. If there is only benevolence and righteousness, then one will not seek profit, but one will never fail to profit."

Mengzi is here elaborating in much more detail a position hinted at by Kongzi, who warned, "If in your affairs you abandon yourself to the pursuit of profit, you will arouse much resentment" (4.12), but also remarked "those who are wise follow Goodness because they feel that they will profit from it" (4.2).

Who is this brilliant but brash defender of the Way of Kongzi?

We have few details about Mengzi's life, other than those contained in his eponymous text, the *Mengzi*. He was born in Zou, a small state near Kongzi's home state of Lu, both of which were in what is now Shandong province. His father died when he was young. In his patriarchal society, this must have left him and his mother in precarious circumstances. However, his mother still managed to send him to study in the Confucian school of Zisi, Kongzi's grandson.

There are several famous stories about Mengzi's mother that are charmingly edifying, whether or not they are true. One is that "Meng's mother moved thrice" (*Mèng mǔ sān qiān* 孟母三遷) in order to find a suitable environment in which her son could grow up. After the death of her husband, she first moved with her son next to a cemetery, and the young sage pretended to perform funeral rituals. Thinking this inappropriate for a child, Mengzi's mother moved to a house near a marketplace, but there her son began imitating someone hawking goods. Still dissatisfied, Mengzi's mother moved to a home beside a school. There Mengzi pretended to be a teacher, which finally pleased his mother.

When Mengzi began attending school, his mother would ask him every day what he had learned. One day his answer showed casual indifference toward his studies. In response, "Meng's mother cut the weft" (*Mèng mǔ duàn jī* 孟母斷機) of the fabric that she had been weaving, thereby ruining it. Her weaving was probably one of their few sources of income, so Mengzi was startled that she would waste a piece of fabric. His mother explained that if he wasted a day of learning it was as bad as her wasting a day of work. Thereafter, Mengzi always applied himself fully in his schoolwork.

As an adult, Mengzi traveled from state to state, trying to find a ruler who would put into effect "benevolent government." By this he meant rule by virtuous "gentlemen" who aimed at the well-being of the people as a whole. Mengzi stressed that most people will engage in crime if they are poor and hungry:

> To lack a constant livelihood, yet to have a constant heart—only a scholar is capable of this. As for the people, if they lack a constant livelihood, it follows that they will lack a constant heart. No one who lacks a constant heart will avoid dissipation and evil. When they

thereupon sink into crime, to go and punish the people is to trap them. When there are benevolent persons in positions of authority, how is it possible for them to trap the people? (1A7; *Readings,* p. 122)

Consequently, it is the obligation of government to ensure that the basic needs of the people are met. Mengzi offered much more specific advice than had Kongzi about how to secure the livelihood of the people, including recommendations about everything from tax rates to farm management to the pay scale for government employees (e.g., 3A3). However, as the references to "a scholar" and "a constant heart" suggest, Mengzi agreed with Kongzi that ethical cultivation is crucial for both individual and social well-being. Thus, Mengzi advocated an educational system that instructs people in how to be a good parent, child, ruler, minister, spouse, and friend (3A4).

We find in Mengzi an emphasis on the five themes that we saw are characteristic of all Confucians: achieving happiness in the everyday world, a revivalistic appropriation of tradition, familial relations as the basis of other ethical obligations and of differentiated caring, ritual as a means of expressing and reinforcing one's ties to others, and the ethically transformative power of education.[1] In addition, Mengzi agreed with Kongzi in regarding war as, at best, a regrettable last resort. In what has become a Chinese proverb, he stated that to try to rule via brute force is as ineffectual as "climbing a tree in search of a fish" (*yuán mù qiú yú* 緣木求魚, 1A7).[2]

However, Mengzi could not simply repeat what Kongzi had said. Confucianism was now under attack by a variety of alternative philosophies. Mengzi saw two positions as the primary competitors to the Way: "the doctrines of Yang Zhu and Mozi fill the world. If a doctrine does not lean toward Yang Zhu, then it leans toward Mozi. Yang Zhu is 'for oneself.' This is to not have a ruler. Mozi is 'impartial caring.' This is to not have a father. To not have a father and to not have a ruler is to be an animal" (3B9; *Readings,* pp. 135–36).

In response to the Mohists, Mengzi argued that the impartiality they demanded was inconsistent with human nature, hence neither practical nor desirable. In this, Mengzi agreed with Yang Zhu. However, Yang Zhu was also wrong, because there is more to human nature than self-interested desires. Rather than being artificial deformations of human nature, benevolence and righteousness are as natural as the fruit that grows from a peach tree. Let's look in more detail at how Mengzi argues for these claims.

---

1. See Chapter 2 for these themes.
2. For more on Mengzi's views on war, see 4A14*, 6B8*, and 7B1*, 7B2*, 7B3, and 7B4*.

I. *The Mohists, Profit, and Impartiality*

We have already seen part of Mengzi's argument against Mohism. When Mengzi chides King Hui "Why must one speak of 'profit (*li*)'?" (1A1) he is also implicitly criticizing the Mohists, who state that "the business of a benevolent person is to promote what is beneficial (*li*) to the world and eliminate what is harmful" (68). For example, the Mohists argue against aggressive warfare on the grounds that it is not beneficial, even to the aggressor state. When Mengzi encounters someone who plans to dissuade rulers from fighting a war by arguing that the war would be unprofitable, he objects,

> Your intention, venerable sir, is indeed great. But your slogan is unacceptable. If you persuade the kings of Qin and Chu by means of profit, the kings of Qin and Chu will set aside the three armies because they delight in profit. This is for the officers of the three armies to delight in being set aside because they delight in profit. Those who are ministers will embrace profit in serving their rulers. Those who are children will embrace profit in serving their fathers. Those who are younger brothers will embrace profit in serving their elder brothers. This is for rulers and ministers, fathers and children, elder and younger brothers to end up abandoning benevolence and righteousness. For people to embrace profit in their contact with one another, yet not be destroyed—such a thing has never happened. (*Mengzi* 6B4*)

As he did with King Hui, Mengzi here argues that aiming to maximize profit or benefit is self-defeating. What would really benefit everyone is a society in which people act in accordance with benevolence and righteousness. But if everyone is thinking only in terms of profit, they will end up betraying and harming other people and groups in the name of what they perceive to be beneficial. Mengzi's critique has something in common with that of modern philosophers who say that our society is so obsessed with quantifiable benefits that we ignore considerations of morality in favor of the bottom line.

Mengzi's most fundamental objection to Mohism is that the impartiality it demands is impractical and perverse because it is contrary to human nature. This comes out most directly in his dialogue with the Mohist Yi Zhi (*Mengzi* 3A5). Mengzi points out that Yi Zhi had himself given his parents elaborate funerals. Yi Zhi's natural attachment to his parents was thus so strong that it led him to ignore his abstract commitment to the Mohist principle of frugal burials.

As we saw, a theoretical weakness of early Mohism is that it regards human motivations as almost infinitely malleable. Yi Zhi holds what seems to be a modified version of Mohism, designed to make it more psychologically plausible. He suggests "love is without distinctions, but it is bestowed beginning with one's parents." Yi Zhi thus seems to be agreeing with the Confucian claim that children first learn to love and have compassion for others in the family (*Analects* 1.2), but argues that this natural compassion should be redirected until it reaches everyone equally, thereby achieving the Mohist goal of "impartial caring."

Mengzi suggests that Yi Zhi's revisionist Mohism still results in a position that is psychologically impractical: "Does Yi Zhi truly hold that one's affection for one's nephew is like one's affection for a neighbor's child?" Mengzi sums up his objection with the aphorism, "Heaven, in producing the things in the world, causes them to have one source, but Yi Zhi gives them two sources." The first source is our innate love for family members (which is naturally stronger for them than for strangers), while the second source is the Mohist doctrine of impartiality. Now, for the Mohists (as much as for the Confucians) the will of Heaven and the Way coincide. So once the Mohists acknowledge that our greater love for family members is part of the nature implanted in us by Heaven, they cannot consistently claim that it is part of the Way to override these motivations in order to achieve impartiality.

In some respects Mengzi's argument against the Mohists is structurally similar to Yang Zhu's. Yang Zhu and Mengzi agree that we should follow our nature, and that the Mohist Way is contrary to that nature. However, Yang Zhu claims that human nature is purely self-interested, while Mengzi argues that human nature is good (6A6). Let's see how.

II. Yang Zhu and Human Nature

In what is perhaps the most famous passage in the *Mengzi,* our philosopher argues for the goodness of human nature with a thought experiment:

> The reason why I say that humans all have hearts that are not unfeeling toward others is this. Suppose someone suddenly saw a child about to fall into a well: everyone in such a situation would have a feeling of alarm and compassion—not because one sought to get in good with the child's parents, not because one wanted fame among their neighbors and friends, and not because one would dislike the sound of the child's cries. From this we can see that if one is without the heart of compassion, one is not a human. (*Mengzi* 2A6)

Mengzi's thought experiment specifies that the situation happens "suddenly." This suggests that the reaction is natural, because one has no time to calculate the potential advantages or disadvantages to oneself. Notice also what Mengzi does *not* say here. He does not claim that anyone would actually act to save the child. A person might freeze in the moment or crisis, or might (after a moment of reflection) think of selfish reasons to allow the child to drown. Mengzi only needs us to share his intuition that any human would have at least a momentary twinge of compassion at the sight of a child about to fall into a well; conversely, "if one is without the heart of compassion, one is not a human."

Mengzi uses a similar thought experiment to argue for the existence of other innate ethical reactions:

> Life is something I desire; righteousness is also something I desire. If I cannot have both, I will forsake life and select righteousness. . . . It is not the case that only the worthy person has this heart. All humans have it. The worthy person simply never loses it.
>
> A basket of food and a bowl of soup—if one gets them then one will live; if one doesn't get them then one will die. But if they're given with contempt, then even a homeless person will not accept them. If they're trampled upon, then even a beggar won't take them. (*Mengzi* 6A10)

The previous passage argued for an innate "heart of compassion," which is the basis of benevolence; this second passage argues that all humans disdain to do certain shameful things that would otherwise benefit them, and this "heart" is the basis of righteousness. So whereas Yang Zhu claimed that human nature consists only of self-interested desires for food, sex, physical comfort, and survival, Mengzi uses these thought experiments to argue that human nature also includes distinctively ethical motivations.

But aren't Mengzi's claims falsified by the simple fact of human wrongdoing? If we are all innately benevolent and righteous, why does anyone ever hurt another person or compromise his integrity? This objection misinterprets Mengzi's position, though. Mengzi does not claim that *humans* are innately good; he claims that *human nature* is innately good. Recall our earlier discussion of the concept of the "nature" of a thing (Chapter 5). It is the nature of a peach tree to bear fruit, but it will fail to realize this nature if denied a healthy environment (with water, sunlight, etc.). It is the nature of a frog to have four legs, but it will never develop them if it is eaten as a tadpole. Mengzi uses a carefully chosen agricultural metaphor to explain how this applies to human nature. He says that the "heart of compassion" (manifested when one sees the child about to fall into a well) is "the *sprout* of benevolence," while the "heart of disdain" (illustrated by the starving beggar who refuses a handout given with contempt) is the "*sprout* of righteousness" (2A6, 6A10). Just as the sprout of a Chinese Juniper is not yet a tree but does have an active potential to develop into a mature tree, so are the "sprout of benevolence" and "sprout of righteousness" potentials for full benevolence and righteousness. But we must develop this potential in order to become fully virtuous. As Mengzi explains when asked to clarify his position, "As for what they genuinely are, humans can become good. That is what I mean by calling their natures good. As for their becoming not good, this is not the fault of their potential" (6A6). Until our potential for virtue is fully developed, the reactions of the sprouts will be haphazard and inconsistent. This is why humans can show great kindness and even self-sacrifice in one situation but stunning indifference to the suffering of others in a slightly different situation.

Fact: *Gunpowder, the magnetic compass, and printing with moveable type were all invented in China long before they were used in the West. It has been said that these are the primary technological breakthroughs responsible for the rise of the modern world.*

Consequently, Mengzi's doctrine that human nature is good is perfectly consistent with the fact that humans often fail to do good. But is Mengzi right in claiming that all humans have at least the *sprouts* of benevolence and righteousness? We are all too familiar with the chilling example of the psychopath: a "human" (such as a serial killer) who lacks ordinary compassion or sympathy. Mengzi's metaphor of Ox Mountain is his explanation for the rare cases of people who seem to lack the sprouts of virtue:

> The trees of Ox Mountain were once beautiful. But because the mountain bordered on a large state, hatchets and axes besieged it. Could it remain verdant? Due to the respite it got during the day or night, and the moisture of rain and dew, it was not that there were no sprouts or shoots growing there. But oxen and sheep then came and grazed on them. Hence, it was as if it were barren. People seeing it barren, believed that there had never been any timber there. Could this be the nature of the mountain?
>
> When we consider what is present in people, could they truly lack the hearts of benevolence and righteousness? That by which they discard their genuine hearts is simply like the hatchets and axes in relation to the trees. With them besieging it day by day, can it remain beautiful? . . . Others see someone who is like an animal, and think that there was never any capacity there. Is this what a human genuinely is? (*Mengzi* 6A8)

Mengzi acknowledges that some people seem to lack the sprouts of virtue. However, this is not "what a human genuinely is" (6A6, 6A8). Mengzi maintains that a bad environment (such as physical deprivation, lack of ethical guidance, or even abusive parenting) destroyed their sprouts.

III. The Virtues

Mengzi agreed with Kongzi that flourishing or living well is something that humans should do while in this world (rather than something to be achieved after death) through life with one's family and friends and participation in communal ritual activities. However, Mengzi gives a much more specific and clear account than does Kongzi of human nature, ethical cultivation, and the virtues. Mengzi identifies four cardinal virtues, each of which is grounded in our innate emotional reactions:

> Humans all have the heart of compassion. Humans all have the heart of disdain. Humans all have the heart of respect. Humans all have the heart of approval and disapproval. The heart of compassion is benevolence. The heart of disdain is righteousness. The heart of respect is propriety. The heart of approval and disapproval is wisdom. Benevolence, righteousness, propriety and wisdom are not welded to us externally. We inherently have them. It is simply that we do not reflect upon them. Hence, it is said, "Seek it and you will get it. Abandon it and you will lose it." (*Mengzi* 6A6)

Benevolence is compassion or sympathy for others. The benevolent person is pained by the suffering of others and takes joy in their happiness. The Mohists also emphasized this term, but for them it is ideally a purely impartial concern for others. For a Confucian like Mengzi, though, compassion should extend to everyone but should be stronger for those tied to one by bonds such as kinship and friendship. Confucian benevolence is thus like the ripples around a stone dropped into a pond, proceeding out from the center but gradually decreasing in strength as they move outward. This is related to the Confucian hypothesis that it is loving and being loved in the family that germinates our capacity for compassion.

Righteousness is the integrity of a person who disdains to demean herself by doing what is base or shameful, even if doing so would reap benefits. So, for example, a righteous person will not accept a gift given with contempt (6A10), beg in order to obtain luxuries (4B33), or cheat at a game (3B1). As with benevolence, the capacity for righteousness is innate, but its growth is first stimulated in the family, where respect for the opinions of one's elders is internalized as an ethical sense of shame. Put in deontological terms, benevolence is a virtue particularly manifested in our *obligations* to help others, while righteousness involves _prohibitions_ against actions that would violate our integrity.

Wisdom has many aspects, each of which is illustrated by the story of the sage Boli Xi (5A9). When the ruler of Yu made foolish concessions to the state of Jin, Boli Xi knew that these policies would result in the destruction of Yu. Recognizing that this ruler was too stubborn to listen to his advice, Boli Xi fled to the state of Qin, whose ruler showed great promise. Boli Xi waited until he was approached respectfully by the ruler of Qin, but then served so ably as his minister that the ruler became illustrious. Boli Xi thus showed great wisdom in judging the characters of the rulers of Yu and Qin. He manifested great skill at instrumental reasoning (i.e., finding the best means to achieve a given end) in the fine advice he gave when he was minister to the ruler of Qin. He revealed his commitment to righteousness by insisting that the ruler of Qin show him respect in requesting an audience. He also demonstrated prudence in fleeing Yu when the situation was hopeless. It may surprise some readers that running away was virtuous in this situation, but keep in mind that a good person does care about her own well-being; she just doesn't care about herself excessively (cf 4B31). Boli Xi thus combines the four parts of wisdom: being a good judge of the character of others, skill at means-end reasoning, an understanding of and commitment to the other virtues, and prudence.

The word rendered "propriety" is the same as the word for "rites" or "rituals." This is appropriate because propriety is the virtue that consists in performing the rites with the proper motivations. In comparison with some other Confucians, Mengzi has relatively little to say about the rites (hence little to say about propriety as a virtue). But one way of conceptualizing propriety is that it is manifested when we express deference or respect to others through ritualized actions (such as bowing, allowing someone else to walk first through a door, etc.).

IV. Ethical Cultivation

Mengzi holds that we are born with only sprouts of the four cardinal virtues. How do we get from the sprouts to the full virtues? As we have already noted, it is the responsibility of a ruler to make sure the people are safe and have the basic necessities of life, because few people will be able to cultivate virtue if subject to hunger, cold, homelessness, and violence. Mengzi also emphasizes two other factors as impediments to the growth of virtue: pernicious doctrines and lack of individual ethical effort.

In Mengzi's era, as in our own, many people either denied that they were capable of virtue or opposed virtue as naive. Mengzi categorizes "those who say 'I myself am unable to dwell in benevolence and follow righteous-ness'" as "throwing themselves away" and "those whose words are opposed to propriety and righteousness" as "destroying themselves" (4A10). Both attitudes are roadblocks to moral growth. So a significant part of Mengzian moral self-cultivation is simply being aware of and delighting in the mani-festations of the sprouts when we do have them. In other words, we rein-force and strengthen our benevolent and righteous motivations when we act out of them with awareness and approval. As Mengzi puts it, "If one delights in them then they grow. If they grow then how can they be stopped? If they cannot be stopped, then without realizing it one's feet be-gin to step in time to them and one's hands dance according to their rhythms" (4A27).

Mengzi more than once says that people fail to develop morally simply because they do not engage in "reflection" (6A6, 6A15). The Chinese term can also mean "to concentrate upon" or "to long for," as when someone longs for an absent loved one (*Analects* 19.6). As Arthur Waley explains, "reflection" refers to

a process that is only at a short remove from concrete observation. Never is there any suggestion of a long interior process of cogitation or ratiocination, in which a whole series of thoughts are evolved one out of another, producing on the physical plane a headache and on the intellectual, an abstract theory. We must think of [reflection] rather as a fixing of the attention . . . on an impression recently im-bibed from without and destined to be immediately re-exteriorized in action.[ii]

Reflection is thus a mental activity with a focus that is both internal and ex-ternal. One reflects upon one's own virtuous feelings, but one also reflects upon the aspects of situations that call forth those feelings.

A much-discussed dialogue between Mengzi and King Xuan of Qi illus-trates the stages of moral development. Mengzi asks the king about how he had spared an ox being led to slaughter because, as the king put it, "I cannot bear its frightened appearance, like an innocent going to the execution ground." Mengzi explains to the king that the kindness he showed to the ox is the same feeling he needs to exercise to be a great king. King Xuan is pleased and replies, "I examined myself and sought it out, but did not under-stand my heart. You spoke, and in my heart there was a feeling of compas-sion." Mengzi helped the king to *reflect upon* and appreciate his own innate kindness. This is an important first step in stimulating the growth of the king's sprouts of virtue. Then Mengzi challenges the king:

In the present case your kindness is sufficient to reach birds and beasts, but the benefits do not reach the commoners. Why is this case alone different? Hence, not lifting one feather is due to not using one's strength. Not seeing a wagon of firewood is due to not using one's eyesight. The commoners not receiving care is due to not using one's kindness. Hence, Your Majesty's not being a genuine king is due to not acting; it is not due to not being able. (*Mengzi* 1A7; *Readings*, p. 120)

This dialogue raises many intriguing and complicated questions. Is Mengzi presenting some sort of *argument* to the king about why he ought to care for the commoners? Perhaps Mengzi is effectively saying to the king: you agree that it is right to show compassion on the suffering ox (Case A), but your people are also suffering due to your exorbitant taxes, wars of conquest, corrupt government, and so on (Case B). Case B is similar to Case A in all relevant respects. Therefore, in order to be consistent, you ought to show compassion on your people. Alternatively, perhaps Mengzi merely wishes to convince the king that he is *capable* of ruling with benevolence: you can show compassion for a simple animal, so certainly you can also show compassion for a suffering human.

My own view is that neither analysis is completely correct. I think Mengzi is leading the king to *reflect upon* relevant similarities between the suffering of the ox and the suffering of his subjects. But this is not an argument for simple consistency. After all, Mengzi also makes clear in the passage that slaughtering animals is ethically permissible, even if "gentlemen" are too kind-hearted to do it themselves. So Mengzi is asking the king to treat his subjects better than he treated the ox, not the same. Mengzi does want the king to recognize his own demonstrated capacity for compassion. However, it is not merely the capacity that Mengzi is getting at. He wants to frame the comparison between the ox and the commoners in a way that encourages the king's compassion to flow from one case to the other. For example, Mengzi reminds the king that he spared the ox because of its "frightened appearance, like an innocent going to the execution ground." He hopes the king will be led from this to reflect upon, and sympathize with, the suffering of his own innocent subjects. In other words, Mengzi is helping the king to achieve cognitive ethical growth as a means to achieving affective ethical growth.[3]

---

3. For more on "reflection," see *Mengzi* 4A1*, 4B20*, 6A6, and 6A15 and *Analects* 2.15 and 15.31.

Mengzi describes this process of ethical growth as "extending" or "filling out" the manifestations of the sprouts. In other words, all of us will have righteous or benevolent reactions to certain paradigmatic situations. We feel love for our parents, which is a manifestation of benevolence, or we disdain allowing ourselves to be addressed disrespectfully, which is a manifestation of righteousness. However, there are other situations in which we do not have these reactions, even though they are in the same "category" (3B3). For example, a person who would find it shameful to have an illicit affair might think nothing of lying to his ruler to achieve some political benefit. "Reflection" is the process by which we identify the relevant similarities between those cases in which we already have the appropriate reactions and other cases in which we do not yet react appropriately. This guides our emotions so that we come to feel similarly about the cases. Or, as Mengzi succinctly put it: "People all have things that they will not bear. To extend this reaction to that which they will bear is benevolence. People all have things that they will not do. To extend this reaction to that which they will do is righteousness" (7B31).

Extension is not a matter of learning to apply a set of explicit rules. Mengzi is not, in other words, a rule-deontologist. Mengzi is similar to Kongzi in having a comparatively particularistic conception of wisdom. For example, a rival philosopher once attempted to trap Mengzi with an ethical dilemma. He began by asking, "That men and women should not touch in handing something to one another—is this the ritual?" When Mengzi acknowledged that it is, his interlocutor asked, "If your sister-in-law were drowning, would you pull her out with your hand?" His opponent thinks that he has Mengzi trapped, but Mengzi replies,

> To not pull your sister-in-law out when she is drowning is to be a beast. That men and women should not touch in handing something to one another is the ritual, but if your sister-in-law is drowning to pull her out with your hand is discretion. (*Mengzi* 4A17)

The ritual Mengzi discusses might initially seem quaint or overly strict. But consider the fact that prudent teachers and bosses in our own society know that it is wise to avoid any unnecessary contact with their students or subordinates. But suppose you were standing near a student who was about to fall from a stepladder. Would you let the student fall or use your discretion and grab her?

This particularism is not relativism. Mengzi thinks that there is a best way to respond in any given situation, and it is not a matter of personal or cultural opinion. So after describing how differently sages of the past have acted,

Mengzi insists that if they "had exchanged places, they all would have done as the others did" (4B29; cf 4B1* and 4B31*). In addition, Mengzi does recognize some absolute ethical prohibitions. When asked if there is anything that all sages have in common, he explains that there is: "if any could obtain all under Heaven by performing one unrighteous deed, or killing one innocent person, he would not do it" (2A2). However, there is much more to the Confucian Way than can be captured in any set of rules.

Mengzi thinks that we generally have the capacity to "extend" to what is ethically required of us. Once, when someone gave him excuses for not immediately doing what is right, Mengzi replied,

> Suppose there is a person who every day appropriates one of his neighbor's chickens. Someone tells him, "This is not the Way of a gentleman." He says, "May I reduce it to appropriating one chicken every month, and wait until next year to stop?" If one knows that it is not righteous, then one should quickly stop. (*Mengzi* 3B8*)

However, Mengzi stresses the importance of acting with appropriate feelings and motivations. Thus, Mengzi praises Sage-King Shun by saying that "he acted out of benevolence and righteousness. He did not act out benevolence and righteousness" (4B19). To force oneself to do what one abstractly believes is right is to treat virtue as "external" (6A4–5). This not only fails to be genuinely virtuous, it is ethically damaging. Mengzi illustrates this using another agricultural metaphor, the story of the farmer from Song:

> One must work at it, but do not aim at it directly. Let the heart not forget, but do not "help" it grow. Do not be like the man from Song. Among the people of the state of Song there was one who, concerned lest his grain not grow, pulled on it. Wearily, he returned home, and said to his family, "Today I am worn out. I helped the grain to grow." His son rushed out and looked at it. The grain was withered. Those in the world who do not "help" the grain to grow are few. Those who abandon it, thinking it will not help, are those who do not weed their grain. Those who "help" it grow are those who pull on their grain. Not only does this not actually help, but it even harms it. (*Mengzi* 2A2; *Readings,* p. 127)

To use a modern illustration, I cannot simply decide today that I will be the next Mother Teresa and expect to suddenly have the unwavering compassion to save the world. If I tried to do so, I would fail, and probably end up being a bitter cynic. Instead, I should begin by showing more consistent kindness to my family and friends and gradually grow into a better person.

V. Cosmology

Mengzi situates his philosophical anthropology in a broader worldview: "To fathom one's heart is to understand one's nature. If one understands one's nature, then one understands Heaven" (7A1). For Mengzi, Heaven is not as anthropomorphic as it was for the Mohists (whose Heaven is as personal as the God of the mainstream Jewish, Christian, and Islamic traditions), but neither is it as naturalized as it was for later Confucians like Xunzi. So, on the one hand, Mengzi sometimes treats Heaven as almost identical with the natural (and amoral) course of events (2B1*, 4A7*). But, on the other hand, Heaven provides a moral standard. Thus, Mengzi approvingly quotes an ode that says: "Heaven gives birth to the teaming people. / If there is a thing, there is a norm" (6A6). We see both the naturalistic and the moral aspects of Heaven in 1B3*, where Mengzi discusses the problem of diplomacy between powerful and weak states: "Those who serve the small with the big delight in Heaven; those who serve the big with the small are in awe of Heaven." In other words, it should be the case (normatively) that the powerful are generous enough to serve the weak. But it is the case (descriptively) that antagonizing powerful states has dangerous consequences.

The complexity of Mengzi's view is also evident in his comments about political justification. He stresses that Heaven is the ultimate source of political legitimacy. However, Heaven primarily manifests itself in the reactions of the common people rather than in any supernatural agency: "Hence, I say that Heaven does not speak but simply reveals the mandate through actions and affairs" (5A5*). Heaven is a causal agent that affects the course of human history: "When no one does it, yet it is done—this is due to Heaven. When no one extends to it yet it is reached—this is fate." (5A6*). Nonetheless, when "gentlemen" find themselves unable to restore order to the world, they must not be "bitter toward Heaven" (2B13). Rather, they must accept Heaven's will while still striving to make the world a better place (7A1).

In order to persevere in the face of adversity without becoming bitter, one must cultivate one's *qi* 氣. This is one of the most intriguing yet difficult-to-understand aspects of Mengzi's thought. *Qi* has been rendered various ways, including "ether," "material force," and "psychophysical stuff." There is really no adequate translation, because this is a concept for which we have no precise analogue. For Mengzi and his contemporaries, *qi* is a kind of fluid, found in the atmosphere and in the human body, closely connected to the kind and intensity of one's emotional reactions. *Qi* therefore straddles the dualism between mind and body that has become a fixture of post-Cartesian philosophy in the West: *qi* is physically embodied emotion. Here are two examples that give an intuitive understanding of *qi*.

1. You are with a group of people in someone's living room, having a pleasant, casual conversation. Someone tries to make an offhand joke, but it sounds like a cutting personal criticism of another guest. It seems as if the literal atmosphere in the room has suddenly changed, like there is something palpably heavy in the air, making further conversation difficult and awkward. That "something" is a kind of negative *qi,* which is both expression and reinforcement of the feelings of those present.[4]

2. Imagine a beautiful April morning. The sun is already bright when you arise. The air smells crisp and fresh. You feel energized for the day ahead. You laugh off any minor problems and annoyances. Your positive mood is partially a product of absorbing some of the vibrant *qi* that circulates on this spring day.[5]

These examples should not lead us to assume that we are purely passive to the influence of the *qi*. Our hearts can resist the effects of negative *qi,* such as when I refuse to allow my fear to dissuade me from doing what I know is right. Mengzi describes this as "maintaining one's will." However, for success in the long run I cannot continue to force myself to act against the promptings of the *qi*. To do so would be to "injure one's *qi,*" eventually producing a person who is dispirited (whose *qi* is "starved"). Instead, one must cultivate an ethically informed *qi* ("a *qi* that harmonizes with righteousness and the Way"). This *qi* gives one the moral stamina to persevere in the face of dangers, challenges, and setbacks. Among the highly cultivated, this reservoir of fortitude is so deep that it is essentially inexhaustible (or "floodlike," as Mengzi puts it). The way to develop this *qi* is simply through the gradual cultivation of the sprouts of virtue (2A2; *Readings,* pp. 126–27).

VI. Historical Significance

Mengzi claimed that he had developed the "floodlike *qi,*" and it turned out that he needed the fortitude that comes with it; he spent much of his adult

---

4. Compare this to Mengzi's example in 7A36* of the effect of an august person's *qi* on how one feels in his presence.

5. Compare this to Mengzi's example in 6A8 of the effects of morning and evening *qi* on restoring one's ethical feelings.

life wandering from state to state, hoping to find a ruler who would put the Way into practice, but his efforts failed. He refused to meet with rulers unless they treated him with the ritual propriety due a distinguished advisor. This might seem arrogant, and his disciples encouraged him to bend his principles in order to obtain audiences with more rulers. However, Mengzi said that there was no hope in transforming a ruler who did not demonstrate that he was willing to accept his guidance: "those who bend themselves have never been able to make others upright" (3B1*; 2B10*). Sometimes rulers did meet with him and praised his teachings but did not give him any official position. He did accept a position as high minister in the state of Qi, but he resigned when it became clear that the king was ignoring his advice (2B6–12*; 2B13).

Mengzi eventually retired from public service and, with the help of some of his disciples, edited his collected sayings and dialogues. Like Kongzi, Gandhi, or Reverend Martin Luther King, Jr., he was a person actively engaged in the struggle for positive social change. However, he never saw the social transformation he worked for, which saddened him. Toward the end of his life, he moaned, "From Kongzi to the present time is a little more than one hundred years. It is not long from the era of a sage, and we are close to the home of a sage. Yet where is he? Where is he?" (7B38*). Nonetheless, Mengzi assured his disciples that he was not bitter: he had faith that Heaven would, in its own time, raise up a sage to bring peace to the world (2B13).

Ironically, it was not until more than a thousand years after Mengzi's death that he achieved his greatest influence. When the movement known in English as Neo-Confucianism revived Confucianism as an alternative to Buddhism, it praised Mengzi as the Second Sage (after only Kongzi himself). Thinkers such as Han Yu, Zhu Xi, and Wang Yangming, although they disagreed about much else, agreed that Mengzi was the one who truly understood the Way that Kongzi transmitted, and made *explicit* many things that were only *implied* in the sayings of Kongzi. In particular, Mengzi's doctrine that human nature is good was implicit in the teachings of Kongzi.

I am not sure the Neo-Confucians were right that Mengzi simply made explicit what was implicit in Kongzi's thought. Although Kongzi says next to nothing about human nature, his comments about the difficulty of cultivating virtue sound much more like those of Xunzi, the later Confucian critic of Mengzi who claimed "human nature is bad" (Chapter 10). Kongzi approves of the comparison between ethical cultivation and the laborious process of grinding and carving jade (1.15), while Xunzi compares ethical cultivation to steaming and bending wood into a wagon wheel, or grinding a metal blade until it is sharp (*Readings*, pp. 256–57). These are precisely the sort of metaphors for ethical cultivation to which Mengzi objects (6A1). I think that the Neo-Confucians were also guilty of anachronism in attributing to Mengzi certain metaphysical concepts that only developed much later in Chinese thought.[iii]

However, I heartily agree with the Neo-Confucians that Mengzi deserves his place as not only one of the greatest Confucian sages but as one of the greatest philosophers in world history. In particular, he provided a unique and inspiring vision of humans as having innate but incipient dispositions toward virtue that require cultivation in order to reach full maturity.

Review Questions

1. According to tradition, "Meng's mother moved thrice" and "Meng's mother cut the weft." Why did she do these things?
2. What does Mengzi mean by "benevolent government"?
3. According to Mengzi, what activity is like "climbing a tree in search of a fish"?
4. Explain Mengzi's argument that aiming at profit or benefit is self-defeating.
5. What is the position of the Mohist Yi Zhi, and why does Mengzi think that it is incoherent?
6. What does Mengzi mean by the claim that "human nature is good"?
7. Explain the thought experiment of the child at the well. What point do you take Mengzi to be arguing for?
8. Explain the story of Ox Mountain. What claim do you take Mengzi to be illustrating with this metaphor?
9. What are Mengzi's four cardinal virtues? Give an example of how each one manifests itself.
10. Explain the story of King Xuan and the ox. What are at least two interpretations of what Mengzi is trying to achieve in his discussion with Xuan?
11. Explain how extension occurs. What is the role of reflection in this process?
12. Explain the story of the farmer from Song. What claim do you believe Mengzi is illustrating with this metaphor?
13. In what ways does Mengzi conceive of Heaven as like a personal God, and in what ways does he conceive of it as simply the impersonal operations of the universe?
14. Give a concrete example to illustrate what qi is. Why does Mengzi think it is important to cultivate one's qi? How does one cultivate it?
15. What later movement praised Mengzi as the Second Sage? What did they think was especially important about him?

▪ 7 ▪

LANGUAGE AND PARADOX
IN THE "SCHOOL OF NAMES"

I left for Yue today but arrived yesterday.
—Hui Shi

Thinkers in the "School of Names" argued for paradoxical conclusions like Gongsun Long's
claim that "a white horse is not a horse."

I. Deng Xi and the Origins of the "School"

Every philosophical tradition has some thinkers who delight in making ingenious arguments for paradoxical conclusions. Sometimes these thinkers are sincere and have serious philosophical purposes. Other times they are more mischievous or playful. In the latter category was Deng Xi, about whom the following anecdote was told:

> The Wei River is very great in size. A wealthy man from Zheng drowned in it, and someone retrieved his body. The wealthy man's family sought to buy it, but the one who found the body was asking a great deal of money. The family reported this to Deng Xi, who said, "Do not worry about it. He certainly can sell it to no one else." The man who found the corpse was anxious about this and reported to Deng Xi, who told him, "Do not worry about it. They certainly will be unable to buy the corpse from someone else."[i]

As this illustrates, Deng Xi advocated the doctrine that "both arguments are acceptable," meaning that either side of any position can be defended equally well. Deng Xi developed his argumentative skills in court, where he would represent people in lawsuits for a fee. He was thus an ancient Chinese attorney. There is an interesting historical parallel here with the Sophists of ancient Greece. The Sophists were paid to write speeches for use in court and at least some of them were happy to defend either side in an argument, but others engaged in and promoted serious, subtle philosophical debate. One of the Greek Sophists was Protagoras, famous for his claim that "humans are the measure of all things," which could be interpreted as a Chinese version of "both arguments are acceptable."

   Deng Xi was the first philosopher in the "School of Names" (sometimes also called the Dialecticians or the Sophists). The "School of Names" is not really an organized movement. It is, instead, a label (coined later in the Han dynasty) for categorizing thinkers who used subtle argumentation to defend paradoxical conclusions. Consequently, we shall always put quotation marks around the name to distinguish it from organized sects with masters and disciples, like the Confucians and Mohists.

   Deng Xi lived near the end of the Spring and Autumn Period, but the two most famous philosophers in the "School of Names," Hui Shi and Gongsun Long, lived much later, in the late fourth and early third centuries BCE. These latter two thinkers brought about a crisis in Chinese philosophy because their paradoxical arguments undermined confidence in the reliability of argumentation and even language itself. This may not have been their intention. Hui Shi in particular seems to have been committed to argumentation as a tool for serious philosophy. However, later thinkers had to respond in some way to Hui Shi and Gongsun Long. At the end of this chapter, we'll look at the Later Mohist attempt to defend and restructure argumentation. In later chapters, we'll examine how Daoists and Confucians reacted.

We have already dealt with many challenging philosophical arguments in this book, but the arguments we'll examine in this chapter are subtle and complicated in a different way. The best way to approach them is to try to have fun with the puzzles and paradoxes.

II. Hui Shi

Hui Shi was particularly intriguing because he combined a career as a statesman with serious philosophical contributions. He rose to prominence as a high official to King Hui of the state of Wei. The ruler admired him so much that he even gave Hui Shi the honorary title of "King's uncle." However, when Wei suffered a decisive military defeat, Hui Shi was forced to flee before officials of the victorious state of Qin could seize him.[1]

As a philosopher, Hui Shi is famous for defending the Ten Theses:

1. There is nothing outside what is supremely large. Call it the "great one." There is nothing inside what is supremely small. Call it the "small one."
2. That which has no thickness cannot be accumulated, yet it can be a thousand leagues large.
3. Heaven and Earth are equally low. Mountains and marshes are on the same level.
4. At the moment that the Sun is at its highest, it is setting. At the moment that something is born, it is dying.
5. When things that are very similar are differentiated from things that are less similar, this is called "small comparison." When the myriad things are all similar and all different, this is called "great comparison."
6. The South is inexhaustible yet exhaustible.
7. I left for Yue today but arrived yesterday.
8. Linked rings can be separated.

---

1. Hui Shi was a contemporary of Mengzi, but Mengzi arrived in Liang (the capital city of Wei) right after Hui Shi fled. Consequently, we will never know what intellectual fireworks would have resulted had they met and debated.

9. I know the center of the world: it is north of Yan and south of Yue.[2]
10. Indiscriminately care for the myriad things. Heaven and Earth are one whole.[ii]

What were Hui Shi's arguments for these theses? We shall never know for sure, because none of Hui Shi's own writings have survived to the present day. However, we can make educated guesses based on what seem to be arguments influenced by Hui Shi in other early texts. The Ten Theses fall into three groups: spatial paradoxes (numbers 1 and 2), paradoxes of perspective (numbers 3–9), and an ethical claim (number 10). Let's look at a possible interpretation of one of the spatial paradoxes and one of the paradoxes of perspective.

The "great one" of Thesis 1 probably refers to the universe as a whole. It is certainly a unique something (hence a "one"), but unlike others entities there is nothing beyond it or bounding it. If there were something outside the universe, that would just be another part of the universe, so it would not really be "outside." The "small one" of the same thesis probably refers to a mathematical point, which has location, but not width, depth, or breadth. We tend to associate the origins of formal mathematics with Western thinkers like Euclid and the Pythagoreans. However, we know from the Later Mohist writings (which we examine in Section IV of this chapter) that Chinese thinkers also had the concept of a point, and saw it as somehow foundational to other spatial dimensions.

The key to understanding the seventh thesis ("I left for Yue today but arrived yesterday") is to notice the relative or relational nature of terms like "today" and "yesterday." Suppose I left for the state of Yue on Tuesday and arrived on Wednesday. On Tuesday, I could truthfully utter, "I left for Yue today," but on Thursday I could truthfully utter, "I arrived in Yue yesterday." The fact is that every day is a today, a yesterday, and a tomorrow, all depending on your perspective.

Below, I will offer one possible interpretation of the other theses and of how they relate to the ethical claim of thesis 10. But before you read on, I invite you to pause and come up with your own interpretation.

Thesis 1: *There is nothing outside what is supremely large. Call it the "great one." There is nothing inside what is supremely small. Call it the "small one."* Do you agree with the interpretation of this thesis given above?

Thesis 2: *That which has no thickness cannot be accumulated, yet it can be a thousand leagues large.* A mathematical point (the "small one" of Thesis 1)

---

2. Yan was a state in the far north, while Yue was a state in the far south.

has no width. If it did, it would be divisible into further points, but there is nothing "inside" a point. Things with no width cannot be combined to produce anything with width. However, a line that is a thousand leagues long is made up of points.

Thesis 3: *Heaven and Earth are equally low. Mountains and marshes are on the same level.* Whether something is low or high depends on where you measure it from. For example, New York City is high relative to Death Valley but low relative to Aspen. Consequently, any location can be taken to be any height, depending on what reference point we take as our start.

Thesis 4: *At the moment that the Sun is at its highest, it is setting. At the moment that something is born, it is dying.* We normally say that the sun is "setting" a little while before it disappears over the horizon. But in actuality the sun is beginning its descent at noon. Consequently, it depends upon our perspective when we judge that it is setting. Similarly, we normally say that someone is "dying" when their death is imminent, but from the moment of birth one is approaching death.

Thesis 5: *When things that are very similar are differentiated from things that are less similar, this is called "small comparison." When the myriad things are all similar and all different, this is called "great comparison."* When we group things together, we focus on some respect in which they are similar to one another and exclude things that are not similar in that particular respect. For example, I might group you and me together as "humans," and distinguish us from Spot, Fluffy, and Tweetie as "animals." However, from another perspective, I might group myself with Spot as members of my household, and group you with Fluffy as members of your household. These are all examples of "small comparison." However, any two things in the universe are similar in at least some respects (or they would not be "things") and different in other respects (or they would not be multiple things). Recognizing this is "great comparison."

Thesis 6: *The South is inexhaustible yet exhaustible.* Hui Shi's argument for this thesis would depend on what he took the shape of the Earth to be. If he thought the Earth was spherical, the south would be "inexhaustible" because someone headed in a southern direction could keep going in the same direction forever (as she circled the globe). However, the south would also be "exhaustible" because the circumference of the Earth would be a specific, limited number.

Thesis 7: *I left for Yue today but arrived yesterday.* I gave one argument for this thesis above, but here is an alternative explanation that illustrates how one might argue for these claims in different ways. Perhaps I cross the border between my state and Yue at precisely midnight, Tuesday evening/Wednesday morning. The border is part of both states, and midnight is part of both days, so I might truthfully state that I left for Yue today (Wednesday) but arrived yesterday (Tuesday).[iii]

Thesis 8: *Linked rings can be separated.* Imagine two intertwined rings held so that they are not touching. In other words, the rings are at right angles to one another, each passing through the center of the other. These rings are still "linked," but you could say they are "separated" because there is space between them.

Thesis 9: *I know the center of the world: it is north of Yan and south of Yue.* The Chinese in Hui Shi's era identified themselves as occupying the "Central States," in contrast with the "barbarians" who lived outside the center. But Hui Shi points out that "center" is relative to your perspective. For the barbarians living up north of Yan, the center of the world is there; for barbarians living south of Yue, the center of the world is there.

Thesis 10: *Indiscriminately care for the myriad things. Heaven and Earth are one whole.* This thesis demonstrates that Hui Shi was not merely fond of abstract paradoxes; there was a serious ethical purpose behind his argumentation. Thesis 10 can be seen as a conclusion that follows from the preceding theses. Generally, people have "differentiated care": we care more for ourselves than for other people, and more for our community than for strangers. In order for this differentiated care to be justified, there has to be some distinction between things that is not purely arbitrary. We might try to distinguish things either spatially or qualitatively. Theses 1 and 2 call into question the practice of dividing things from one another spatially, while Theses 3 through 9 call into question qualitative divisions.

Consider spatial differentiation. We typically think that one entity is distinguished from another (like you from me) because there is a spatial separation between us. But Theses 1 and 2 draw our attention to the fact that space is infinitely divisible, so there are no spatial "gaps" to individuate one thing from another. Consider a point, P1, which is supposedly at the boundary of my body. For any point we pick, P2, which is on the other side of this boundary, there will be another point P3, which is in between P1 and P2. We can then find another point, P4, between P1 and P3, and so on. Since there is no point that is "next" after P1, the attempt to set a spatial boundary must be conventional and arbitrary. Consequently, if we are to distinguish one individual from another or one community from another, and if that distinction is supposed to give us a justification for different treatment of the two, it cannot be on the basis of spatial separation alone. Any division between things that justifies differential treatment must be based on a qualitative distinction.

Theses 3, 4, and 7 attempt to illustrate how qualitative distinctions—such as whether a city is high or low; when the Sun starts setting or a person begins dying; whether we think of Tuesday as tomorrow, today, or yesterday—depend upon the arbitrary assumption of a perspective. Thesis 5 generalizes these examples to make a claim about the dependence of all differentiation upon perspective: for any two things, we can take the perspective from which they are different (which is merely "small comparison") or the perspective from which they are similar ("great comparison").

Rather than emphasize how you are different from me (in social class, education, family, etc.), I can choose to emphasize how you are similar to me (in being human, in needing food, in suffering when injured). There is no reason to prefer "small comparison," so there is no justification for differentiated caring.

Fact: The British civil service examinations and their later U.S. counterparts were consciously modeled on the civil service examinations of premodern China. In both cultures, there is a long-standing debate about whether the exams, intended to select people based on merit rather than family background, are fair and accurate.

- Some of Hui Shi's theses may be intended as political analogies. This is most obvious in the case of thesis 9, because it calls into question the privileging of Chinese civilization as occupying the "center" of the world. But thesis 8 may also have a political point: just as linked rings can be seen as either connected or separated, so can the king and the lowliest peasant. The latter are separated by spatial distance, wealth, and social status, but they are also connected, because the king depends upon the peasants to grow food, while the peasants depend upon the king to disburse food from the granaries during a famine. We might make a similar point about the separation between me and the person half a world away who picks the beans that end up being used for my morning coffee.

In summary, the overall point of Hui Shi's philosophy is that we should "indiscriminately care" for everyone and everything, because all spatial and qualitative distinctions among things are arbitrary and, hence, unjustified. Of course, this is just one way of understanding Hui Shi's paradoxes and how they are related. I hope you will try to come up with other and perhaps more plausible interpretations of your own. In particular, one possibility is that we should group theses 1 through 4 together as spatial paradoxes, and theses 5 through 8 as qualitative paradoxes. This makes the arrangement of the theses less arbitrary, because each section would begin with a general introductory thesis (1 and 5, respectively).

Hui Shi is a fascinating figure but frustrating to study because we must guess what his arguments were. We are in a much better position with the next major figure in the "School of Names," Gongsun Long.

III. *Gongsun Long*

Gongsun Long is best known for a philosophical dialogue, "On the White Horse," which survives to the present day (*Readings,* pp. 363–68). "On the White Horse" is reminiscent in style of the Socratic dialogues of Plato. It presents a debate between two unnamed figures who are conventionally referred to as the Advocate and the Objector. The Advocate defends the acceptability of the claim that "A white horse is not a horse," while the Objector argues against it. One of the Advocate's arguments is a reductio ad absurdum. He claims that if it were true that a white horse is a horse, wanting a white horse would be the same as wanting a black or yellow horse.

> B: If one wants a horse, that extends to a yellow or black horse. But if one wants a white horse, that does not extend to a yellow or black horse. Suppose that a white horse were a horse. Then what one wants [in the two cases] would be the same. If what one wants were the same, then white [horse] would not differ from horse. If what one wants does not differ, then how is it that a yellow or black horse is sometimes acceptable and sometimes unacceptable? (*Readings,* p. 365)

We might paraphrase the Advocate's argument like this:

> B* (paraphrase of B): If you went to a stable and asked simply for a horse, the stable hand could bring you any color horse: yellow, black, etc. But if you asked for a white horse, the stable hand could not bring you a yellow or black horse. However, suppose it were true that "a white horse is a horse." In that case, if you went to a stable and asked for a white horse, it would be perfectly acceptable for the stable hand to bring you a black horse. If you complained, the stable hand could reply, "A white horse is a horse, so to want a white horse is to want a horse. A black horse is also a horse, so to give you a black horse is to give you a horse. Therefore, you wanted a horse, and I gave you a horse."

Obviously, there is some sort of dialectical sleight of hand going on here, but the trick is to identify where it occurs, because each individual step in the Advocate's argument has some plausibility to it.

There is a linguistic claim underlying the Advocate's argument:

> A: "Horse" is that by means of which one names the shape. "White" is that by means of which one names the color. What names the color is not what names the shape. Hence, I say that a white horse is not a horse. (*Readings*, p. 364)

All of this seems true and unobjectionable up until the "Hence, I say. . . ." Why does the Advocate think this conclusion follows from what he has said? The key is an assumption that the Advocate does not state here (but does make explicit later in the dialogue, in section C): "A white horse is a horse and white." With this assumption in mind, we can paraphrase the Advocate's argument as follows:

> A* (paraphrase of A): The term "white" refers to a color and the term "horse" refers to a shape. (The expression "white horse" refers to a combination of color and shape.) Since color is not the same as shape, "white horse" and "white" refer to different things. Hence, a white horse is not a horse.

The Objector tries to isolate the mistake the Advocate is making:

> E.1: If there are white horses, one cannot say that there are no horses, because of what is called the separability of white. Only according to those people who do not separate can having a white horse not be said to be having a horse. Hence, the reason we think there are horses is only that we think that "horse" is "there are horses." It is not that we think "there are white horses" is "there are horses." Hence, because of the reason that there are horses, one cannot say that a white horse is not a horse. (*Readings*, pp. 366–67)

In other words,

> E.1* (paraphrase of E.1): If there are white horses, then there are horses. This is because of the "separability of white." (According to the "separability of white," in the expression, "white horse," we can separate out the term "white" or the term "horse.") Hence, the reason we go from "there are white horses" to "there are horses" is that we separate out "horses" in the first expression. It is not that we think the expressions "there are white horses" and "there are horses" are the same. Hence, we say that a white horse is a horse for the same reason: we just separate out "horse" from the expression "white horse."

However, the Advocate insists that one cannot always separate the term "horse" from the expression "white horse":

> E.2: "Horse" is indifferent to color. Hence [if you only wanted a horse], a yellow or black horse would each be appropriate. "White horse" does select for color. So [if you wanted a white horse,] a yellow or black horse would be rejected on account of its color. Hence, only a white horse alone would be appropriate. That which does not reject [like "horse" does not exclude a white, yellow, or black horse] is not what does reject [like "white horse," which does exclude a black or yellow horse]. Hence, I say that a white horse is not a horse. (*Readings,* p. 367)

The key to understanding this dialogue is an ambiguity in a particular grammatical construction. Fortunately, the same ambiguity exists in English, so you don't need to read Classical Chinese to understand it. What does it mean to state "X is not Y"? This might seem very straightforward, but consider the difference between saying "Batman is not a bat" and "Batman is not Jimmy Olsen." The former sentence denies that one thing is part of a particular group, while the latter sentence denies that one thing is identical with another thing. You don't generally notice this distinction, because context normally makes clear what sense is intended. Now consider "white horses are not horses."[3] This could have two meanings:

1. The group of things that are both white and horses is *not a part of* the group of things that are horses.
2. The group of things that are both white and horses is *not identical* to the group of things that are horses.

We could express these senses using formal symbols:

1*. NOT [{white things} ∩ {horses} ⊆ {horses}]
2*. NOT [{white things} ∩ {horses} ≡ {horses}]

The first claim in each pair is obviously false. However, the second claim in each pair is true. When the Advocate asserts "a white horse is not a horse," it seems as though he is asserting claim 1, and this is the claim that the Objector argues against. However, the Advocate is actually defending claim 2! The Advocate's arguments all make perfect sense if you interpret "a white horse is not

---

3. The original Chinese sentence can be translated as either "a white horse is not a horse" or "white horses are not horses." I have switched the translation here because it is easier to see the semantic structure of the latter sentence.

a horse" in this way. Consequently, the Objector's arguments have no force against the Advocate's position. There are two important lessons here: Make sure that you understand a position before you start criticizing it. In addition, during the course of an argument, be on the lookout for the possibility that you may have misunderstood your opponent's position.

It may be that the Advocate is intentionally exploiting this ambiguity in the expression "a white horse is not a horse." Recall that the thesis the Advocate is defending is that it *can be* that a white horse is not a horse. We might also translate this as: It is *acceptable* that a white horse is not a horse. In other words, the Advocate is only arguing that "a white horse is not a horse" *could* be true, given a certain interpretation. He might acknowledge that, in another interpretation, "a white horse *is* a horse." So perhaps the Objector and the Advocate would agree if they fully understood each other's position.

Then again, perhaps not. Notice that the Objector asserts "it *cannot* be that a white horse is not a horse" (D; *Readings,* p. 366). What many people found so disorienting and even dangerous about the "School of Names" is that it seemed to undermine our confidence in the possibility of using language and argumentation to guide our actions and describe the world. The Objector may be desperate to rule out the possibility that "a white horse is not a horse" is true on *any* interpretation. If we can legitimately assert outlandish claims like "I left for Yue today but arrived yesterday" and "a white horse it not a horse," then perhaps it really is true that "both arguments are acceptable" on every topic.

IV. The Later Mohists

As we saw in Chapter 4, the early Mohists pushed argumentation to new levels of sophistication. However, they opposed the use of argumentation to arrive at paradoxical conclusions, like those defended by Hui Shi and Gongsun Long. Consequently, the movement known as Later Mohism developed in opposition to the "School of Names." The Later Mohist writings are fascinating works of philosophy. In addition to combating what they see as sophistries, they explore issues in the philosophy of language, dialectics (the theory of argumentation), the foundations of ethics, and even natural sciences, including geometry, optics, and mechanics. Unfortunately, the Later Mohist writings have come down to us in a fragmentary and difficult-to-interpret form. Consequently, I will frequently paraphrase rather than quote them in this section. In addition, the Later Mohists do not typically identify whom a given argument is directed against. However, we often understand their arguments better if we see them as replies to particular positions.

1. Resolving the Paradox of Deng Xi

Recall Deng Xi's thesis that in any debate "both arguments are acceptable." This can be interpreted in a number of ways, and the Mohists respond to several specific formulations. Thus, if one claims that *neither side in an argument is the correct one,* the Later Mohists reply,

> There are cases in which two alternatives can both be correct or both be incorrect. For example, if you call this thing a "dog" and I call it a "canine," we are both correct. Or if you call a dog a "horse" and I call it an "ox," we are both wrong. However, genuine argumentation is over exclusive alternatives, such as whether this particular thing is "ox" or "not ox." One and only one of these options can be true.[iv]

Every statement is true; no statement is false. The Later Mohists reply,

> It is self-contradictory to deny that some statements are false. Either you deny the falsity of your own position or not. If you deny the falsity of your own position, then you do not deny falsity (because you admit that the denial of your position is false). If you do not deny the falsity of your own position, then you do not deny falsity (because you admit that your own position is false). In either case, you deny your own statement.[v,4]

Every statement is self-contradictory. The Later Mohists reply,

> It is self-contradictory to regard every statement as self-contradictory. If you assert this, either your words are true or not. What is self-contradictory is not true. So if your statement is true, it is not self-contradictory. If it is not true, it is certainly not plausible.[vi]

When we turn to Zhuangzi (in Chapter 9), we'll consider another way of understanding Deng Xi's thesis, which the Mohists may not have successfully answered.

2. Resolving the Paradoxes of Hui Shi

In reply to the spatial paradoxes of Hui Shi, the Later Mohists state,

> A "point" is "the dimensionless unit which precedes all others." Since a point is the endpoint of a line segment, there is no paradox in the fact that lengths are composed of points.[vii]

----

4. This argument is remarkably similar to one that Plato gave against Protagorean relativism.

This does not undermine Hui Shi's underlying contention that spatial division is arbitrary. However, I think that with this argument the Mohists simply wanted to show that the notion of a "point" is not paradoxical. They had a serious interest in the sciences of geometry, optics, and mechanics, so it was important to them that the notion of a mathematical "point" not be undermined.

It was Hui Shi's paradoxes of perspective that the Later Mohists were most concerned about defusing. They used "this" and "that" as examples of perspectival terms. Suppose that I am lecturing in a classroom and I refer to "this" lectern in front of me. You, sitting a few rows back, would refer to the same thing as "that" lectern. "This" and "that" appear to be contrasting terms, but it is also true that one entity is both "this" and "that," depending upon one's perspective. However, the Mohists argue that there is no paradox or contradiction here:

> Terms like "that" and "this" can switch what they refer to. But as long as we refer to this as "this," we have to refer to that as "that." If we change and refer to this as "that," we must also change and refer to that as "this." This presents no difficulties as long as we confine ourselves for the moment to one or the other way of speaking.[viii]

In other words, a person can correctly talk about "this" lectern *and* can correctly talk about "that" lectern but cannot correctly call it both "this" and "that" lectern in the same context. We must "confine ourselves" to one or the other manner of speaking at a time.

It might not be immediately clear why this argument is so important, but notice that all of Hui Shi's paradoxes of perspective have the same form as the case of "this" and "that." For example, I can truthfully say that "I left for Yue today" and that "I arrived in Yue yesterday," but I cannot truthfully say them both in the same context. Again, we must "confine ourselves" to one or the other manner of speaking at a time. Hui Shi's paradoxes 3–9 can all be dealt with in the same way.

3. Resolving the White Horse Paradox

The Mohist solution to the White Horse Paradox lies in noticing a structural parallel between the sentence "white horses are not horses" and the sentence "oxen and horses are not horses."

> "Oxen and horses are not oxen" and "oxen and horses are oxen" are both acceptable, because the oxen and horses form a group. Suppose you deny that "oxen and horses are oxen" because some of them are

not oxen, or you deny that "oxen and horses are *not* oxen" because some of them *are* oxen. You would then have to admit that "oxen and horses *are* oxen" because some of them are oxen. Moreover, an ox is not two, and a horse is not two, but an ox and a horse are two (so what is true of oxen need not be true of oxen and horses). Hence, even though we cannot deny that "oxen are oxen" and "horses are horses," there is no problem with it being the case that "oxen and horses are not oxen" and "oxen and horses are not horses."[ix]

In other words, we can say that "oxen and horses are not oxen" because the group of oxen *and* horses is not identical with the group of oxen; however, it is equally legitimate to state that "oxen and horses *are* oxen" because some members of the former group are part of the latter group.

How is this relevant to the White Horse Paradox? What makes this paradox so troubling is that it appears to make it false that "a white horse is a horse." However, the Later Mohist argument suggests that we must draw the same conclusion about "white horses are not horses" that we would draw about "oxen and horses are not horses." Specifically, we can say that "a white horse is not a horse" (because the group of white horses is not identical with the group of horses), but it is equally legitimate to state that "white horses are horses" (because the members of the former group are part of the latter group).

It might seem to be problematic for the Mohists, opponents of paradox and sophistry, to accept both "a white horse is a horse" and "a white horse is *not* a horse." However, they can appeal here to their resolution of Hui Shi's perspectival paradoxes. Just as Tuesday can be either "yesterday" or "today," we can say that, in one sense (the standard one), a white horse is a horse, but in another sense a white horse is not a horse. There is no contradiction here so long as we "confine ourselves" to one sense or the other at a time.

4. The New Foundation of Mohist Ethics

In addition to responding to the "School of Names," the Later Mohists significantly revised the foundation of their ethics. Instead of characterizing "benefit" in terms of wealth, populousness, and order, they provide a more psychological definition:

- "Benefit" is what one is pleased to get.

- "Harm" is what one dislikes getting.

However, this does not mean that anything a person happens to want is a benefit for them:

- "Desire" is either immediate or having weighed the benefits.

- "Dislike" is either immediate or having weighed the harms.

Something that one would dislike "immediately" may be what one desires once one has weighed the long-term consequences:

> The wrong alternative when weighed becoming the right, and the wrong rejected as the wrong, are the "weighed" and the "immediate." Cutting off a finger to save an arm is choosing the larger among benefits and the smaller among harms. . . . One desires it because there is no alternative; it is not that one desires it immediately.ˣ

Based on these considerations, the specifically ethical terms can easily be defined:

- "Caring" is [desiring to benefit individuals].[5]

- "Benevolence" is caring for individuals.

- "Righteousness" is benefiting.

- To act "for the sake of" others is to give the most weight to their desires when one knows all there is to know.

- A "sage" is one who a priori desires or dislikes things for the sake of people.ˣⁱ

"A priori" refers to what can be known independently of sensory experience. It is often contrasted with "a posteriori," which refers to things that can be known only through experience. Western philosophers may be surprised or suspicious about the use of this phrase in translating an ancient Chinese text. However, it is clear that the Mohists distinguish between something like a priori and a posteriori knowledge:

> "Knowledge" is either by report, by explanation, or by experience. "By report" is when you get it second hand. "By explanation" is like "if it is square, it will not rotate." "By experience" is when you are a witness yourself.

Another illustration of knowing by explanation is understanding what a circle is:

---

5. The Later Mohist text contains the heading "caring" (or "love") in the midst of the other definitions, but the accompanying characterization is missing. A number of scholars agree, though, that the original definition is something like what I have supplied in brackets.

- "Circular" is having the same lengths from a single center.

- The circle stays even after we "jump the city wall." By the things that follow upon or exclude each other we know a priori what it is.[xii]

To "jump the city wall" is to be unable to directly observe something. The point is that even if we are unable to see a particular circle, we know that it is circular because of the "explanation" of what a circle is; similarly, we know that a square will not rotate easily against a surface whether or not we can directly observe it.

The Later Mohists thus reformulated ethics in a manner that is startlingly close to a deductive system based on a set of interlocking definitions. Nonetheless, it would be a mistake to attribute to the Mohists formal logic as we understand it in the West.

5. The Limits of Logic

What is formal logic? Consider this argument:

1. All humans are mammals.
2. All mammals are warm-blooded.
3. Therefore, all humans are warm-blooded.

If the premises (1 and 2) are true, then the conclusion (3) must also be true. This might seem too obvious to be worth stating, but Aristotle made a huge conceptual breakthrough when he noticed that sentences like this are a special example of a general pattern:

1. All A are B.
2. All B are C.
3. Therefore, all A are C.

Aristotle realized that there are many such patterns, that we can categorize them, and that doing so will enable us to understand and evaluate much more complex chains of reasoning. Formal logic has advanced a long way since Aristotle, but it all began with these insights.

The Later Mohists were keenly interested in argumentation, but they never developed formal logic. Some historians see this as a regrettable failing. However, I offer two reasons why we should not think less of Chinese philosophy because it did not develop formal logic. First, one does not need formal logic to argue rationally or logically (in a broad sense of that term). Even in the West, Parmenides, Zeno, Socrates, and Plato produced rational arguments without needing to wait for Aristotle's logic. So-called informal reasoning can be very powerful. Indeed, speaking as someone trained in and conversant with contemporary Western philosophy, I am struck by how small a role technical formal logic actually plays in most philosophy.

Furthermore, one of the reasons the Later Mohists did not develop formal logic is that they had a deep insight into an aspect of ordinary language that was only fully appreciated by Western philosophers over two millennia later. Consider these sentences:

1. A white horse is a horse.
2. To ride a white horse is to ride a horse.

It might seem that we could generalize this to the following pattern:

P1. X is Y
P2. To do A to X is to do A to Y.

However, the Later Mohists noted that, while the previous example of this pattern is reliable, there are other instances that are not:

3. Jane's brother is a handsome man.
4. For Jane to love her brother is for Jane to love a handsome man.

The problem with this second instance is that if we say "Jane loves a handsome man," it sounds like Jane is *in love with* someone, and that certainly does not follow from the fact that she loves her brother. The Mohists give another illustration of how the pattern fails:

5. Robbers are people.
6. Having lots of robbers is having lots of people.[xiii]

We might have a very low population but a very high percentage of robbers, so it would be true that we have "lots of robbers," but false that we therefore have "lots of people."

The Mohists describe sentence pairs such as 1 and 2 as cases in which "it is this and that is so"; Western philosophers call sentences like 2 "transparent contexts." Sentence pairs like 3 and 4, or 5 and 6 are labeled by the Mohists as cases in which "it is this, but that is not so"; Western philosophers refer to sentences like 4 and 6 as "opaque contexts." Opaque contexts are those in which, if you substitute two terms that refer to the same thing, you cannot be sure you will preserve the truth of the sentence.[6] The existence of opaque

---

6. The examples that have particularly engaged recent Western philosophers are belief contexts, like "Lois Lane believes that Clark Kent is a mild-mannered reporter." Despite the truth of this sentence and the truth of the claim that "Clark Kent is Superman," it does not follow that "Lois Lane believes that Superman is a mild-mannered reporter."

contexts frustrates the effort to identify patterns of inference that will *always* be reliable. Or, as the Later Mohists put it, "The parallelism of sentences is exact only up to a certain point."[xiv] Thus, it was not a failure of rigor that kept Chinese philosophy from developing formal logic; it was a deep insight into the limitations of truth-preserving patterns in ordinary language.

V. Historical Significance

Hui Shi sought to use his subtle argumentation for constructive philosophical purposes. In addition, responding to the paradoxes of Deng Xi, Hui Shi, and Gongsun Long led to sophisticated discussions of dialectic and the philosophy of language by the Later Mohists and others. However, for many (including the Confucians) the lesson to be learned from the "School of Names" was to simply refuse to engage in abstract discussions that are not grounded in everyday life. This attitude is well illustrated by the story of what happened when Gongsun Long won a debate in which he argued that a human has three ears. The ruler in front of whom the debate was conducted was initially very impressed. However, the ruler's advisor (who was the one defeated in the debate) remarked,

> May I put a question to your lordship? The claim that a human has three ears is difficult to argue because it is actually wrong, whereas the claim that a human has two ears is easy to argue because it is actually right. I wonder whether your lordship will follow what is easy and right, or what is difficult and wrong?

The next day, the ruler told Gongsun Long to stop pestering his advisor: "In him, the way things are triumphs over rhetoric, while in you rhetoric triumphs over the way things are."[xv] It is possible that many people in China had a similar distaste for abstruse and unintuitive argumentation, because the "School of Names" disappeared by the end of the Warring States Period.

   In contrast with Chinese philosophy, the tradition of using complex arguments for surprising conclusions lived on in Western philosophy. It began with Parmenides and continues through recent philosophers like Saul Kripke. Plato may have been crucial in keeping this particular tradition alive, because he wrote inspiring philosophical dialogues that wove subtle metaphysical argumentation and a challenging ethical ideal into a beautiful literary style. Bertrand Russell (one of the founding figures of contemporary Anglo-American philosophy) expressed this approach to philosophy when he remarked, "the point of philosophy is to start with something so simple as not to seem worth stating, and to end with something so paradoxical that no one will believe it."[xvi]

While the Later Mohists attempted to sharpen rational argumentation in order to defuse the paradoxes of the "School of Names," others like the Confucians chose to evade the debate by sticking with "common sense." A third reaction to the dizzying paradoxes of the "School of Names" was a general suspicion about the reliability of argumentation and even ordinary language. This approach is seen in the mysticism of Daoist texts like the *Daodejing* and the *Zhuangzi*. It is to these approaches that we turn in the next two chapters.

Review Questions

1. Why do we consistently put "School of Names" in quotation marks but not Mohism or Confucianism?

2. For what thesis is Deng Xi famous? What does it mean?

3. Explain Hui Shi's thesis that "I left for Yue today but arrived yesterday."

4. What are the two possible meanings of "a white horse is not a horse"? Explain why it is true on one of those interpretations and why it is false on the other.

5. How did the Mohists reply to the claim that "every statement is true"?

6. How did the Mohists use the example of "this" and "that" to reply to the perspectival paradoxes of Hui Shi?

7. Explain the distinction between "a priori" and "a posteriori."

8. Give an example of the sort of patterns that formal logic studies.

9. Give one example of an opaque context and one example of a transparent context.

■ 8 ■

THE *DAODEJING* AND MYSTICISM

Ways can be spoken, but they are not constant Ways.
Names can be named, but they are not constant names.
—Daodejing

Laozi is said to have grown disillusioned with society and left China riding
on an ox.

I. Myth and Reality

The *Daodejing*, attributed to Laozi, is one of the most famous classics of world literature. Along with the Bible and the Bhagavad Gita, it is one of the three most widely translated works ever and the extent of its cultural influence is immense. *The Simpsons* has referenced it. Director Sam Peckinpah's controversial, ultraviolent film *Straw Dogs* takes its title from it. Ronald Reagan quoted it in one of his State of the Union Addresses. Architect Frank Lloyd Wright drew inspiration from it. The seminal German philosopher Martin Heidegger collaborated on a translation of it.[i]

However, the *Daodejing* is especially prone to misinterpretation and misappropriation. This is due in part to the fact that, although it has been rendered in many languages, the *Daodejing* is often badly mistranslated. Indeed, it is amazingly common for people to "translate" the *Daodejing* without knowing how to read Chinese.[ii] Furthermore, because the *Daodejing* is written in such an enigmatic style, people tend to project onto it whatever meaning they want to find. Even within the Chinese tradition, a considerable body of myth has grown up around both the *Daodejing* and Laozi. So let's begin with some often-overlooked facts about Daoism.

• Daoism did not exist in ancient China.

• Laozi, the author of the *Daodejing*, did not exist either.

• The *Daodejing* is not about being mellow, following your bliss, or just taking life easy. And it has nothing to do with Winnie the Pooh.[1]

Let's take these facts in turn. During the period covered in this book, Daoism was not an organized movement (or group of related sects), the way Confucianism and Mohism were. The term "Daoism" was coined much later, during the Han dynasty, as one of several labels to categorize thinkers with similar views. Also during the Han, Daoism became an organized religion, with elaborate rituals, clergy, and scriptures. However, the doctrines of this religion often differed from those of classic "Daoist" texts from the Warring States Period. For example, later Daoism was frequently associated with efforts to achieve physical immortality through the use of elixirs.

Laozi was identified as the founder of this later Daoist religion and the author of the *Daodejing*. However, this story is suspicious for many reasons.

---

1. *The Tao of Pooh* by Benjamin Hoff (reprint, New York: Viking Press, 1983) is a charming work that has attained a wide readership. There is nothing wrong with enjoying it for itself. But it reveals much more about how the *Daodejing* has been appropriated to illustrate Western Romanticism than it does about the *Daodejing* itself. (See later in this section for more on Romanticism.)

Though he was supposedly a contemporary of Kongzi (in the Spring and Autumn Period), there are no references to him in any texts until about three centuries later (late in the Warring States Period). Furthermore, the earliest Chinese historian to write a biography of Laozi reports sharply conflicting accounts of his actions, his lifetime, and even his name. "Laozi" really means "Old Master" and does not appear to be an actual name. No wonder this historian sighs, "Our generation does not know the truth of the matter."[iii] Many modern scholars are drawn to a simple explanation for these discrepancies: stories about several different "old masters" coalesced to form the legend of "Laozi."

Mythical or not, a couple of the stories about Laozi are sufficiently intriguing and influential that they are worth repeating. Laozi was supposedly a scribe in the Zhou dynasty archives. Kongzi went to see him, hoping to learn more about the Zhou rituals. However, Laozi rebuked Kongzi on three grounds. First, Kongzi asked about the mere "words" of those who have "already rotted away." Second, a gentleman simply "moves on like a tumbleweed" if his era is not receptive to his message (instead of trying to obtain an official position as Kongzi did). Third,

Myth: *"The Great Wall is the only human creation visible from space."*

Fact: *Although this myth is repeated countless times, even in documentaries and news reports, it is impossible to see the Great Wall from space with the unaided eye. It still is a great wall, though.*

Kongzi's efforts only show his arrogance. Laozi therefore dismisses Kongzi, saying, "What I have to tell you is this, and nothing more."[iv] We can see why later Daoists would like this story, because it presents Laozi as having the upper hand in his one exchange with Kongzi.

Seeing that the Zhou dynasty was continuing to decline, Laozi got on an ox and headed off to the "uncivilized" regions to the West. Gentlemen normally traveled in a carriage or chariot, so the image of this sage riding an ox is striking. When he arrived at the pass leading into the mountains, the border guard implored him to write down his teachings before leaving. To satisfy this official, Laozi casually jotted down the *Daodejing* before riding off. This myth helps explain why Laozi—who after all warned Kongzi against mere "words"—bothered to write down any work at all.

If the preceding stories are myths, who *did* write the *Daodejing*? No one wrote it. Philological and historical studies of the *Daodejing* suggest that it is an anthology that records a variety of oral sayings and did not become something like the book we recognize until the third century BCE. In Chinese, this book is most commonly referred to as the *Laozi*, after its supposed author. But in order to emphasize the fact that we have a text without a single creator, I shall refer to it by its alternative title, the *Daodejing*, which means the *Classic of the Way and Virtue.* Although the Way and Virtue are important concepts in the work, the title seems to be taken simply from the first words of the first and second books of the text. In recent decades, alternative versions of all or part of the *Daodejing* have been unearthed from ancient tombs (near the villages of Mawangdui and Guodian). But the translation found in *Readings in Classical Chinese Philosophy* is based largely on what has been the traditional version of the *Daodejing* in China for two millennia.[2]

Although it lacks a single author, there do seem to be enough common and interrelated themes in the *Daodejing* that we can treat it as a coherent text. Nonetheless, we must acknowledge that it has a very fractured and enigmatic style. Because of this, the *Daodejing* often functions like a Rorschach test, in which readers find what they want to find. Wang Bi, a Han dynasty philosopher who wrote one of the most influential commentaries on the *Daodejing,* noted that some of his contemporaries found Confucian elements in the work and labeled it "Confucian," while others noted Mohist elements in it and called it "Mohist." Wang Bi concludes, "They adjust the name they apply to it in accordance with what they find and insist on interpreting it in terms of what they like."[v]

We see a similar trend in the West. In particular, contemporary Westerners often project onto the *Daodejing* the assumptions of Romanticism. In reaction against the emphasis on reason that was characteristic of the Enlightenment, Romanticism championed the importance and wisdom of one's passions. But the dichotomy of reason and passion is Western, not Chinese, and the individualism characteristic of some forms of Romanticism is quite alien to the *Daodejing.* Consequently, we should be on the lookout for how Romantic preconceptions can distort our appreciation of the text.[3]

There are five major themes that give coherence to the *Daodejing.* (1) Like most of the other philosophies of this era, the *Daodejing* expresses outrage at the corruption, violence, and suffering of the contemporary world. However, unlike Confucianism and Mohism, the *Daodejing* seeks a return to the primitive society that existed prior to the so-called achievements of civilization. This precivilized time was supposedly a utopia in which people enjoyed a simple, preliterate, honest, contented life. (2) In contrast, contemporary society is marked by hypocrisy and self-aggrandizement. To return to the ancient ideal, rulers and their subjects must practice "nonaction": acting without self-conscious or self-aggrandizing desires. (3) One of the keys to achieving nonaction is escaping fixation on the often-arbitrary distinctions embodied

---

2. Citations of the *Daodejing* are by chapters, rather than by page numbers.

3. This is an illustration of the hermeneutic circle between the reader and the text, discussed in Appendix A.

in language. We will cease to covet and contend when we let go of words like "wealth" and "poverty," "success" and "failure." (4) The proper source of guidance for human action is neither self-conscious choice nor the social conventions embodied in language but a transcendent entity that sustains the world. Although this entity is beyond all language, it can be called the "Way" for want of a better term. (5) Since the highest kind of knowledge transcends language, the *Daodejing* advocates a kind of mystical knowledge.

II. Five Themes

1. Social Ills and Their Solution

Many Westerners have a preconception of the *Daodejing* as otherworldly. In reality, the text has an urgent practical concern, rooted in the chaotic situation of the Warring States Period:

> The court is resplendent;
> Yet the fields are overgrown.
> The granaries are empty;
> Yet some wear elegant clothes;
> Fine swords dangle at their sides;
> They are stuffed with food and drink;
> And possess wealth in gross abundance.
> This is known as taking pride in robbery.
> Far is this from the Way! (53)

The *Daodejing* is similar to Confucianism and Mohism in that it preaches peace but stops short of endorsing complete pacifism:

> Wherever an army resides, thorns and thistles grow.
> . . .
> Weapons are inauspicious instruments, not the instruments of a
>   cultivated person.
> But if given no choice, the cultivated person will use them.
> Peace and quiet are the highest ideals;
> A military victory is not a thing of beauty. (30–31)

The solution the *Daodejing* offers for the corruption and violence of contemporary life is to return to a primitive, agrarian utopia—the human condition before the corrupting influences of culture, literature, urbanization, laws, and advanced technology:

The more taboos and prohibitions there are in the world, the poorer the
people.
The more sharp implements the people have, the more benighted the
state.
The more clever and skillful the people, the more strange and perverse
things arise.
The more clear the laws and edicts, the more thieves and robbers. (57)

How are we to return to the utopia of the distant past? The *Daodejing* shares
with Confucianism a belief in the transformative power of a good ruler's
Virtue:

If you deeply accumulate Virtue, nothing can stand in your way.
If nothing can stand in your way, no one will know your limits.
If no one knows your limits, you can possess the state. (59)

However, unlike Confucianism, the *Daodejing* rejects the effort to cultivate
virtues like benevolence, righteousness, wisdom, and propriety. In fact, it suggests that this effort is one of the sources of social decay. To *try* to be virtuous
will lead only to artificiality and hypocrisy:

When the great Way is abandoned, there are benevolence and
righteousness.
When wisdom and intelligence come forth, there is great hypocrisy.
When the six familial relationships are out of balance, there are kind
parents and filial children.
When the state is in turmoil and chaos, there are loyal ministers. (18)

The *Daodejing* implicitly criticizes Mohist doctrines as well. The Mohists
were brilliant debaters, but the *Daodejing* warns, "The good do not engage
in disputation; / Those who engage in disputation are not good" (81). The
Mohists championed intelligent rulers who sought to maximize profit, but
the *Daodejing* advises, "Cut off cleverness, abandon profit, and robbers and
thieves will be no more" (19). For the *Daodejing,* the fundamental problem
with both the Confucians and the Mohists is that they engage in action,
rather than "nonaction."

2. Nonaction

Nonaction is not the same as not acting. If I slump in my chair listlessly and
brood over my problems, I am not acting, but I am doing the very opposite

of nonaction. A professional basketball player, at the top of his game, dribbling down the court, dodging and weaving around his opponents, passing to his teammates, then performing a well-timed jump shot is quite active, yet he is engaging in nonaction. In the former case, brooding in my chair, I am focused on myself; in the latter case, running down the court, the basketball player is focused on the game. Generally speaking, nonaction is action that is non-self-conscious yet perfectly responsive to the situation.

Although the term "nonaction" is new to us, it refers to something we are quite familiar with from everyday life. Consider learning to ride a bicycle. At first, you are very conscious of yourself, the bike, and the various rules and bits of advice that you have been given. Someone who already knows how to ride a bicycle may give you a verbal account of "the Way of the bicycle." But this "Way that can be spoken" is of only limited usefulness:

> "How do I ride a bike without falling down?"
> "You have to pedal fast enough to maintain balance."
> "How fast is that?"
> "Uhm, I dunno. Just develop a feel for it."
> "How do I corner?"
> "Turn the handlebars and lean into the turn."
> "How far do I turn the handlebars and how far do I lean?"
> "It depends on how sharp you have to corner. The sharper the corner the more you turn and lean."
> "But how much?"
> "Look, just do it and you'll get it eventually."

What is the "it" that you are trying to "get"? It is "the Way to ride a bike," which is not captured in any set of rules you have memorized. Now, in this case, there is a linguistic account that completely expresses what you are doing when you successfully ride a bicycle. A physicist could tell you precisely how fast you have to go and precisely how far you need to lean in order for the gyroscopic force of the wheels to be in equilibrium with gravity. But this information is not necessary to ride a bike, and knowing it would not be sufficient to ride a bike.

Recent Western philosophers have expressed this point with the distinction between "knowing how" and "knowing that." *Knowing that* is a matter of believing in linguistic claims with rational justification. *Knowing how* is a matter of ability. You *know that* Paris is the capital of France, but you *know how* to ride a bicycle.

Throughout most of its history, Western philosophy has emphasized *knowing that*. The *Apology*, one of the foundational texts of Western philosophy, presents Socrates on a quest to find someone who possesses real knowledge. He interrogates politicians, poets, and craftspeople. In each case, they fail his test for knowledge because they cannot give a linguistic account of why what they say is true. The implicit response of the *Daodejing* to Socrates' challenge would be to agree that no one has the kind of knowledge Socrates seeks, but that he is looking for the wrong kind of knowledge.

Imagine I have lost my wallet and you find it. You will, I hope, return it to me. But why will you do so? It would show no virtue if your only motivation is that you expect some reward for returning my wallet. What would be a virtuous motivation for returning my wallet? Different philosophers will give different answers. For Mengzi, to follow the Way is to return the wallet out of a "feeling of compassion" for my suffering and a "feeling of disdain" to do something shameful like stealing (*Mengzi* 2A6). In sharp contrast, Immanuel Kant would argue that acting out of compassion or ethical disdain is not moral. It is not that such feelings are *im*moral. Kant acknowledges that such emotions are useful and worth cultivating for the assistance they give us in motivating us to do the right thing. But for Kant feelings are morally neutral because we have (he thinks) no control over them. You cannot choose to be sympathetic to my loss, but you can choose to follow the moral law. Consequently, for Kant, returning my wallet has moral value only if it is done out of respect for the moral law. The moral law dictates that we act only on principles that we could consistently will to universalize. Kant would argue that we cannot consistently will that others keep what *we* lose (because that would be to will that our own goals, whatever they are, be frustrated). Consequently, we cannot will that we keep what *others* lose.

The *Daodejing* suggests that both Mengzi and Kant are wrong. You are only genuinely following the Way when you return the wallet because it simply does not cross your mind to keep it; this is nonaction, naturalness, and the simplicity of "unhewn wood" (28). As soon as I label my action as "righteous" or "benevolent," my motivation has become artificial, unnatural, and in violation of the Way. This is what the text means when it says,

> Those of highest Virtue do not strive for Virtue and so they have it.
> Those of lowest Virtue never stray from Virtue and so they lack it.
> Those of highest Virtue practice nonaction and never act for ulterior
>   motives.
> Those of lowest Virtue act and always have some ulterior motive.
> Those of highest benevolence act, but without ulterior motives.
> Those of highest righteousness act, but with ulterior motives.
> Those who are ritually correct act, but if others do not respond, they
>   roll up their sleeves and resort to force. (38)

It seems very likely that the *Daodejing* has Confucians in mind as "those of lowest Virtue . . . who are ritually correct." However, there is an ancient tradition that Confucians agree with Daoists in recognizing nonaction as the highest embodiment of the Way. We do find in the *Analects* a passage in which Kongzi praises Sage-King Shun as "an example of someone who ruled by means of nonaction" (15.5). In addition, although I presented Mengzi above to draw a contrast with the *Daodejing*, it is certainly true that Mengzi advocated developing one's compassion for suffering and disdain for wrongdoing to the point that they would manifest themselves spontaneously, without premeditation, "like a fire starting up, a spring breaking through" (2A6). Admittedly, the *Analects* and the *Daodejing* do seem to be very different works, but Han-dynasty commentator Wang Bi explained their fundamental agreement by saying, "The Sage [Kongzi] *embodied* nothingness, so he also knew that it could not be explained in words. Thus he did not talk about it. Master Lao, by contrast, operated on the level of being. This is why he constantly *discussed* nothingness; he had to, for what he said about it always fell short."[vi]

Whatever similarities there may be between some aspects of Confucian thought and the *Daodejing*, there is a clear contrast with Mohist political theory, with its emphasis on praise, prosperity, and promotions as tools by which rulers encourage good behavior. Such methods lead the people away from nonaction and toward artifice:

> Not paying honor to the worthy leads the people to avoid contention.
> Not showing reverence for precious goods leads them to not steal.
> Not making a display of what is desirable leads their hearts away from chaos. (3)

Nonaction dictates a more subtle approach to governing:

> The greatest of rulers is but a shadowy presence;
> Next is the ruler who is loved and praised;
> Next is the one who is feared;
> Next is the one who is reviled.
> . . .
> When their task is done and work complete,
> Their people all say, "This is just how we are naturally." (17)

The ruler who practices nonaction transforms the people through his Virtue, without the need for manipulative policies.

> After they are transformed, should some still desire to act,
> I shall press them down with the weight of nameless unhewn wood.

> Nameless unhewn wood is but freedom from desire.
> Without desire and still, the world will settle itself. (37)

"Unhewn wood" is one of the central metaphors of the *Daodejing*. Just as a tree is mutilated by a human's axe, so is everything natural mutilated by self-conscious human desires.

> When unhewn wood is carved up, then there are names.
> Now that there are names, know enough to stop! (32)

But why are "names" so problematic?

3. The Teaching That Is without Words

The *Daodejing* suggests that humans and the languages they use project artificial distinctions onto the world:

> To have and to lack generate each other.
> Difficult and easy give form to each other.
> Long and short offset each other.
> High and low incline into each other.
> Note and rhythm harmonize with each other.
> Before and after follow each other.
> This is why sages abide in the business of nonaction,
>   and practice the teaching that is without words. (2)

"Have" and "lack," "difficult" versus "easy," "long" as opposed to "short": we think of these as natural distinctions. But if I pride myself on having stylish clothes, it can only be because someone else lacks stylish clothes. I find it onerous to do difficult tasks only because they have been labeled as such, in contrast to those that are easy. Consider how much of our thinking and feeling is artificially produced by society and its linguistic distinctions. Would people crave being thin if our society did not invidiously distinguish it from being fat? Why would anyone worry about the trappings of success (a fancy education, a prestigious job, etc.) unless our language distinguished success from failure? What makes some people beautiful other than the fact that society labels them "beautiful," as opposed to "ugly"?

For earlier philosophers such as the Confucians and Mohists, one of the key senses of "Way" is a linguistic account of the right way to live and organize society. Consequently, the *Daodejing* opens with what would have seemed a startling paradox: "Ways can be spoken, but they are not constant Ways. / Names

can be named, but they are not constant names" (1*). The paradoxes of the
"School of Names" had helped pave the way for this challenge to the "con-
stancy" of language and disputation. How can we take philosophical debate or
even words seriously if it is possible to argue successfully that "White horses are
not horses" and "I left for Yue yesterday and arrived yesterday"? The *Daodejing*
embraces paradox as the best kind of language for getting close to expressing
knowledge. This is what accounts for the enigmatic style of the text. However,
it stresses that the highest kind of knowledge cannot be fully expressed using
words: "Those who know do not talk about it; / Those who talk about it do not
know" (56). But if the Way is not a doctrine, what is it?

4. The Way

The *Daodejing* goes beyond earlier philosophers in positing an entity that
generates and guides Heaven, earth, and the myriad creatures:

> There is a thing confused yet perfect, which arose before Heaven and earth.
> Still and indistinct, it stands alone and unchanging.
> It goes everywhere yet is never at a loss.
> One can regard it as the mother of Heaven and earth.
> I do not know its proper name;
> I have given it the style "Way."
> . . .
> People model themselves on the earth.
> The earth models itself on Heaven.
> Heaven models itself on the Way.
> The Way models itself on what is natural. (25)

A "style" is a formal nickname used to respectfully address those with whom
one is not intimately familiar. Notice that the text is explicit about the fact
that it is appropriating the term "Way" and using it in a new way as a nickname for this thing, "which arose before Heaven and earth." This innovative
understanding of the Way, *dao,* is why "Daoists" are given this name.
     This Way is not constant, it cannot be captured by any fixed doctrines,
because the world is ever changing:

> The Way of Heaven, is it not like the stretching of a bow?
> What is high it presses down;
> What is low it lifts up.
> It takes from what has excess;
> It augments what is deficient. (77)

Of course, there is a paradox in using language to talk about the Way, which transcends all language. One technique the *Daodejing* uses to address this paradox is the *via negativa* ("negative way," also referred to as apophatic discourse or apophasis). Found in many forms of Western and Eastern philosophy, the *via negativa* gestures at something by using terms that suggest emptiness and absence, on the grounds that they are less misleading than positive descriptions.

> Looked for but not seen, its name is "minute."
> Listened for but not heard, its name is "rarified."
> Grasped for but not gotten, its name is "subtle."
> These three cannot be perfectly explained, and so are confused and
>   regarded as one.
> Its top is not clear or bright.
> Its bottom is not obscure or dark.
> Trailing off without end, it cannot be named. (14)

In Chinese as well as English, negative terms often have a connotation that is, well, "negative." But the *Daodejing* points out that emptiness and absence are often valuable or even essential:

> Thirty spokes are joined in the hub of a wheel.
> But only by relying on what is not there, do we have the use of the
>   carriage.
> By adding and removing clay we form a vessel.
> But only by relying on what is not there, do we have the use of the
>   vessel.
> By carving out doors and windows we make a room.
> But only by relying on what is not there, do we have the use of the
>   room. (11)

This passage is a metaphor for how the Way can seem to be nothing yet be essential for everything else to exist. To say that the Way is "empty" or "nothing" is not to suggest that it is absolute nonexistence. The Way is nothing in the sense that it is no particular thing and lacks any particular qualities. According to Wang Bi, it is precisely because the Way is formless and nameless that it "is capable of serving as the progenitor and master of things in all their different categories": "If it were warm, it could not be cold; if it were the note *gong*, it could not be the note *shang;* if it had a form, it would necessarily possess the means of being distinguished from other things."[vii]

If the Way were "something," it would have some particular content that we should always intentionally adhere to in an inflexible manner. But because the Way is "nothing," it can only be followed through nonaction, action that is non-self-conscious and infinitely flexible. The Way is itself a paradigm of nonaction. Consequently, descriptions of the Way are often implicit descriptions of the sage:

> How expansive is the great Way!
> Flowing to the left and to the right.
> The myriad creatures rely upon it for life, and it turns none of them away.
> When its work is done it claims no merit.
> It clothes and nourishes the myriad creatures, but does not lord it over them.
> Because it is always without desires, one could consider it insignificant.
> Because the myriad creatures all turn to it and yet it does not lord it over them, one could consider it great.
> Because it never considers itself great, it is able to perfect its greatness. (34)

5. Mysticism

Because it emphasizes a kind of knowledge that is nonlinguistic, the *Daodejing* may be classified as a mystical work. Broadly speaking, mysticism is the view that there is

1. a kind of knowledge
2. that cannot be adequately expressed in words
3. but is important to human life in general.[viii]

Every major religious tradition has mystical strands of thought, including Buddhism, Christianity, Hinduism, Judaism, and Islam. In addition, many great philosophers have mystical elements in their thought, from Plato, the most seminal thinker in the Western tradition, to Martin Heidegger and Ludwig Wittgenstein, perhaps the two most influential philosophers of the twentieth century. Consequently, it would actually be quite surprising if there were *not* a significant mystical element in early Chinese thought. It might seem that, because they deny that the knowledge they seek can be expressed in words, all forms of mysticism are the same. However, traditions assign different roles to mystical experience, depending upon their overall philosophical framework. For example, in the classic Christian tradition (a) mystical knowledge is a sort of spiritual *vision* or *feeling* that (b) reveals a realm of existence (God) that transcends the ordinary world. This experience is intrinsically valuable and it may indirectly support being a good person, because it strengthens the faith, hope, and love needed for true virtue. However, Christian mystics generally insist that (c) the content of the experience neither adds to nor detracts from ordinary ethics. Part of what is so fascinating about Daoist mysticism (and the Daoist-influenced Buddhism of Zen) is that it denies each of these claims. For Daoists, (a′) mystical knowledge is embodied in certain practical activities that are (b′) performed in the everyday world. Furthermore, Daoists insist that (c′) the manifestation of mystical knowledge in practical action *is* the highest ethical activity.

Try to imagine watching someone who is having a mystical experience. If you have any preconceptions about this at all, you probably are envisioning something like a Christian nun kneeling in prayer or a Buddhist monk sitting cross-legged in the full lotus position. There is some truth to both images. "Quiet sitting" (*zazen,* as it is known in contemporary Zen) is a significant part of East Asian mysticism, and there is some evidence that it was practiced even in the era of the *Daodejing*. However, representative images of a Chinese mystic would include someone collecting kindling and gathering water, engaging in the calisthenics of *tàijíquán* 太極拳 *(t'ai-chi ch'üan),* or engaged in some other practical activity. In short, Daoism is a mysticism not through *vision* but through *action,* not of *transcendence* but of *immanence.*

The *Daodejing* hints at techniques for cultivating oneself; unsurprisingly, these are different from those of the Confucians. Kongzi's key cultivation metaphor is to reshape oneself, "as if cut, as if polished; / as if carved, as if ground" (*Analects* 1.15), similar to the way that a piece of rough jade is made into a beautiful statue. Mengzi's key metaphor is cultivating one's heart as one would cultivate a sprout into a mature plant (*Mengzi* 2A6). This difference is reflected in their respective views on *qi*.[4] Kongzi warns that

> when he is young, and his blood and *qi* are still unstable, [the gentleman] guards against the temptation of female beauty; when he reaches his prime, and his blood and *qi* have become unyielding, he guards against being contentious; when he reaches old age, and his blood and *qi* have begun to decline, he guards against being acquisitive. (*Analects* 16.7)

The *qi* is here presented as something that must be carefully controlled and resisted. Mengzi would acknowledge that this sort of resistance to the *qi* (which he would describe as "maintaining your resolution") is sometimes necessary. However, he would insist that continually doing this would "starve" our *qi*. Instead, Mengzi recommends cultivating the ethical inclinations in

---

4. *Qi,* as explained in Chapter 6, is the fluid that circulates through humans and their environment, embodying our feelings and motivations.

our heart. We can thereby develop a "floodlike *qi*" that will provide us with the strength of character to persevere through any challenge (*Mengzi* 2A2).

The *Daodejing* flips both Kongzi's image of the laboriously reworked jade and Mengzi's metaphor of the carefully tended plant, encouraging us to be "Honest, like unhewn wood" (15). Furthermore, the *Daodejing* warns that "When the heart is used to guide the *qi*, this is called 'forcing things'" (55*). The *Daodejing* encourages us to empty our hearts so that we can accumulate the *qi* within ourselves and be guided by it:

> Embracing your soul and holding on to the One, can you keep them
>   from departing?
> Concentrating your *qi* and attaining the utmost suppleness, can you
>   be a child?
> Cleaning and purifying your enigmatic mirror, can you erase every
>   flaw? (10)

"Concentrating your *qi*" refers to a process of refining the *qi* through guided breathing exercises (a common technique of *zazen* familiar to contemporary Buddhists). The result is a state of equanimity in which one can experience the Way. One's heart then becomes an "enigmatic mirror" that reflects the world without perturbation. Achieving this state is not a goal in itself, though. The ultimate goal is to model oneself on the Way, "holding on to the One," while engaging in nonaction in one's everyday activities:

> To produce without possessing;
> To act with no expectation of reward;
> To lead without lording over;
> Such is Enigmatic Virtue! (10)

If one can achieve this state, one's Virtue will manifest itself, subtly but powerfully, in a wide variety of contexts, whether one is king or commoner.

III. Historical Significance

Ideas from the *Daodejing* have been applied in a wide variety of contexts. When Buddhists came to China in the first century CE, they saw Daoist works as anticipating many of their own philosophical concepts, such as *śūnyatā*, "emptiness." Some Chinese Daoists even suggested that, when Laozi left China for the Western wilderness, he continued on into India, where he became known as "the Buddha."[ix] It is a deep and vexing question to what extent Daoism and Buddhism are really similar in their original formulations. However, it is undeniable that the practice-oriented mysticism and the veneration of naturalness characteristic of Daoism influenced the direction that Chinese Buddhism took, particularly in the case of Chan Buddhism (better known in the West by its Japanese name, Zen). In fact, the metaphor of the mind as mirror from *The Platform Sutra of the Sixth Patriarch,* a seminal text of Zen Buddhism, is drawn ultimately from image of the "enigmatic mirror" of *Daodejing* 10.

Another style of interpretation is to read the *Daodejing* as a work of ingenious and subtle strategy. Han Feizi, whom we shall discuss in more detail in Chapter 11, saw the *Daodejing* in these terms:

> The Way lies in not being seen, its use lies in not being known. Remain empty, still, and without concern, so that you may secretly observe the defects of others. See others but do not allow yourself to be seen; hear others but do not allow yourself to be heard; know others but do not allow yourself to be known. . . . Cover your tracks, conceal your starting points, and your subordinates will not be able to see where you are coming from. Get rid of wisdom, dispense with ability, and your subordinates will not be able to guess your intentions. (*Han Feizi* 5; *Readings,* p. 315)

Although such a reading is far from the understanding of the text I have presented in this chapter, there is some support for it:

> Why was this Way so honored in ancient times?
> Did they not say that through it,
> "One could get what one seeks and escape punishment for one's crimes"? (62)

In a different way, the Japanese martial arts of judō and aikidō also show the influence of strategic ideas gleaned from the *Daodejing*. As the founder of judō, Jigorō Kanō explains,

> let us say a man is standing before me whose strength is ten, and that my own strength is but seven. If he pushes me as hard as he can, I am sure to be pushed back or knocked down, even if I resist with all my might. This is opposing strength with strength. But if instead of opposing him I give way to the extent he has pushed, withdrawing my body and maintaining my balance, my opponent will lose his balance. Weakened by his awkward position, he will be unable to use all

his strength. It will have fallen to three. Because I retain my balance, my strength remains at seven. Now I am stronger than my opponent and can defeat him by using only half my strength, keeping the other half available for some other purpose. Even if you are stronger than your opponent, it is better to give way. By doing so you conserve energy while exhausting your opponent.[x]

This is a practical application of the advice of the *Daodejing:*

> In all the world, nothing is more supple or weak than water;
> Yet nothing can surpass it for attacking what is stiff and strong.
> And so nothing can take its place.
> That the weak overcomes the strong and the supple overcomes the
>   hard,
> These are things everyone in the world knows but none can practice. (78)

If you watch an Olympic judō match, you will see what Kanō means. The competitors seem to do nothing at first because a judō master can easily exploit any direct lunge by an opponent, pulling the opponent off balance into a decisive takedown. So the judōka wait until they spot a miniscule movement or opening, then take advantage of their opponent's own momentum, typically with explosive consequences.

Judō is a grappling martial art, but the emphasis is on striking with the hands and feet in the Chinese martial art of kung fu; however, here too Daoist ideas have application. In the film *Enter the Dragon,* which established Bruce Lee as an international star, we find the following exchange between Lee's character and his Master:

> *Master:* "What is the highest technique you hope to achieve?"
> *Lee:* "To have no technique."
> *Master:* "Very good. What are your thoughts when facing an opponent?"
> *Lee:* "There is no opponent."
> *Master:* "And why is that?"
> *Lee:* "Because the word 'I' does not exist. . . . A good martial artist
>   does not become tense, but ready; not thinking, yet not dreaming;
>   ready for whatever may come. When the opponent expands, I
>   contract. When he contracts, I expand. And when there is an
>   opportunity, I do not hit. It hits all by itself."

To the uninitiated, this might sound like pseudo-profound gibberish. But Lee was both an outstanding martial artist and a student of philosophy who knew that the most advanced style was nonaction: perfect responsiveness to one's situation not limited by any narrow technique.

A larger-scale application of Daoist principles is found in guerilla warfare. History has shown again and again that a smaller, less-well-equipped force can defeat a huge, professional army.[5] Because a guerilla army is small, it is easy to support and easy to hide. "This is called a formation without form" (69). In contrast, the large size of a conventional army means that it always has many fixed vulnerable points (supply lines, barracks, etc.). "A weapon that is too strong will not prove victorious; / A tree that is too strong will break" (76). The guerilla army "wins" as long as it is not eliminated, and it will not be eliminated as long as a significant portion of the populace supports it, allowing it to successfully hide among them. "Sages blend into the world and accord with the people's hearts" (49). It is perhaps not a coincidence that one of the most successful practitioners of guerilla warfare was Chinese leader Mao Zedong.

Although aspects of it have been appropriated in many ways, we must not lose sight of the social concern at the heart of the *Daodejing*. It presents a touching image of the ideal society:

> Reduce the size of the state;
> Lessen the population.
> Make sure that even though there are labor-saving tools, they are never used.
> Make sure that the people look upon death as a weighty matter and never move to distant places.
> Even if they were to have ships and carts, they would have no use for them.
> Even if they were to have armor and weapons, they would have no reason to deploy them.
> Make sure that the people return to the use of the knotted cord.
> Make their food savory,
> Their clothes fine,
> Their houses comfortable,
> Their lives happy.
> Then even though neighboring states are within sight of each other,
> Even if they can hear the sounds of each other's dogs and chickens,
> Their people will grow old and die without ever having visited one another. (80)

---

5. The failure of the former Soviet Union in Afghanistan and of the United States in Vietnam are two recent illustrations.

Only the heartless could fail to be moved by this vision of a simple, happy life in a small community. But does this vision give us practical guidance today? It already seemed quaint in the agrarian society of ancient China. When Wang Bi presented the philosophy of the *Daodejing* to a high government official of his era, the official simply laughed at him.[xi] Then again, "If they did not laugh at it, it would not really be the Way" (41). It seems even more quixotic to hope for a return to simple agrarian life in the Information Age of the twenty-first century. However, Zhuangzi, a philosopher who has also been labeled a "Daoist," offered a Way not tied to any particular government, economic, or technological system. To him we turn in the next chapter.

Review Questions

1. What are three surprising facts about Daoism, Laozi, and the *Daodejing*?
2. What is the story of Kongzi's meeting with Laozi?
3. According to tradition, what did Laozi do when he saw the decline of the Zhou dynasty?
4. According to the *Daodejing,* how should society change?
5. What is nonaction and how does it differ from not acting?
6. Explain the distinction between "knowing how" and "knowing that." Give an example of each.
7. Why are names potentially problematic?
8. What is mysticism in general? How does Daoist mysticism differ from classical Christian mysticism?
9. What distinctive innovation did the *Daodejing* make involving the concept of the Way?
10. Explain the *via negativa.*
11. How is the metaphor of "unhewn wood" an implicit criticism of the Confucianism of Kongzi and Mengzi?
12. Discuss how strategic concepts drawn from the *Daodejing* have been applied in other areas of human experience.

■ 9 ■

ZHUANGZI'S THERAPEUTIC
SKEPTICISM AND RELATIVISM

*Where can I find someone who's forgotten words so I can have a word
with him?*

—Zhuangzi

"She changes into a bird named Breeze. No one knows how many thousand leagues
across she is. She ruffles and flies, and her wings are like clouds hanging from Heaven."

I. Zhuangzi's Context

We know very little about Zhuangzi, except that he lived in the state of Song during the mid-fourth century BCE. This makes him a younger contemporary of Mengzi, but the Confucian makes no reference to him. Perhaps Mengzi was simply unaware of Zhuangzi and his writings. Another hypothesis is that Mengzi lumped Zhuangzi together with Yang Zhu, as someone who preached self-preservation and escape from social convention. But to do this is to greatly oversimplify Zhuangzi's Way. Yang Zhu emphasizes protecting the self; Zhuangzi suggests that we must let go of the self. Yang Zhu (and the *Daodejing*) preach leaving the evils of advanced civilization behind; Zhuangzi teaches us to be *in* the world but not *of* the world, so that we can flourish in any social structure.

Although Mengzi never adverts to Zhuangzi, Zhuangzi does critique many other philosophers, including Confucians and Mohists. These philosophers claim to know the Way. But Zhuangzi presents challenging arguments in favor of skepticism (the view that we cannot know the Way) and in support of relativism (the claim that the Way depends on one's perspective). As we shall see, it is not obvious how to reconcile these arguments. If you don't know anything, how do you know the Way depends on your perspective? In other passages, Zhuangzi suggests that we *do* know certain things: we *know that* love of parents is instilled in children's hearts; a skillful butcher *knows how* to carve up an ox.[1] It seems that Zhuangzi is always defying our expectations and assumptions. He does not do this out of carelessness or mischievousness, though. Rather, Zhuangzi shares the view expressed in the *Daodejing* that the highest human knowledge goes beyond words. He uses language to disorient us so that he can then reorient us. Zhuangzi's philosophy can thus be understood as therapeutic rather than doctrinal.

The *Zhuangzi* is divided into three parts. Most scholars today would agree that only the first seven sections (the Inner Chapters) can be reliably attributed to one author, but the Outer and Miscellaneous Chapters sometimes shed light on the core vision. The *Zhuangzi* is written in a wide variety of styles—short stories, dialogues, philosophical argumentation, verse—and Zhuangzi is a master of them all. Zhuangzi himself figures as a character in several incidents in the text. However, to read these as autobiographical is to miss the point; what he says about himself is no more intended to be factually accurate than are his stories about giant fish who turn into giant birds, petulant talking monkeys, or the conflicting words he puts into the mouth of

---

1. We discussed the distinction between *knowing how* and *knowing that* in Chapter 8.

"Kongzi" at different points in the text. One of the great classics of world literature and philosophy, the *Zhuangzi* is humorous and deadly serious, lighthearted and morbid, precisely argued and intentionally confusing, as protean as the Way it gestures toward.

II. Skepticism

In the West, skepticism is the doctrine that we cannot know the truth. Using the concepts of Warring States China, skepticism would be the view that we cannot know what the Way is: we cannot know what is so or is not so, what is right or wrong. Zhuangzi presents some arguments that would be immediately recognized as skeptical by Western philosophers:

> Once you and I have started arguing, if you win and I lose, then are you really right and am I really wrong? If I win and you lose, then am I really right and are you really wrong? Is one of us right and the other one wrong? Or are both of us right and both of us wrong? If you and I can't understand one another, then other people will certainly be even more in the dark. Whom shall we get to set us right? Shall we get someone who agrees with you to set us right? But if they already agree with you how can they set us right? Shall we get someone who agrees with me to set us right? But if they already agree with me, how can they set us right? (*Zhuangzi* 2; *Readings,* p. 223)

Suppose you are an ancient Chinese ruler listening to an argument between Confucians and Mohists over "differentiated caring" versus "impartial caring." You find the arguments of the Mohists persuasive, so you consider them the winners of the debate. Now, the Confucians continue to be persuaded by their own arguments for a contrary conclusion. Because you disagree with the Confucians, you have to admit that the fact that someone is persuaded by an argument is no guarantee that it is right. But, by the same reasoning, the fact that the Mohists have won the debate does not show they are right. It simply shows that they persuaded you that they are right. What criteria independent of your own perspective can we use to determine whether you were right to be persuaded by the Mohists? We could ask other people, but all they can tell us is that they are or are not persuaded by the arguments that persuade us, which we have already agreed does not show that they are right.

Zhuangzi also appeals to dreams to undermine our confidence in our values and beliefs:

How do I know that loving life is not a mistake? How do I know that hating death is not like a lost child forgetting its way home? Lady Li was the daughter of the border guard of Ai. When the duke of Jin got her, her tears fell until they soaked her collar. But once she reached the royal palace, slept in the king's bed, and ate the meats of his table, she regretted her tears. How do I know that the dead don't regret that they ever longed for life?

One who dreams of drinking wine may weep in the morning. One who dreams of weeping may go for a hunt the next day. In the dream, you don't know it's a dream. In the middle of a dream, you may interpret a dream within it. Only after waking do you know it was a dream. Still, there may be an even greater awakening after which you will know that this, too, was just a greater dream. (*Zhuangzi* 2; *Readings*, pp. 222–23)

This is extremely reminiscent of the dream argument of René Descartes (seventeenth century CE). Descartes, the founder of modern Western philosophy, noted that we sometimes dream without knowing that we are dreaming. Since we cannot be certain that we are not dreaming now, it is possible to doubt every aspect of the external world. Descartes was not ultimately a skeptic, though. He raised doubts as part of an epistemological project of trying to find something indubitable, something that survived even the most rigorous skeptical arguments. He hoped to use this as an absolutely certain foundation upon which to reconstruct human knowledge. He thought he found this in his knowledge of his own thoughts, whose existence he could not doubt. Since he could not doubt that he had thoughts, he could not doubt his own existence: "I think, therefore I am." But Zhuangzi is not primarily interested in epistemology (the general theory of knowledge). Zhuangzi is like the Hellenistic Skeptics of the ancient West in that there is a practical point to his doubt. Part of the point of doubting is to relieve us of certain kinds of fear or anxiety. Death is less frightening if we realize that we really don't know it would be bad.

III. Relativism

In the West, relativism is the doctrine that truth depends upon one's perspective. For a relativist, "true" functions like directional terms, such as "left" or "above." The second floor is above in relation to the first floor but below in relation to the third floor. From the professor's perspective at the front of the classroom, the door is on the left, but from the students' perspective, the door is on the right. There is no objective fact about whether something is left or right, above or below, independently of perspective. Similarly, the relativist argues, there is no objective fact about whether a claim is true or false. Put in the terms of ancient China, relativism would be the view that the Way depends upon one's perspective: the correct use of terms like "is so" and "is not so," "right" and "wrong," depends upon who is using them.

Zhuangzi uses an ambiguity that exists in Classical Chinese to illustrate relativism:

> How is the Way obscured that there are genuine and fake? How are words obscured that there are *shi,* "right," and *fei,* "wrong"? Where can you go that the Way does not exist? How can words exist and not be okay? The Way is obscured by small completions. Words are obscured by glory and show. So we have the rights and wrongs of the Confucians and Mohists. Each calls right what the other calls wrong and each calls wrong what the other calls right. But if you want to right their wrongs and wrong their rights, it's better to throw them open to the light.
> There is nothing that cannot be looked at that way.
> There is nothing that cannot be looked at this way.
> But that is not the way I see things;
> Only as I know things myself do I know them.
> Hence it is said, "*Bi,* 'that,' comes from *shi,* 'this,' and this follows from that." . . . What is this is also that, and what is that is also this. That is both right and wrong. This is also both right and wrong. So is there really a this and a that? Or isn't there any this or that? (*Zhuangzi* 2; *Readings,* p. 217)

The Chinese term *shi* 是 can be a demonstrative pronoun meaning "this"; in this sense it contrasts with *bi* 彼, which means "that." "This" is a good example of a relative term. The professor might refer to "this lectern" in front of her, but the student sitting in the back of the classroom would call it "that lectern." If the professor and the student got into a heated dispute over whether it was *really* "this lectern" or "that lectern," we'd laugh at their foolishness. "For this reason the sage does not follow this route but illuminates things with Heaven's light" (217).

However, *shi* can also be a verbal adjective meaning "is right"; in this sense it contrasts with *fei* 非, meaning "is wrong." By juxtaposing the two contrasts marked with *shi* ("this and that," "right and wrong"), Zhuangzi is suggesting the ethical evaluations of *right* and *wrong* are as perspective-dependent as the distinction between *this* and *that.* This point seems even more compelling in Classical Chinese, because *shi* and *fei* can also be used as transitive verbs, meaning *to regard as right* and *to regard as wrong*. So it seems a natural move to suggest that what is right (*shi*) is simply what is regarded as right (*shi*), and what is wrong (*fei*) is what is regarded as wrong (*fei*). But obviously what is *regarded as right* depends upon who is doing the regarding.

Zhuangzi's thesis here is clearly influenced by Hui Shi, his older contemporary, who appealed to relative terms in his argument for paradoxes like "I went to Yue today and arrived yesterday" (see Chapter 7). But we shall see that Zhuangzi took this emphasis in a different direction from Hui Shi.

What difference does it make whether relativism is true? You might be surprised to learn that most contemporary Western relativists say that their doctrine makes no practical difference at all. They point out that even if ethics is relative to your perspective, you need not stop making ethical judgments. After all, you don't stop using words like "left" and "right," "today" and "yesterday" just because they're relative. And, because relativism applies to all ethical systems, it does not support one ethics over another. You could, with equal consistency, be a relativist humanitarian or a relativist fascist. Relative to the former, compassion and generosity would be "right," and relative to the latter intolerance and aggression would be "right."[i]

Zhuangzi, though, clearly thinks that something deeply important is at stake here. His skepticism and relativism are intended to reduce or even eliminate our commitment to conventional evaluations. He explains the implications via a humorous story:

> When the monkey trainer was passing out nuts he said, "You get three in the morning and four at night." The monkeys were all angry. "All right," he said, "you get four in the morning and three at night." The monkeys were all pleased. With no loss in name or substance, he made use of their joy and anger because he went along with them. So the sage harmonizes people with right and wrong and rests them on Heaven's wheel. This is called walking two roads. (*Zhuangzi* 2; *Readings*, p. 218)

The monkey trainer knows that nothing is fundamentally altered about the world whether the monkeys get three or four of their seven nuts in the morning, but he accommodates the monkeys' insistence that it does make a difference. Similarly, the sage knows that it doesn't change anything about the world whether we call impartial caring "right" (as the Mohists do) or "wrong" (as the Confucians do). He goes along with ordinary distinctions to make people happy.[2]

---

2. The expression "three in the morning, four at night," *zhāo sān mù sì* 朝三暮四 became an idiom in Chinese, originally having the sense of "to trick someone," but nowadays generally used to mean "to change one's mind easily."

IV. Detachment in Society, Not from Society

Just as the trainer does not abandon the monkeys even though he recognizes the pointlessness of their distinctions, likewise the sage's insight into the limitations of human knowledge and language does not lead him to abandon society or life with other humans. Unlike Yang Zhu and the *Daodejing*, which in their different ways both advocate rejecting contemporary civilization, Zhuangzi teaches us a Way of being detached within whatever kind of civilization and social roles we finds ourselves.

The *Zhuangzi* reports that the Duke of She came to Kongzi to ask for advice when the king sent him on an extremely important and dangerous mission. The Duke explains that he is "already shaking" with fear and has been gulping ice water because he feels like he's burning up inside. In our terms, the Duke is really stressing out. Kongzi, who is often used as a spokesman for Zhuangzi's perspective, replies with advice that at first glance is very conventional:

> In this world, there are two great concerns. One is destiny. One is righteousness. Children's love for their family is destiny: you can't undo it in your heart. The service of subjects for their rulers is righteousness: there is nowhere you can go and not have rulers, nowhere you can escape between Heaven and earth. These are great concerns. To serve your family, wherever they go, is the perfection of filial piety. To serve your rulers, whatever they ask, is the height of loyalty. To serve your own heart, so that sorrow and joy aren't constantly revolving in front of you, knowing what you can't do anything about and accepting it as though it were destiny, is the perfection of Virtue. As a subject or a child, there will certainly be things you can't avoid. As long as you stick to the actual job and forget about yourself, what leisure do you have to love life or hate death? You'll be able to do it. (*Zhuangzi* 4; *Readings*, p. 230)

There is no hint, either here or in the rest of the passage, of irony. Zhuangzi seems to be presenting it as honest, straightforward advice. Although none of us today are dukes going on missions for kings, Zhuangzi has framed the advice so that it has universal applicability—whether you are an attorney faced with an important case, a doctor treating an urgent medical condition, a student facing finals, or a businessperson whose boss has said, "You *must* close the deal at this meeting." What is the advice? You must accept that you have obligations because of the personal and social roles you happen to occupy. These obligations can be a source of agitation, but attempting to escape the world is not a real solution. Wherever you go and whatever you do, there will be dangers of some kind.

The futility of trying to escape the world is expressed in a story about Zhuangzi himself. Zhuangzi was out hunting near a restricted game preserve, bow in hand, when an unusually large magpie flew right in front of him, grazing him with its wings. Curious about the bird (and perhaps also seeing a chance to shoot some supper), Zhuangzi followed the bird and encountered a troubling sight:

> He saw a cicada forgetting itself in a pretty bit of shade. A praying mantis took advantage of the cover to grab for it, forgetting its own body at the sight of gain. The strange magpie was right behind, eyeing the prize and forgetting its truth. Zhuangzi shuddered. "Eeeee! Things certainly entangle one another, each one dragging in the next!" (*Zhuangzi* 20; *Readings*, p. 248)

Zhuangzi's lesson did not end there, because in pursuing the magpie he had wandered into the restricted game preserve: "He threw down his bow and ran back the way he came—but then the warden of the grove saw and pursued him, cursing." Seeing the magpie hunt the mantis, which hunts the cicada, which does nothing while enjoying a bit of shade, Zhuangzi sees the dangers inherent in the world. However, Zhuangzi realizes that he, too, is both predator and prey. There is no escape from this, wherever he goes. He concludes by citing the adage, "Out in the world, follow its rules."

Consequently, unless you change yourself, you will carry your problems with you wherever you go and whatever you do:

> You hide your boat in a gully or your net in a swamp and call them secure. But in the middle of the night a strong man could still take them on his back and leave, and you would be asleep and not know. Hiding the small in the large seems fitting, but still you lose. But if you hid the world in the world, you would have nothing to lose. . . . So the sage wanders in what exists everywhere and can't be lost. He likes growing old and he likes dying young. He likes the beginning and he likes the end. (*Zhuangzi* 6; *Readings*, p. 236)

To "hide the world in the world" is to achieve a detached acceptance of it. On the one hand, we are detached from our judgments of good and bad, gain and loss. After all, we do not know that they are accurate. "How do [we] know that loving life is not a mistake?" Our judgments seem to be mere projections of our personal perspectives. "Each calls right what the other calls wrong and each calls wrong what the other calls right." But to be detached from our evaluations is not to cease making them. After all, there is "nowhere you can escape between Heaven and earth" from engagement with other people and the world. So you must accept that the tasks associated with your role are something beyond your control. "Nothing is as good as fulfilling your destiny" (213). The combination of detachment and acceptance allows you to face the world with equanimity, "so that sorrow and joy aren't constantly revolving in front of you." Zhuangzi encapsulates his advice in a memorable aphorism: "To stop leaving tracks is easy. Not to walk upon the ground is hard" (229). To stop leaving tracks would be to do nothing. One can certainly just sit there, but that is not a practical plan for life. To not walk upon the ground is to be active in the world yet detached from it. This is the real achievement.

While Zhuangzi does not advocate withdrawal from society, he does warn us that there is no reason to seek social prominence. When Hui Shi complained that Zhuangzi's talk was useless, like a tree with a trunk so gnarled and branches so twisted that it could not be made into anything, Zhuangzi shot back,

> Haven't you seen a weasel? It bends down then rises up. It springs east and west, not worrying about heights or depths—and lands in a snare or dies in a net. . . . You have a big tree and are upset that you can't use it. Why not plant it by a nothing-at-all village in a wide empty waste? You could do nothing, dilly-dallying by its side, or nap, ho-hum, beneath it. It won't fall to any axe's chop and nothing will harm it. Since it isn't any use, what bad can happen to it? (*Zhuangzi* 1; *Readings,* p. 213)

This story has special poignancy when we recall that Hui Shi rose to be a high official in the state of Wei but had to flee for his life when Wei was invaded. Perhaps Hui Shi should have followed Zhuangzi's example. When the king of Chu offered to make Zhuangzi prime minister, Zhuangzi noted that the king had sacred turtle bones that were revered and kept in a place of honor in his ancestral hall.[3] "Now," Zhuangzi asked, "would that turtle rather have its bones treasured in death, or be alive dragging its tail in the mud? . . . Go! I'll keep my tail in the mud, too" (247). So Zhuangzi recommends that we do not seek prominence. But as we saw from the advice he gives those who are already in positions of prominence, he does not encourage us to try to escape the roles we are already in.

---

3. These are the oracle bones explained in Chapter 1.

How does this apply to you? If you are reading this, one of your social roles is probably that of a student. Being a student is often fun but also stressful. You worry about getting papers finished and being prepared for exams. Some of you are concerned about flunking out of school, while others of you are just as anxious about getting a B+ rather than an A–. The pressure can seem overwhelming. Zhuangzi would ask why you are so convinced it would be bad to get an F (or a B+). After all, they're just letters on a piece of paper. Opinions and words (including grades) do not change the underlying reality of the world for good or bad. "But grades affect my future opportunities," you might protest. Even if your grades keep you out of a particular graduate school or job, how do you know that would be bad? Many people spend years studying to be an attorney or medical doctor only to discover that they really *hate* the profession once they enter it. A "bad" grade (another conventional label) may have been hugely beneficial for you, for all you know. Zhuangzi would hope that these reflections would make you more detached from the evaluations that lead to fear, anxiety, and suffering.

Fact: The words for "tea" in most of the world's languages are derived either from the Chinese words chá *(like the Hindi* chai*) or* tê *(like the English "tea").* Chá *is the word for tea in the Cantonese dialect, while* tê *is used in the Hokkien dialect (which is spoken in Fujian Province).*

It might be tempting to conclude that you should drop out of school (the *Daodejing* might counsel this) or at least make the bare minimum effort to get by while enjoying yourself (this is like Yang Zhu's Way). But Zhuangzi would note that if you drop out you would just be in a different social context. Most of the jobs you can get without a college degree are not *less* stressful; they're just stressful in different ways. The real answer is to accept your role and do your best at it. It might seem that trying to do your best is precisely what gave you anxiety in the first place. However, paradoxically, by focusing on the tasks that accompany your role, you turn attention away from yourself and your fixation on success and failure. In the previous chapter, we learned a name for immersing oneself so completely in one's task that one loses all sense of self: nonaction.

V. Nonaction

Zhuangzi is much more explicit about what nonaction is and how it is achieved than was the *Daodejing*. He provides us what is perhaps the most memorable illustration of nonaction in all of Chinese philosophy:

A butcher was cutting up an ox for Lord Wenhui. Wherever his hand touched, wherever his shoulder leaned, wherever his foot stepped, wherever his knee pushed—with a zip! with a whoosh!—he handled his chopper with aplomb, and never skipped a beat. He moved in time to the *Dance of the Mulberry Forest,* and harmonized with the *Head of the Line Symphony.* Lord Wenhui said, "Ah, excellent, that technique can reach such heights!"

The butcher sheathed his chopper and responded, "What your servant values is the Way, which goes beyond technique. When I first began cutting up oxen, I did not see anything but oxen. Three years later, I couldn't see the whole ox. And now, I encounter them with spirit and don't look with my eyes. Sensible knowledge stops and spiritual desires proceed. I rely on the Heavenly patterns, strike in the big gaps, am guided by the large fissures, and follow what is inherently so. I never touch a ligament or tendon, much less do any heavy wrenching!" (*Zhuangzi* 3; *Readings,* pp. 224–25)

The butcher's description of learning to carve an ox will be familiar at some level to anyone who has acquired a complex physical skill. Consider someone learning to box. She is told, "don't square off, don't load up your punches, don't drop your guard, don't lead with your chin." She tries to pay attention to all of this at once, though she finds it overwhelming (like the cook who still "sees the whole ox"). If she perseveres, she begins to internalize the Way of boxing, so she doesn't have to think about following it any more. If she becomes a master boxer, we say that it has become second nature to her, that she has an intuitive grasp of it. Zhuangzi's butcher is expressing a similar phenomenon in saying, "I encounter them with spirit and don't look with my eyes."

As impressive as skillful action is, the butcher stresses that what he really values "is the Way, which goes beyond technique." How is carving up an ox carcass related to the Way? We see a key in the butcher's explanation that he never chips his blade because he relies on the "Heavenly patterns" of the ox's body. The butcher is so effective because he has learned to intuitively follow the inherent, natural structure of the world. So carving the ox carcass skillfully is a small illustration of following the Way throughout one's life. This is why Lord Wenhui exclaims, "Excellent! I have heard the words of a butcher and learned how to care for life!"

A story that Zhuangzi fabricates about Kongzi and his most promising disciple, Yan Hui, brings together the themes of skillfulness and detached engagement, along with suggesting what sort of meditative techniques are useful in understanding the Way. Yan Hui asks permission to try to reform the ruler of Wei, who "is so careless with people's lives that the dead fill the state like falling leaves in a swamp. The people have nowhere to turn" (226). Kongzi replies, "Sheesh! You're just going to get yourself hurt" (227). He then interrogates Yan Hui about his strategy for approaching the ruler, shooting down every proposal. Finally, Yan Hui says, "I have nothing else to offer. May I ask what to do?" Kongzi replies that Yan Hui must engage in "the fasting of the heart":

> Unify your intention. Do not listen with your ears but listen with your heart. Do not listen with your heart but listen with your *qi*. Listening stops with the ear. The heart stops with signs. *Qi* is empty and waits on external things. Only the Way gathers in emptiness. Emptiness is the fasting of the heart. (*Zhuangzi* 4; *Readings,* p. 228)

To achieve emptiness we must focus our concentration. As a first approximation to achieving this focus, we turn inward, listening with our heart rather than our ears. (Our ears can only hear the competing doctrines of the various philosophers.) However, we ultimately must transcend our individual heart as well. We "fast" it (rather than cultivating it), so that it achieves "emptiness," allowing us to be guided by the *qi* that flows through the world.

Yan Hui replies, "Prior to receiving this instruction, I was full of thoughts of Hui. But having applied it, it's as though Hui never existed. Is this what you mean by emptiness?" Kongzi exclaims,

> Perfect! Let me tell you. You can wander in his cage without being moved by his fame. If you're getting through, sing. If not, stop. No schools of thought. No prescriptions. Dwell in unity and lodge in what cannot be helped, and you're almost there. (*Zhuangzi* 4; *Readings,* p. 229)

As a member of the scholar class, involvement in government is a part of Yan Hui's role, and Kongzi does not encourage him to try escaping it. Instead, he advises performing his role, but with detachment from the self: nonaction.

VI. Doctrine or Therapy?

How do the various things that Zhuangzi says fit together? Zhuangzi seems to advocate skepticism in some passages and relativism in others. But these views are actually inconsistent. If I do not know what is right or wrong (skepticism), how do I know that right and wrong depend upon one's perspective (relativism)? The proper conclusion to draw from skepticism is that the Way *might* depend upon one's perspective (relativism), or there *might* be one right Way (objectivism), but we can't know which. Since we can't know, there is no reason to favor relativism over objectivism.

And how do we reconcile skepticism with Zhuangzi's praise of the butcher? The butcher's skill certainly seems to show that he has knowledge. But perhaps Zhuangzi is only skeptical about *knowing that* certain things are true (like knowing whether impartial caring is right or wrong). The butcher's *knowing how* to carve up the ox is a different kind of knowing. This only pushes back the problem one step, though. The butcher's skill is explained by his ability to "rely on the Heavenly patterns . . . and follow what is inherently so" (225). This explanation assumes that there *are* inherent Heavenly patterns. How do we know that? And how do we know that it is better to be skillful than clumsy? To paraphrase Zhuangzi: How do I know that loving skillfulness is not a mistake? How do I know that hating clumsiness is not like a lost child forgetting its way home?

Similar problems arise for understanding the role of relativism in Zhuangzi's thought. The sage smirks at the Confucians and Mohists because he sees that their judgments of right and wrong are merely expressions of their own perspectives. But if this somehow invalidates their evaluations, why is the sage any better when he decides it is best to humor conventional people (like the monkey trainer) and better to avoid positions of prominence (like Zhuangzi "dragging [his] tail in the mud")?

One resolution to the apparent tension between the different strains in Zhuangzi's thought is to regard his philosophy as therapeutic rather than doctrinal. A doctrinal philosophy aims to convince you of certain specific conclusions. Doctrinal philosophies do not have to be indifferent to behavior and motivations. Confucianism and Mohism are most fundamentally concerned about getting people to willingly follow the Way (as each conceives it). However, Mohists give arguments for the doctrine of impartial caring, while Confucians try to convince you to accept differentiated caring instead.

A therapeutic philosophy, in contrast, does not try to get you to trade your current beliefs for a different set. Therapeutic philosophers use language and argumentation only as instruments to alter your behavior and attitudes. An example of a therapeutic use of language (although not a philosophical one per se) is reading *The Cat in the Hat* to children. There is no moral or doctrine we expect children to learn from this story. (What would it be? "Let in a stranger while your parents are away and you'll have lots of fun. Let him make a mess and break things, because he'll clean it up before he leaves.") So why do generations of parents read this story out loud? It helps children internalize the feel and sound of English verse. They can learn to recognize simple words on the page. It develops their imagination. Listening quietly will help them relax at bedtime. Most important of all, it makes children happy.

But any therapy must serve some purpose. Zhuangzi's purpose is to help us follow the Way. Like the *Daodejing*, Zhuangzi treats the Way as something that guides yet transcends the world: "The Way has an essence and can be trusted. But it takes no action and has no form. . . . Before Heaven and earth existed, it spiritualized the ghosts and gods, and gave birth to Heaven and earth" (236). Zhuangzi acknowledges the uses of various kinds of language, but suggests that the Way is beyond all of them:

> The sage acknowledges what is beyond the six directions but does not discuss it. He discusses what is within the six directions but does not deliberate on it. He deliberates on the springs and autumns of successive generations and the records of former kings but does not debate about them. (*Zhuangzi* 2; *Readings*, p. 220)

So Zhuangzi is ultimately a mystic. A mystic thinks that there is a kind of knowledge important to human life that cannot be expressed in words. However, this does not mean that words have no use in attaining mystical insight. Language can help loosen fixed beliefs and preconceptions that are impediments to understanding the Way.

Words can also gesture toward the Way, to help those struggling to grasp it, as long as they do not become fixated on these words:

> A trap is for fish: when you've got the fish, you can forget the trap. A snare is for rabbits: when you've got the rabbit, you can forget the snare. Words are for meaning: when you've gotten the meaning, you can forget the words. Where can I find someone who's forgotten words so I can have a word with him? (*Zhuangzi* 26; *Readings*, p. 250)

There is a suggestive similarity here between Zhuangzi's approach and some comments by Ludwig Wittgenstein, a twentieth-century philosopher who has also been interpreted as therapeutic:

> My propositions are elucidatory in this way: he who understands me finally recognizes them as senseless, when he has climbed out through them, on them, over them. (He must so to speak throw away the ladder, after he has climbed up on it.)[ii]

Interpreting Zhuangzi as a therapeutic mystic helps shed light on his disagreement with Hui Shi. Zhuangzi had learned from Hui Shi the philosophical interest of relative terms. However, Hui Shi was ultimately a doctrinal philosopher who hoped to convince everyone to "indiscriminately care for the myriad things," because "Heaven and Earth are one whole." For Zhuangzi, any doctrine was just a stepping-stone on the path to something beyond it.

If you read Zhuangzi's arguments for skepticism and become convinced that you do not know anything, you are carrying around a ladder after you have already climbed to the roof. If you are convinced that relativism is right and objectivism is wrong, you are trying to fry up the fish trap rather than the fish. The point of Zhuangzi's writings is to open us up to new ways of relating to the world, not to talk us out of one fixation and into another.

VII. Conventional or Radical?

If Zhuangzi's therapy works on us, how different will we be? For Confucians, sages do not leave their humanity behind, they perfect it: "The unicorn among beasts, the phoenix among birds, Mount Tai among hills, and rivers and seas among flowing waters are all of a kind. The sage among people is also of the same kind" (*Mengzi* 2A2). Mengzi explains that, whether sage or tyrant, humans share the same "essence": the hearts of compassion, disdain, respect, right and wrong (6A6). To lose the heart's commitment to right and wrong is to cease being human (2A6). It is a tragedy, like the stripping of the trees and vegetation from Ox Mountain (6A8). In contrast, Zhuangzi suggests that sages intentionally lose what Mengzi values so much: "They have human form but not human essence. Since they have human form, they flock with people. Since they lack human essence, right and wrong do not get to them" (234).

Hui Shi no doubt had a very different conception of the human essence than Mengzi. However, he questions whether it is even possible for humans to lose it:

> "But if you call them 'people,' how can they have no essence?"
> Zhuangzi said, "Rights and wrongs are what I mean by 'essence.' By 'no essence,' I mean people not letting in good and bad to hurt them. Follow the natural and do not help life along."
> Hui Shi said, "How can people exist without helping life?"
> Zhuangzi said, "The Way gave them a face, Heaven gave them a form—by not letting likes and dislikes in to do harm, that's how."
> (*Zhuangzi* 5; *Readings,* p. 235)

Losing one's "essential" human tendency to make evaluations of right and wrong is to achieve the sort of detachment that Zhuangzi advocates. How different does this make Zhuangzi's sage from the rest of us? Sometimes Zhuangzi suggests that losing the human "essence" radically changes one's motivations and experiences. One of the most striking illustrations is the morbid story of Master Chariot, who vividly describes his illness: "How extraordinary of the maker of things to knot me up like this. My back is hunched out. My organs are all out of order. My chin is hidden in my navel. My shoulders are peaked. And my neck bones point to Heaven" (238). Gazing at his horrific reflection in a pool of water, Master Chariot remarks, "Sheesh! The maker of things really is knotting me up." When his friend, Master Sacrifice, asks whether he dislikes what is happening to him, Master Chariot replies:

> Not at all. What is there to dislike? If, in time, he turns my left arm into a rooster, I'll use it to crow the day. If he turns my right arm into a bow, I'll shoot down a dove for roasting. If he turns my buttocks into wheels, and my spirit into a horse, I'll climb aboard. What better carriage? You get something when it's time. You lose it when it's passed. If you are content with the time and abide by the passing, there's no room for sorrow or joy. (*Zhuangzi* 6; *Readings*, p. 238)

Because he lets go of parochial human judgments of good and bad, gain and loss, Master Chariot accepts with equanimity the changes his body is undergoing and his eventual death. They are just aspects of the endless transformations of the world. It's easy to succumb to the charm of this story without feeling its full impact, so let's use a contemporary example. Imagine what it is like to be one of the people who needs a complete face transplant. Such people undergo such extreme surgery for a simple reason: their faces are *gone*, destroyed as a result of traumatic injury. How would you feel in this situation? Could you really be as nonchalant as to think, "What is there to dislike?" How could any *human* be that nonchalant?

This superhuman indifference applies equally to the loss of our friends and loved ones. When Zhuangzi's wife died, Hui Shi came to mourn her only to find Zhuangzi singing and beating on a tub like it was a drum. Hui Shi protests that such behavior is wrong: "You lived with this person, raised children, and grew old together." But Zhuangzi explains,

> When she first died, don't you think I was like everyone else? But then I considered her beginning, before she was alive. . . . In all the mixed-up bustle and confusion, something changed and there was *qi*. The *qi* changed and there was form. The form changed and she had life. Now there was another change and she died. It's like the round of the four seasons: spring, summer, fall and winter. She was resting quietly, per-

fectly at home, and I followed her crying "Boo-hoo!" It seemed like I hadn't comprehended fate. So I stopped. (*Zhuangzi* 18; *Readings,* p. 247)

One interpretation is that this story is not as radical as it might seem: Zhuangzi does cry for the loss of his wife, but he eventually moves on (as we might put it), taking comfort in the thought of the circle of life. Perhaps all Zhuangzi is warning against is the excessive, forced mourning of the Confucians.

However, other stories seem to reinforce the more extreme interpretation. When Master Mulberry-door died, his friends sang happily over his corpse and continued about their daily business (239–40). Another person is praised for going through with the external forms of mourning, but without a deep commitment to them: "When Mengsun Cai's mother died, he cried without tears. In his inner heart he did not mourn. And conducting the funeral, he did not grieve" (240). This Mengsun Cai seems similar to the monkey trainer Zhuangzi describes, who is unmoved by the distinctions that so engage the monkeys but humors them by acting in accordance with their distinctions.

Do we really want to become the kind of person who could be indifferent to the decay of his own body, his death, and the loss of his friends and loved ones? And is it even possible for us to become that sort of person? Zhuangzi often uses the figure of Kongzi to address the latter question. Kongzi appears in the *Zhuangzi* in three main roles. Sometimes (but rarely) Kongzi is the representative of smug, conventional thinking.[4] Other times, Kongzi is a spokesman for Zhuangzi's vision of the Way (as in the long dialogue between Kongzi and Yan Hui, discussed earlier). Why does Zhuangzi, the consummate anti-Confucian, use Kongzi as a spokesman? There are passages in the *Analects* that resonate with themes in the *Daodejing* and *Zhuangzi*. Beliefs in the transformative power of Virtue and nonaction as the ultimate form of agency are common to all three works. In addition, Zhuangzi self-consciously fabricates statements by Kongzi to suggest that Confucians unknowingly fabricate their own Kongzi. If he were challenged that he was not being faithful to the historical Kongzi, Zhuangzi might reply, "You Confucians disagree among yourselves about what the Way of Kongzi was. How do you know that he *didn't* say these things?"

The third and perhaps most interesting persona of Kongzi is the "wistful Daoist," someone who recognizes the existence of true sages and learns something from their example but also knows that he is incapable of fully realizing their Way. Kongzi's disciple Zigong is outraged when the friends of Master

---

4. In a portion of *Zhuangzi* 5 not included in *Readings,* Kongzi is presented as arrogantly dismissive of someone whose feet had been amputated as punishment for a previous crime.

Mulberry-door seem unperturbed by their friend's death. However, Kongzi explains to him,

> Those are men who wander outside the rules. I am one who wanders within them. Inside and outside don't meet, and it was rude of me to send you to mourn. They are about to join with the generator of things in being human and wander in the single breath of Heaven and earth. They think of life as a hanging tumor and a dangling mole and of death as a wart falling off or a boil bursting. People such as this, how can they say whether death and life are ground gained or lost? They commit themselves to different things but trust to their all being one body. (*Zhuangzi* 6; *Readings,* pp. 239–40)

Puzzled, Zigong asks, "So why then does my master follow rules himself?" Kongzi replies, "Me, I am one of those who are punished by Heaven." In other words, given his personality and character traits, it is not possible for Kongzi to be like the friends of Master Mulberry-door. He sees the grandeur and the value of the Way that they follow, but he cannot bring himself to completely let go of benevolence and righteousness. I suspect that most of us are more like the figure of Kongzi as wistful Daoist than we are like the friends of Master Mulberry-door (or Master Chariot), but a wistful Daoist can still benefit from whatever lesser degree of detachment she is able to achieve.

A contemporary wistful Daoist might want to go to a top law school. If she does not get in, she will be disappointed but she will not be distraught: she does not take society's and her own evaluations seriously enough for that. When she goes to a less prestigious law school instead, she will submerge herself in her work, and she will be better at it than many of her peers because of her level of commitment but also because she is less fearful of failure. Her approach will be the same when she becomes an attorney; however, she will avoid high-profile cases that might get her face on television. Part of her wants to be famous, but she knows that overall the costs of celebrity are not worth it.

The most famous passage from the *Zhuangzi* is the butterfly dream. It is a profound story that is interpreted in many ways. But I think it expresses how a wistful Daoist can get an intimation of the perspective of the true sage:

> One night, Zhuangzi dreamed of being a butterfly—a happy butterfly, showing off and doing as he pleased, unaware of being Zhuangzi. Suddenly he awoke, drowsily, Zhuangzi again. And he could not tell whether it was Zhuangzi who had dreamt the butterfly or the butterfly dreaming Zhuangzi. But there must be some difference between them!

This is called "the ~~transformation of things.~~" (*Zhuangzi* 2; *Readings*, p. 224)

We have seen that Zhuangzi does sometimes appeal to dreams to argue for skepticism. The butterfly dream story is sometimes interpreted along similar lines. However, notice that the story is supposed to illustrate "transformation." Transformation is not primarily about what we know; it is about what something becomes. Transformation is the kind of change by which a caterpillar becomes a butterfly, and Zhuangzi earlier uses it to describe how the giant fish, Minnow, "transforms into a bird named Breeze" (208*). Breeze is a metaphor for the sage. Zhuangzi says elsewhere of the ancient sages: "Sometimes they took themselves for horses. Sometimes they took themselves for cows" (242). Similarly, Zhuangzi's difficulty in distinguishing between himself and the butterfly, while initially disorienting, gives him a taste of the perspective of the sage, for whom all things are part of a potentially harmonious whole.

The butterfly dream story comes at the end of the chapter "On Equalizing Things," and a later commentator, Zhu Boxiu, explains how it summarizes the rest of the chapter: "One realizes that the myriad things share one form, the myriad things are one process of transformation, the myriad things have one spirit. . . . Which is the thing and which is me? This is what the chapter means by the great 'equalizing' [of things]."[iii]

VIII. Historical Significance

Zhuangzi influenced later East Asian culture in myriad ways. Here I will only touch on two of them, one literary and one philosophical. Parables and metaphors certainly exist before Zhuangzi, but he is the first major author of self-conscious fiction. Consequently, later novelists, short-story writers, and poets appealed to Zhuangzi as a historical precedent for their art. In differing ways and to various extents, poets from the Seven Worthies of the Bamboo Grove to Li Bai (Li Po) tried to embody in their verse and their own lives what they saw as Zhuangzi's unconventionality, his reclusiveness, and his appreciation of the natural world. Witness the Zhuangzian themes in this celebrated poem by Tao Qian:

> I built my hut beside a traveled road
> Yet hear no noise of passing carts and horses.
> You would like to know how it is done?

With the mind detached, one's place becomes remote.
Picking chrysanthemums by the eastern hedge
I catch sight of the distant southern hills:
The mountain air is lovely as the sun sets
And flocks of flying birds return together.
In these things is a fundamental truth
I would like to tell, but lack the words.[iv]

The influence of Zhuangzi was also significant in Japan. Haiku poets such as Bashō admired what they saw as Zhuangzi's ability to use humor for serious purposes and to create spontaneously but in a manner that was uncontrived.[v]

Zhuangzi's vision that one can be put into contact with the Way via skillful activity ramified through many aspects of later thought. In *Dream of the Red Chamber,* the greatest of the classic Chinese novels, the character of Lin Daiyu explains the true meaning of playing the Qin (a kind of zither) in Zhuangzian terms: "I realized that playing the Qin is a form of meditation and spiritual discipline handed down to us from the ancients."[vi] She adds that when you play the Qin, your "Soul may now commune with the Divine, and enter into that mysterious Union with the Way."[vii] Two of the recurring characters in *Dream of the Red Chamber* are a Daoist priest and a Buddhist monk, who often travel together. This reflects the mutual influence in China of Buddhism and Daoism, noted in the previous chapter. One of the most significant contributions of Chinese Buddhism is Chan (better known in the West by its Japanese name, Zen). At the risk of oversimplifying, Chan can be seen as a fusion of Buddhist and Zhuangzian ideas. For example, Chan accepts the belief that even mundane and unexalted activities, if done through selfless nonaction, can put one in touch with the Way. Because they are vegetarians, you will not find Chan Buddhists slaughtering oxen, but monks are told that they should see everyday tasks like fetching water, cooking rice gruel, and sweeping the floor as opportunities for enlightenment.

I noted at the beginning of this chapter that Mengzi and Zhuangzi are contemporaries. Both are profound philosophers with compelling literary styles. However, they offer arguments for strikingly different conclusions. If you agree that the butcher's skillful dismemberment of the ox puts him in touch with the Way (224–25), you must disagree with Mengzi's suggestion that "gentlemen keep their distance from the kitchen" (1A7). If you accept Mengzi's argument that we must cultivate "the sprout of benevolence" and "the sprout of righteousness" that are part of our nature (2A6), you must reject Zhuangzi's argument that "the sprouts of benevolence and righteousness and the pathways of right and wrong are all snarled and jumbled" (222). And either you can cultivate the heart so that it functions as the "commander" of the *qi* (2A2) or you can achieve "emptiness" by "the fasting of the heart," so that you "do not listen with your heart but listen with your *qi*" (228).

Beyond these disagreements over detail there is a more fundamental difference in their visions of living well. Mengzi offers us a life rich in deep commitments to other humans. Our friendships, familial relations, and obligations to others are at the center of our existence. We engage in political activity because we hope to improve society for our fellow humans, freeing them from fear of war, theft, and assault, making sure they are clothed and fed. There is much to admire in that, but the result is a life that is very vulnerable. Shun sobs because his parents don't love him. Yu works himself to exhaustion, feeling personally responsible for every person he does not save. Kongzi is almost murdered at one point and nearly starves at another. In contrast, Zhuangzi's detachment insulates one from loss. The true sage can watch with amused curiosity as his body rots or humor others by performing a funeral service that means nothing to him. The wistful Daoists "punished by Heaven," whose personalities prevent them from completely letting go of benevolence and righteousness, can still achieve a degree of protection insofar as they recognize the limitations of human evaluations. Their lack of attachment also keeps them from pursuing the extremes of fame, wealth, and power that so often lead to trouble. The Zhuangzian ideal is not purely negative, though. There is a particular kind of joy that comes from recognizing and accepting the endless transformations of the universe. And there does seem to be something exquisitely beautiful about skillful activity that goes beyond its simple efficacy.

Mengzi and Zhuangzi are not the only two philosophical options, of course. The next major philosopher, Xunzi, was a Confucian, but he disagreed with Mengzi's claim that human nature is good. Xunzi accepts Zhuangzi's view that human evaluations are artificial fabrications, not privileged by Heaven and earth. However, Xunzi argues that we have good reason to commit ourselves to the construct that is human civilization. We turn to this syncretic thinker in the next chapter.

Review Questions

1. What is skepticism?
2. Explain one of Zhuangzi's arguments for skepticism.
3. What is relativism?
4. Explain how Zhuangzi exploits an ambiguity in the word *shi* to suggest relativism.
5. Tell the story of "three in the morning, four at night." What do you think this story illustrates?

6. Tell the story of the butcher carving up the ox. What do you think this story illustrates?

7. What is one significant similarity between the philosophy of the *Daodejing* and that of the *Zhuangzi*? What is one important difference?

8. Why are sages like Master Chariot unafraid of illness and death?

9. Explain the difference between the most radical vision of sagehood and the "wistful Daoist."

10. Tell the story of the butterfly dream. What do you think this story illustrates?

11. Apply your understanding of Zhuangzi to the story of Minnow and Breeze that opens the text. How could you interpret it as suggesting relativism? How could you read the story as skeptical? How might you interpret it as contrasting the perspective of the sage with that of ordinary people?

■ 10 ■

XUNZI'S CONFUCIAN NATURALISM

Since people's nature is bad, they must await teachers and proper models, and only then do they become correct in their behavior.

—Xunzi

中国邮政 CHINA

古代思想家 — 荀子

2000 – 20

(6 – 6) J

2.80元

Xunzi is one of the most systematic Confucian philosophers.

I. Xunzi's Context

Xunzi lived near the end of the Warring States Period (403–221 BCE) and may have seen the unification of China under the Qin dynasty. Xunzi's extensive and wide-ranging writings discuss ethics, metaphysics, epistemology, the philosophy of language, and psychology, and he is acknowledged today as one of the greatest ancient philosophers. He spent a significant portion of his career at the Jixia Academy, a think tank created by the ruler of Qi to bring together the greatest minds of his era to study, teach, and provide advice to the state.

At the Academy, Xunzi learned much from the views of other philosophers. Like the Mohists, Xunzi employs the expository essay style as a vehicle for philosophy and appeals to a state-of-nature argument to justify government. Like Yang Zhu, Xunzi holds that human nature is ultimately self-centered and that the Confucian Way is artificial. Like Zhuangzi, Xunzi takes the activity of craftspeople as a model for following the Way: Zhuangzi's butcher and Xunzi's sage both gradually learn to act in accordance with the pattern of the world. Above all, though, Xunzi is a Confucian. He brilliantly synthesizes elements from other philosophers into a defense of the Way of Kongzi. For Xunzi, the most important elements of Kongzi's thought are his emphases on ritual, learning, and the arduousness of transforming human motivations, like working jade: "As if cut, as if polished; / As if carved, as if ground" (*Analects* 1.15). However, Xunzi did not hesitate to criticize his fellow Confucian Mengzi, whose claim that human nature is good "does not match the test of experience" (303). The reality, Xunzi claims, is that "people's nature is bad, and their goodness is a matter of deliberate effort" (298).

II. Naturalism and Ritual

Metaphysics is the branch of philosophy that attempts to answer the question: What are the most fundamental types of things that exist? Naturalism is the metaphysical view that all that exists is ultimately reducible to the entities studied by natural science (physics, chemistry, biology, etc.). If we accept that definition, Xunzi cannot be classified as a naturalist, because he lived before the development of the natural sciences as we now understand them. However, Xunzi does share one of the core commitments distinctive of naturalism. He denies teleology (the view that the universe has some intentional goal): "The activities of Heaven are constant. They do not persist because of Yao. They do not perish because of Jie" (269).

Since nature is not goal directed, we must reject the appeal to omens and spiritual entities to explain phenomena:

> If stars fall or trees cry out, the people of the state are filled with fear and say, "What is this?" I say: It is nothing. These are simply rarely occurring things among the changes in Heaven and earth and the transformations of *yin* and *yang*. To marvel at them is alright, but to fear them is not. Eclipses of the sun and moon, unseasonable winds and rains, unexpected appearances of strange stars—there is no age in which such things do not occur. (*Xunzi* 17; *Readings,* pp. 271–72)

Mengzi did not express any interest in omens, but he did have a teleological view of Heaven. He saw it as guiding history so that, in the long run, those with Virtue will rule, bringing peace and prosperity to the people (*Mengzi* 2B13). Another aspect of Mengzi's teleology was his view that Heaven implants in us our virtuous nature (*Mengzi* 7A1). We'll see that Xunzi challenges this second aspect of Mengzi's thought as well.

Because the universe does not have a teleological structure, rituals cannot be instrumental to achieving their superficial goals. However, they may serve an alternative purpose:

> One performs the rain sacrifice and it rains. Why? I say: There is no special reason why. It is the same as when one does not perform the rain sacrifice and it rains anyway. When the sun and moon suffer eclipse, one tries to save them. When Heaven sends drought, one performs the rain sacrifice. One performs divination and only then decides on important affairs. But this is not for the sake of getting what one seeks, but rather to give things proper form. Thus, the gentleman looks upon this as proper form, but the common people look upon it as connecting with spirits. (*Xunzi* 17; *Readings,* p. 272)

We quoted this passage in Chapter 2, where we noted that it suggests functionalism, the position developed millennia later in the West, according to which the best way to understand rituals is in terms of the social and psychological needs that they meet. Xunzi clearly sees one of the functions of ritual as providing a means for giving form to and expressing one's emotions:

> When the feelings that come to him stir him greatly but are deprived of an outlet and stopped, then with regard to the refined expression of remembrance he will feel anguished and unsatisfied, and his practice of

ritual and proper regulation will be lacking and incomplete. And so, the former kings accordingly established a proper form for it, and thereby was set what is righteous in venerating those esteemed and loving those intimate. Thus I say: The sacrificial rites are the refined expression of remembrance and longing. (*Xunzi* 19; *Readings,* p. 284)

Xunzi illustrates this by explaining the expressive purpose behind certain rituals:

> The standard practice of funeral rites is that one changes the appearance of the corpse by gradually adding more ornamentations, one moves the corpse gradually further away, and over a long time one gradually returns to one's regular routine. Thus, the way that death works is that if one does not ornament the dead, then one will come to feel disgust at them, and if one feels disgust, then one will not feel sad. (*Xunzi* 19; *Readings,* pp. 279–80)

Rituals do not just provide an outlet for emotions we already have. One of the most important functions of ritual is to reshape our motivations. Xunzi uses a state-of-nature argument to justify the importance of ritual for this purpose:

> From what did ritual arise? I say: Humans are born having desires. When they have desires but do not get the objects of their desires, then they cannot but seek some means of satisfaction. If there is no measure or limit to their seeking, then they cannot help but struggle with each other. If they strugle with each other then there will be chaos, and if there is chaos then they will be impoverished. The former kings hated such chaos, and so they established rituals and the standards of righteousness in order to allot things to people, to nurture their desires, and to satisfy their seeking. They caused desires never to exhaust material goods, and material goods never to be depleted by desires, so that the two support each other and prosper. This is how ritual arose. Thus, ritual is a means of nurture. (*Xunzi* 19; *Readings,* p. 274)

The Mohists had earlier used state-of-nature arguments, but Xunzi starts from different assumptions and therefore arrives at a different conclusion. The Mohists held that human motivations are highly malleable. For them, conflict in the state of nature results from the fact that in the absence of central authority, humans will have widely varying conceptions of righteousness.[1]

---

1. *Yì* 義, rendered "norms" in the translation of *Mozi* 11; *Readings,* pp. 65–68.

In contrast, Xunzi held that we share a common human nature and that it is characterized primarily by self-interest:

> As for the way that the eyes like pretty colors, the ears like beautiful sounds, the mouth likes good flavors, the heart likes what is beneficial, and the bones and flesh like what is comfortable—these are produced from people's inborn dispositions and nature. (*Xunzi* 23; *Readings,* p. 300)

Because the objects of desire are always limited, each of us seeking to benefit ourselves without restraint will lead to chaos in the state of nature:

> Liking what is beneficial and desiring gain are people's inborn dispositions and nature. Suppose there were brothers who had some property to divide, and that they followed the fondness for benefit and desire for gain in their inborn dispositions and nature. If they were to do so, then the brothers would conflict and contend with each other for it. (*Xunzi* 23; *Readings,* p. 301)

In order to address this conflict and save the people from their own natures, the ancient sage-kings

> set up the power of rulers and superiors in order to control them. They made clear ritual and the standards of righteousness in order to transform them. They set up laws and standards in order to manage them. They multiplied punishments and fines in order to restrain them. As a result, they caused all under Heaven to become well ordered and conform to the Way. (*Xunzi* 23; *Readings,* p. 302)

Rituals and the standards of righteousness coordinate human desires and material goods in two ways. First, they establish rules for who is entitled to which of the limited material resources available. For example, it is traditional that the eldest brother, not a younger brother, inherits the land that belonged to his father. Similarly, kings are entitled to palaces and regal clothes, while farmers have simple huts and functional work clothes. Elders are served first and get the choicest foods, while youngsters must wait their turn. Consequently, rituals justify differential treatment and privileges. However, everyone is better off with rituals and righteousness than they would be without them, because they allow us to escape the chaotic state of nature.

The rituals do not merely set rules for entitlement, though. They are effective because they reshape human motivations. Xunzi's argument is that because humans are innately self-interested they have to be transformed via ritual or they will never successfully live in harmony. The Mohist political program will fail, Xunzi suggests, because it ignores our innate motivations and the effort required to transform them. Xunzi illustrates this with the example of music:

> Music is joy, an unavoidable human disposition. So, people cannot be without music; if they feel joy, they must express it in sound and give it shape in movement. . . . So, people cannot be without joy, and their joy cannot be without shape, but if it takes shape and does not accord with the Way, then there will inevitably be chaos. (*Xunzi* 20; *Readings,* p. 285)

As we saw in Chapter 4, the Mohists condemn musical performances as wasteful and suggest eliminating them (see *Mozi* 32; *Readings,* pp. 105–10). They see no difficulty in achieving this because they assume human motivations are highly malleable. Xunzi counters that humans are recalcitrant: we cannot change the fact that humans wish to express emotions in music. But while our motivations are innate, the Way is not. Consequently, we must re-shape our dispositions through ritual and particular forms of music so that we can live harmoniously together in society:

> And so, if a person puts even one measure of effort into following ritual and the standards of righteousness, he will get back twice as much. If he puts even one measure of effort into following his nature and inborn dispositions, he will lose twice as much. And so, the Confucians are those who will cause people to gain twice as much, and the Mohists are those who will cause people to lose twice as much. (*Xunzi* 19; *Readings,* p. 275)

III. History and Objectivity

If humans need to be reshaped by the rituals and standards of righteousness developed by the sages, how did the sages develop them in the first place? Xunzi frequently draws analogies between the sages and craftspeople. Let's follow out that analogy in more detail. Humans need sharp implements for hunting, butchering, and warfare. In ancient times, a craftsperson surmised that a blade made out of bronze would be superior to the flint ones in use at the time, because the bronze blades could have a larger cutting surface and would be less brittle. The craftsperson smelted the bronze, then used a hammer and anvil to forge it. The result was the beginning of the Bronze Age, which offered superior solutions to human needs.

Similarly, the ancient sages recognized a problem that humans faced: "people were deviant, dangerous, and not correct in their behavior, and they were unruly, chaotic, and not well ordered" (302). As a result of this, "the strong would harm the weak and take from them. The many would tyrannize the few and shout them down" (302). Even those who were momentarily dominant lived in fear, knowing that their position was always unstable. Using their imagination and intelligence, the sages invented a solution to save people from this problem: "They made clear ritual and the standards of righteousness in order to transform them" (302). Just as creating and using bronze blades was a better answer to the human need for a cutting implement, so was creating and using ritual and standards of righteousness a better way to live than the chaotic state of nature.

Neither the craftsperson nor the sage creates according to some innate pattern. (After all, our brain is not hardwired with the knowledge of how to smelt bronze and forge it into blades.) Their products are the result of "deliberate effort":

> Thus, when the potter mixes clay and makes vessels, the vessels are produced from the deliberate efforts of the craftsman; they are not produced from people's nature. Thus, when the craftsman carves wood and makes utensils, the utensils are produced from the deliberate efforts of the craftsman; they are not produced from people's nature. . . . So, ritual and standards of righteousness and proper models and measures are produced from the deliberate efforts of the sage; they are not produced from people's nature. (*Xunzi* 23; *Readings,* p. 300)

Does Xunzi want us to view the invention of ritual and the standards of righteousness as something that happened all at once in the distant past, or as something that gradually accumulated over many generations? The craftsperson analogy suggests the latter, since technology develops piecemeal and over time. Just within the few centuries since Kongzi, Xunzi's world had seen the transition from the Bronze Age to the Iron Age. There are some passages that indicate Xunzi had a similar view of the Way: "The sages *accumulated* reflections and deliberations and practiced deliberate efforts and reasoned activities in order to produce ritual and standards of righteousness and to establish proper models and measures."[2] This invites us to imagine a gradual accumula-

---

2. You will find a version of this sentence on p. 300 of *Readings,* but in the translation there the subject of the sentence is singular, "the sage," and the central verbs are in the

tion of rituals and standards of righteousness over time. Perhaps the earliest sages recognized only that everyone would be happier and civilization would be more likely to survive if we adopted a standard of righteousness in warfare: "It is wrong to kill the children of your enemy." Over many generations, sages built upon this, adding more and more rituals and standards of righteousness, until they reached what they considered to be the ideal form.

The craftsperson analogy also adopts ideas taken from Zhuangzi to construct a response to his relativistic and skeptical arguments. Zhuangzi suggests (at least sometimes) that just as "this" and "that" depend upon one's perspective, so is the Way nothing more than a matter of what one "regards as right" or "regards as wrong." However, Zhuangzi also indicates that we can learn "how to care for life" by observing the almost miraculous effectiveness of craftspeople, like the butcher who slaughters an ox. The butcher's skill results from the fact that he is able to "rely on the Heavenly patterns," the natural makeup of the ox's body, as he carves. Because of how the butcher, his blade, and the ox carcass relate to one another, there is a right way (and many wrong ways) for him to carve. And this is not simply a matter of perspective.[3]

Xunzi appeals to the same language of "patterns" to describe how the sage develops the Way: "benevolence, righteousness, lawfulness, and correctness have patterns that can be known and can be practiced" (304). He says of ritual in particular that "[i]n its differentiations of things, it is the utmost in patterning. In its explanations, it is the utmost in keen discernment. Those under Heaven who follow it will have good order. Those who do not follow it will have chaos" (276). So while Xunzi agrees with Zhuangzi and Yang Zhu that the Confucian Way is the result of artifice, he argues that, just as there is a best way for a butcher to carve an ox, so there is a best set of practices and institutions to regulate and transform humans so that they can live harmoniously with each other and their environment. Because he sees ritual as a pattern of such power and scope, Xunzi waxes rhapsodic about it:

> By ritual, Heaven and earth harmoniously combine;
> By ritual, the sun and moon radiantly shine;
> By ritual, the four seasons in progression arise;
> By ritual, the stars move orderly across the skies;
> . . .

---

present tense, "accumulates" and "practices." Both translations are possible, because Chinese grammar does not mark number or tense. The issue is whether the sentence refers primarily to a process sages in each generation engage in to transform themselves and others, or to a gradual development that occurred over many generations, through the piecemeal accomplishments of the sages.

3. See the discussion of the butcher in Chapter 9.

By ritual, for love and hate proper measure is made;
By ritual, on joy and anger fit limits are laid.
By ritual, compliant subordinates are created,
By ritual, enlightened leaders are generated. (*Xunzi* 19; *Readings,* p. 276)

How does Xunzi reconcile his suggestion that ritual governs the transformations of the four seasons and the motions of the stars with his comparison of
ritual to the fabrications of craftspeople? After all, the former image implies
that rituals are cosmic principles that humans discover, while the latter suggests that they are invented. There does not need to be a tension between the
two views, though. A bronze sword is an invention, a product of the deliberate effort of the craftsperson, but its invention is not arbitrary. It is based on
the human purposes it is intended to serve and the characteristics and ca-
pacities of bronze. This is why the Bronze Age dawned in multiple civilizations independently, despite the fact that our primate brains are not hard-wired
to smelt bronze. Similarly, human rituals are invented, but they are based
upon the patterns of Heaven, earth, and humans. Xunzi is explicit that sages
bring all three into harmony:

When the grasses and trees are flowering and abundant, then axes
and hatchets are not to enter the mountains and forests, so as not to
cut short their life, and not to break off their growth. When the
turtles and crocodiles, fish and eels are pregnant and giving birth,
then nets and poisons are not to enter the marshes, so as not to cut
short their life, and not to break off their growth. Plow in the spring,
weed in the summer, harvest in the fall and store in the winter. . . .
Cutting and nurturing are not to miss their proper times, and then
the mountains and forests will not be barren, and the common people will have surplus materials. (*Xunzi* 9; *Readings,* p. 268)

Thus, we can metaphorically think of larger cosmic phenomena as extensions
of the patterns of ritual. The comparison of ritual to the rules governing the
motions of the stars suggests that both are eternal and unchangeable. Xunzi
does seem to embrace this conclusion: "Is not ritual perfect indeed! It estab-
lishes a lofty standard that is the ultimate of its kind, and none under Heaven
can add to or subtract from it" (276).

IV. Human Nature and Psychology

Xunzi sketches an account of how the sages invented the Way. But if our innate dispositions are opposed to the Way, how is it possible for anyone to

learn to follow it? Part of Xunzi's answer is that humans do not necessarily follow their own desires. He illustrates this with the example of those who sacrifice their lives for the sake of righteousness:

> Life is what people most desire, and death is what people most despise. However, when people let go of life and bring about their own death, this is not because they do not desire life and instead desire death. Rather, it is because they do not approve of living under these circumstances, but do approve of dying under these circumstances. (*Xunzi* 22; *Readings,* p. 297)

What is the distinction that Xunzi wishes to draw between desire and approval? Paradigmatic desires are our largely innate cravings, especially for the objects of the senses. Approval is a kind of evaluation, so it is based on a conception of the Way.

The passage above seems to be a response to *Mengzi* 6A10, which claims that people choose to die only because they desire righteousness even more than they desire life. The centrality of desire to human motivation is not an ethical problem for Mengzi, though, because he thinks we innately desire righteousness. Our task in self-cultivation is to develop and strengthen these desires so that we act consistently in accordance with them. Xunzi regards our innate desires as self-interested, though, so Mengzi's solution is not open to him. Instead, Xunzi postulates that we are capable of overriding our desires. We do not necessarily follow our desires but instead act out of what our heart approves, which is based on our conception of the Way. Because this attributes an ethical capacity to the heart, it might seem to be equivalent to Mengzi's position. However, for Mengzi, the innate motivations of the heart have specific content: we all sometimes show disdain for shameful behavior; we all sometimes manifest compassion for the suffering of others.

Fact: *The English expression "gung ho," meaning "very or overly enthusiastic," is originally Chinese. True, but the story is complicated. In World War II, a U.S. officer hoped to inspire in his soldiers the same team spirit and dedication he saw among his Chinese friends, so he adopted an expression he thought meant "work together in harmony." Unfortunately, the Chinese gōnghé 工合 is actually an abbreviation for Association of Industrial Cooperatives.*

Xunzi's position seems to be that the approval of the heart is empty until it is given a specific content. One person might be taught by his culture that possessing wealth is identical with living well, so he will pursue wealth far beyond what is necessary for the satisfaction of his physical desires. Think of the contemporary celebrities who own a dozen mansions around the world, each with swimming pools, a garage for a dozen cars, and a score of bedrooms. It seems unlikely that anyone actually has physical desires that can only be satisfed by this level of consumption. Instead, they are motivated by their conception of how they ought to live. "When the desire is lacking but one's action surpasses it, this is because the heart compels it. If what the heart approves misses the proper patterns, then even if the desires are few, how would it stop short of chaos?" (297).

In contrast, another person might long for some fine clothes that he cannot afford to buy. But if he has learned from the Way of the sages to disapprove of stealing, he will not act on this desire. "Thus, when the desire is excessive but one's action does not match it, this is because the heart prevents it. If what the heart approves conforms to the proper patterns, then even if one's desires are many, what harm would they be to good order?" (297).

In Xunzi's terminology, approval is a kind of "deliberation," the heart's choice among desires:

> The feelings of liking and disliking, happiness and anger, and sadness and joy in one's nature are called the "dispositions." When there is a certain disposition and the heart makes a choice on its behalf, this is called "deliberation." When the heart deliberates and one's abilities act on it, this is called "deliberate effort." That which comes into being through accumulated deliberations and training of one's abilities is also called "deliberate effort." (*Xunzi* 22; *Readings,* p. 292)

If I have a desire to eat a second piece of cheesecake for dessert, this is a disposition of my nature. My heart will deliberate on this disposition and may choose to disapprove of it (if I have learned a Way that endorses moderate consumption of sweets). Forgoing the cheesecake is an example of deliberate effort, and it may prove difficult to do at first, but by repeatedly engaging in deliberate effort, I can train myself so that I am no longer tempted to have the second piece of cheesecake.

So, our physical desires are certainly part of our nature. It is not clear whether Xunzi regards the heart's *capacity* to deliberate as also part of our nature. He might acknowledge this. However, given what he says elsewhere, it is clear that the deliberate effort of the heart and its products are not part of one's nature. Through deliberate effort, we transcend our nature and establish social distinctions. Xunzi claims that these distinctions are what sets humans apart from other animals:

> Thus, that by which humans are human is not that they are special in having two legs and no feathers, but that they have distinctions. The

birds and beasts have fathers and sons but not the intimate relationship of father and son. They have the male sex and the female sex but no differentiation between male and female. And so among human ways, none is without distinctions. Of distinctions, none are greater than social divisions, and of social divisions, none are greater than rituals, and of rituals, none are greater than those of the sage-kings. (*Xunzi* 5; *Readings,* p. 266)

Arguably, social animals like ants and wolves *do* have recognizable social distinctions, so Xunzi may have failed to specify a characteristic unique to humans. However, what is most important is his claim that such distinctions are artificial yet essential to human life.

Xunzi's slogan to describe his position is "human nature is bad," which he formulates as a denial of Mengzi's claim that human nature is good. However, there has been extensive debate about exactly what Xunzi means by this and whether he really disagrees with Mengzi. One thing is clear: Xunzi does not wish to assert that human nature is *evil.* Philosophers like Augustine who claim that human nature is evil hold that people are innately capable of doing evil for the sake of evil. In his *Confessions* Augustine notes that humans sometimes do wrong in order to obtain some good for themselves, like stealing to obtain expensive luxuries. Augustine argues that it is always a mistake to do wrong. Someone who steals obtains a lesser good (like the temporary admiration of one's contemporaries for one's fine clothes) at the expense of a greater good (the health of one's eternal soul). Nonetheless, motivations of greed and lust manifest a sort of limited reasonableness. We know *why* someone is doing wrong. However, Augustine argues, appealing to his own experiences, that humans sometimes do wrong even when it does not benefit them. When he was a teenager, Augustine and some of his friends stole some pears from a nearby orchard even though they were not hungry and had access to better fruit than the ones they took. They simply threw the pears away after they stole them. Thus, Augustine and his friends did not satisfy any sensual desire or benefit themselves in any way by stealing the pears. So why did they do it? They did it because it was forbidden. Augustine is aware that this youthful action was hardly a serious crime. But he is disturbed by what he thinks the action reveals: *humans can do wrong simply because it is wrong.* This is what Augustine means in claiming that human nature is evil.

Xunzi suggests nothing quite as dire as this. Part of what Xunzi means by saying that human nature is bad is that if we follow our innate dispositions, they will lead us to do wrong: if we all try to benefit ourselves and satisfy our sensual desires without any constraints, we will end up in a state of conflict and chaos.

Would Mengzi actually disagree with this? When Mengzi states that human nature is good, he means that we have innate but incipient tendencies toward virtue, but he stresses that we must cultivate these tendencies in order to achieve full virtue: "It is the way of people that if they are full of food, have warm clothes, and live in comfort, but are without instruction, then they come close to being animals" (*Mengzi* 3A4). Perhaps Xunzi misinterpreted Mengzi's stance on human nature. Further support for this hypothesis comes from consideration of the specific arguments that Xunzi directs against Mengzi:

> Mengzi says: When people engage in learning, this manifests the goodness of their nature. I say: This is not so. . . . In every case, the nature of a thing is the accomplishment of Heaven. It cannot be learned. It cannot be worked at. . . . Now people's nature is such that their eyes can see, and their ears can hear. The keenness by which they see does not depart from their eyes, and the acuity by which they hear does not depart from their ears. Their eyes are simply keen, and their ears are simply acute; it is clear that one does not learn these things. (*Xunzi* 23; *Readings,* pp. 299–300)

Xunzi argues that human nature cannot be good, because if it were, goodness could not be something that we can get better at through ethical education. If human nature were already good, then "what use would there be for sage-kings? What use for ritual and the standards of righteousness?" (302). Notice, though, that Mengzi means something very different by "human nature." For Mengzi, the nature of a sprout is to grow into a mature plant and produce its own sprouts. It is a *process* for the sprout to realize its nature, requiring a supportive environment, which is not something it possesses automatically. Similarly, when Mengzi states that human nature is good, he means that humans have an active potential to become good, not that they are good already.

So, in the interpretation above, the views of Mengzi and Xunzi do not directly conflict, because they mean different things by "human nature." This is certainly part of the story. But Xunzi would disagree with Mengzi even if he had understood more clearly what he meant. It is not that Xunzi agrees about the existence of the "sprouts" of virtue but simply does not wish to refer to them as "human nature." Xunzi denies that we have even the incipient tendencies toward virtue in our nature. Contrast Mengzi's sprout metaphors with Xunzi's preferred metaphors for ethical cultivation:

> Through steaming and bending, you can make wood straight as a plumb line into a wheel. And after its curve conforms to the compass, even when parched under the sun it will not become straight

again, because the steaming and bending have made it a certain way. Likewise, when wood comes under the ink-line, it becomes straight, and when metal is brought to the whetstone, it becomes sharp. The gentleman learns broadly and examines himself thrice daily, and then his knowledge is clear and his conduct is without fault. (*Xunzi* 1; *Readings*, pp. 256–57)

Xunzi suggests that bringing our nature into conformity with the Way is like the forced bending of a plank of wood into a wheel. This is precisely the model that Mengzi rejects in his debate with Gaozi (*Mengzi* 6A1). Mengzi objects to its unappealing consequence, that to follow the Way we must warp our nature (just as the nature of the wood is warped when we carve it into cups and bowls). But Xunzi embraces this conclusion. Indeed, Xunzi seems to accept Gaozi's basic claim: "The desires for food and sex are nature" (6A4).

The differences between Mengzi and Xunzi are crucial for interpreting the so-called ladder of souls passage:

Water and fire have *qi* but are without life. Grasses and trees have life but are without awareness. Birds and beasts have awareness but are without standards of righteousness. Humans have *qi* and life and awareness, and moreover they have standards of righteousness. And so they are the most precious thing under Heaven. (*Xunzi* 9; *Readings*, p. 267)

Water and fire represent two complementary kinds of *qi:* water is a paradigm of what is *yin* (dark, passive, cool, flowing downward, etc.), while fire is an exemplar of *yang* (light, active, hot, rising upward, etc.). Plants have *qi,* but are also alive; animals have *qi* and life but also awareness of their surroundings. Humans have *qi,* life, awareness but also standards of righteousness. This last phrase is a translation of the Chinese *yi,* which is usually rendered simply as "righteousness." The translation used in *Readings* reflects the view that Mengzi and Xunzi understand righteousness very differently. For Mengzi, righteousness is an expression of our innate but incipient virtuous inclinations. For Xunzi, righteousness is an artificial construct, invented by the sages to meet the human need for society. After presenting the ladder of souls, Xunzi notes that humans

are not as strong as oxen or as fast as horses, but oxen and horses are used by them. How is this so? I say: It is because humans are able to form communities while the animals cannot. Why are humans able to form communities? I say: It is because of social divisions. How can social divisions be put into practice? I say: It is because of standards of righteousness. (*Xunzi* 9; *Readings,* p. 267)

This understanding of "righteousness" as referring to *standards* of righteousness fits what Xunzi says in other contexts, especially since he very frequently pairs ritual and righteousness. Ritual is also an external construct of the sages. However, there is an alternative interpretation. Perhaps "righteousness" in the ladder of souls passage refers to a <u>capacity to learn a Way,</u> but a *contentless* capacity, in the sense that it does not innately favor any particular Way. Xunzi's comparison of ethical cultivation to language acquisition suggests this interpretation: "The children of the Han, Yue, Yi, and Mo peoples all cry with the same sound at birth, but when grown they have different customs, because teaching makes them be this way" (257). At birth, humans have a capacity to acquire a language, but they are not born knowing a language or even with a disposition to speak any one particular language. Similarly, Xunzi believes, we are born with a capacity to learn ritual and to guide our innate desires with it. But we are not born with a disposition toward any particular set of rituals. Xunzi may use the term "righteousness" to refer to this contentless capacity to learn ritual.

Another puzzling passage for understanding the differences between Mengzi and Xunzi occurs in the latter's discussion of mourning rituals:

Among all the living things between Heaven and earth, those that have blood and *qi* are sure to have awareness, and of those that have awareness, none does not love its own kind. Now if one of the great birds or beasts loses its group of companions, then after a month or a season has passed, it is sure to retrace its former path and go by its old home. . . . Among creatures that have blood and *qi,* none has greater awareness than man, and so man's feeling for his parents knows no limit until the day they die. (*Xunzi* 19; *Readings,* p. 283)

Both in this passage and in *Mengzi* 3A5, the origin of funerals or mourning is the affection of the living for the deceased; both passages suggest that these feelings are nearly universal. Xunzi seems to acknowledge here that there is more to human nature than just self-interested desires for things like food and sex. <u>Humans innately</u> love their parents and thus have an <u>innate need to grieve over their loss in some way.</u>

Is Xunzi really a Mengzian, whether he knows it or not? Xunzi's position seems different from that of Mengzi in at least one important respect. For Mengzi, our feelings of familial affection are intrinsically virtuous: they are our "best capability" and our "best knowledge" (*Mengzi* 7A15). For Xunzi, our feelings are too inchoate and unstructured to be considered virtuous. We must reshape even emotions like familial love in accordance with ritual. Some people are insufficiently cognizant of the debt that they owe their ancestors: "Those who have died that morning they forget by that evening" (283). Others are excessive in their mourning.

> If one simply acquiesces in this, then mourning would continue without end. Therefore, the former kings and sages accordingly established a middle way and fixed a proper measure for it, such that once mourning is made sufficient to achieve good form and proper order, then one stops it. (*Xunzi* 19; *Readings*, p. 283)

Thus, Xunzi has what Mengzi refers to contempuously as a two source view of the Way. In Xunzi's view,

> human nature is the original beginning and the raw material, and deliberate effort is to pattern and order it and make it exalted. If there were no human nature, then there would be nothing for deliberate effort to be applied to. If there were no deliberate effort, then human nature would not be able to beautify itself. . . . For Heaven can give birth to creatures, but it cannot enforce distinctions among creatures. (*Xunzi* 19; *Readings*, pp. 281–82)

Mengzi would reply, "Heaven, in producing the things in the world, causes them to have one source" (*Mengzi* 3A5).

V. Ethical Cultivation

The disagreement between Mengzi and Xunzi over human nature is reflected in their views on ethical cultivation. As we noted in Chapter 2, one of the longstanding disagreements among Confucians is over the comparative importance of learning and thinking in ethical cultivation. Because he believes that human nature is good, Mengzi emphasizes thinking: "Benevolence, righteousness, propriety, and wisdom are not welded to us externally. We inherently have them. It is simply that we do not reflect upon them" (6A6).

In contrast, Xunzi's conception of human nature and the importance of deliberate effort leads him to emphasize learning: "I once spent the whole day pondering, but it wasn't as good as a moment's worth of learning" (257). Xunzi presents an inspiring but challenging image of learning:

> Where does learning begin? Where does learning end? I say: Its order begins with reciting the classics, and ends with studying ritual. Its

purpose begins with becoming a noble man, and ends with becoming a sage. If you truly accumulate effort for a long time, then you will advance. Learning proceeds until death and only then does it stop. (*Xunzi* 1; *Readings,* p. 258)

Xunzi's methodology of learning is very teacher centered: "In learning, nothing is more expedient than to draw near to the right person" (259). The "right person" is a teacher who can guide your understanding of the ancient texts and rituals. This is necessary because, as Xunzi acknowledges, they are difficult to interpret and apply to contemporary situations.

Based upon one's level of learning, Xunzi identifies a hierarchy of character types. At the bottom is the person who has no commitment to learning and remains like a "beast" (258). He is "barbaric, obtuse, perverse, vulgar, and unruly" (262). Only slightly better is the "vulgar scholar" (259). This person pursues learning but does not live up to the values embodied in what he studies; he will only "learn for the sake of impressing others." If you become a vulgar scholar, "you will simply be learning haphazard knowledge and focusing your intentions on blindly following the *Odes* and *History.*" Xunzi no doubt has such vulgar scholars in mind when he remarks, "The learning of the petty person enters through his ears and passes out his mouth. From mouth to ears is only four inches—how could it be enough to improve a whole body much larger than that?" In contrast, the "learning of the gentleman enters through his ears, fastens to his heart, spreads through his four limbs, and manifests itself in his actions. His slightest word, his most subtle movement, all can serve as a model for others" (259).

Xunzi distinguishes among serious learners based on how deeply they have grasped the Way:

> He who likes the right model and carries it out is a man of good breeding. He who focuses his intention upon it and embodies it is a gentleman. He who completely understands it and practices it without tiring is a sage. If a person lacks the proper model, then he will act recklessly [like a beast]. If he has the proper model but does not fix his intentions on its true meaning, then he will act too rigidly [like a vulgar scholar]. If he relies on the proper model and also deeply understands its categories, only then will he act with comfortable mastery of it [like a sage]. (*Xunzi* 2; *Readings,* p. 264)

It is fruitful to compare Xunzi's typology with that found in Aristotle's *Nicomachean Ethics,* where he distinguishes between the bestial person (who has no commitment to virtue), the incontinent person (who knows what is virtuous, but succumbs to temptation), the continent person (who feels temptation but acts virtuously through strength of will), and the fully virtuous person (who is no longer tempted to do wrong).

Learning is a kind of "deliberate effort" (*wěi* 偽), a term that has a positive connotation for Xunzi. It is the self-conscious activity that humans engage in to transform themselves from their natural state into someone virtuous. This puts Xunzi in sharp contrast with the view of the "Robber Zhi" dialogue (369–75), which repeatedly uses the same word to condemn Kongzi for being "artificial" (*wei*). The *Daodejing* also seems to be at odds with Xunzi, because of its frequent condemnation of self-conscious action: "Everyone knows that when the good strives to be good, it is no good" (*Daodejing* 2). The case of Zhuangzi is more complex. It took the butcher years of what was initially deliberate effort to learn how to skillfully carve oxen. The ultimate goal of the butcher's practice is to act effortlessly, but then so does Xunzi hope to produce a gentleman who effortlessly follows the Way:

> He makes his eyes not want to see what is not right, makes his ears not want to hear what is not right, makes his mouth not want to speak what is not right, and makes his heart not want to deliberate over what is not right. He comes to the point where he loves it, and then his eyes love it more than the five colors, his ears love it more than the five tones, his mouth loves it more than the five flavors, and his heart considers it more profitable than possessing the whole world. (*Xunzi* 1; *Readings*, pp. 260–61)

VI. Historical Significance

Xunzi's quasi-naturalistic Confucianism is ingenious, and many aspects of it are plausible from our contemporary perspective. However, a serious limitation of Xunzi's philosophy seems to be that it claims the sages invented the one right Way to organize society. Surely there are rituals (for funerals, weddings, birth, and other major life events) that are just as good as those of ancient China. Furthermore, we think that some version of democracy is a better form of government than the benevolent paternalism Xunzi envisioned. However, taking Xunzi's craftsperson metaphor seriously may allow us to develop a Xunzian philosophy acceptable for the modern world. The sages developed rituals and standards of righteousness to meet human needs, just like craftspeople developed bronze tools. But as the Bronze Age succeeded the Stone Age, so did the Iron Age succeed the Bronze Age. None of the fundamental commitments of Xunzi's philosophy prevent him from acknowledging that the Way continues to develop in a similar manner. Interestingly, a much later Confucian, Zhang Xuecheng (1738–1801), argued explicitly that the Way evolved gradually over time in response to concrete human needs. Zhang did not see himself as following in the steps of Xunzi, but his work provides a detailed account of how we might historicize Confucianism.[i]

Within the Chinese tradition, Xunzi's influence has waxed and waned. His emphasis on learning became the dominant trend in Confucianism for much of its history. Particularly during the Han dynasty (202 BCE–220 CE), Confucianism was known for its almost obsessive emphasis on the study of texts and ritual. During this period, the government appointed experts to interpret each of what came to be known as the *Five Classics*. Xunzi would certainly have approved of this policy:

> In learning, nothing is more expedient than to draw near to the right person. Rituals and music provide proper models but give no precepts. The *Odes* and *History* contain ancient stories but no explanations of their present application. The *Spring and Autumn Annals* is terse and cannot be quickly understood. (*Xunzi* 1; *Readings,* p. 259)

The works that Xunzi cites here became three of the *Five Classics*. The other members of the *Five Classics* were the *Changes,* a work whose cosmological speculations only became important during the Han, and the *Record of Rites*.

Xunzi later came in for criticism, though, from the so-called Neo-Confucians of the Tang (618–906 CE) and Song (960–1279 CE) dynasties. Although they were very critical of Buddhism, the Neo-Confucians had been deeply influenced by the view that we all share an underlying virtuous Buddha-nature that is obscured by selfish desires. Against such an intellectual background, Mengzi's doctrine that human nature is good resonated with the Neo-Confucians. As a result, thinkers like Zhu Xi (1130–1200 CE) identified Mengzi as the true inheritor of the Way of Kongzi and criticized Xunzi for his doctrine that human nature is bad. Zhu Xi also de-emphasized the *Five Classics* in ethical education, arguing that they encouraged an overly scholastic approach to learning. Some interpreters then tried to defend Xunzi by arguing that he did not really disagree with Mengzi. On this complementarian interpretation, Xunzi is simply stressing the obstacles to ethical cultivation, while Mengzi emphasizes the potential to overcome these obstacles. To use a Western metaphor, Xunzi notes that the glass is half empty, while Mengzi observes that it is half full. We have seen that there are some passages in which Xunzi sounds like Mengzi, and these might be read as support for a complementarian reading, but overall Xunzi seems to be very clear in rejecting Mengzi's view. Still other scholars have suggested that Xunzi did not really write the essay "Human Nature Is Bad." But this essay reflects ideas found in many passages in the rest of Xunzi's writings.

Ironically, Xunzi also came under criticism because of his most brilliant pupil, Han Feizi. Han Feizi learned much from his teacher but developed a philosophy that was avowedly anti-Confucian. Han Feizi's ideas, in turn, influenced the policies of the state of Qin. He was blamed for the excesses of the Qin government, and Xunzi was faulted for producing such a student. But to know whether the criticism of Han Feizi is accurate, we need to understand the details of his philosophy. To this topic we turn in the next chapter.

Review Questions

1. What is "naturalism"? Why would we say that Xunzi cannot be a naturalist? What is an important commitment that Xunzi shares with naturalism?

2. How does Xunzi's conception of Heaven differ from that of Mengzi?

3. Consider a ritual in which we leave out offerings of food and drink for the spirits of our ancestors. How would Xunzi say a gentleman should understand this ritual?

4. Explain how Xunzi uses a state-of-nature argument to justify rituals and standards of righteousness.

5. How does Xunzi disagree with the Mohist version of the state-of-nature argument? Specifically, how do the two versions make different assumptions about innate human motivations, and how does this lead them to different conclusions?

6. Xunzi compares the actions of the sages to those of craftspeople. How does this comparison suggest that there can be a "right" Way even though it is not part of human nature?

7. Xunzi writes, "By ritual, the stars move orderly across the skies." Why does this seem to conflict with Xunzi's craftperson metaphor? How might we reconcile the two?

8. Explain the difference between desire and approval. Why is approval important in self-cultivation?

9. According to Xunzi, what is it that distinguishes humans from other animals?

10. What is the difference between Xunzi's view that human nature is bad and Augustine's view that human nature is evil?

11. What is the difference between Xunzi's definition of human nature and that assumed by Mengzi? Why might this difference lead us to think that

Xunzi and Mengzi do not really disagree? Why might we still think that they do disagree?

12. Use the example of wood to illustrate the difference between Xunzi's conception of ethical cultivation and that of Mengzi.

13. Paraphrase the ladder of souls passage.

14. Xunzi notes that, of creatures "that have awareness, none does not love its kind." Why does this seem to commit Xunzi to a position on human nature much like that of Mengzi? How might the passage be interpreted to preserve the disagreement between them?

15. In the "Robber Zhi" dialogue the term *wei* is translated as "artificial," while in the *Xunzi* it is rendered "deliberate effort." How do these differing translations reflect the different attitudes of the two works toward transforming human nature?

■ 11 ■

HAN FEIZI

People naturally grow arrogant when loved, and become obedient only through coercion.

—Han Feizi

This decorated axe head symbolizes punishment, one of Han Feizi's "two handles" of government.

I. Life and Context

Han Feizi's life was tragic.

Born into one of the noble families of his home state of Han, Han Feizi was expected to enter into an official career. However, he had a stutter, which made public speaking difficult for him. Perhaps by way of compensation, he became one of the greatest writers of the Chinese tradition. As a young man, he went to study with Xunzi. We shall see that Xunzi's influence is evident in Han Feizi's philosophy; however, Han Feizi became one of the most incisive critics of Confucianism. Xunzi had another student around the same time, Li Si, and, according to an early Chinese historian, "Li Si himself thought that he was not the equal of Han Fei."[i] This feeling of intellectual inferiority would have serious consequences later.

Han Feizi believed that state of Han was in danger because its king was promoting unworthy sycophants to positions of authority. He wrote essays and memoranda to try and persuade the king to changes his policies, but to no avail. However, some of Han Feizi's writings came to the attention of the ruler of the state of Qin, who was deeply impressed. As it turned out, Han Feizi's former classmate Li Si was now a high minister in Qin, and he initially encouraged the ruler to meet Han Feizi. When Han Feizi arrived as an official emissary from the state of Han, the ruler of Qin took a liking to him. In fact, the ruler admired Han Feizi so much that Li Si began to think of Han Feizi as a threat to his own position. Li Si told the ruler of Qin that Han Feizi could not be trusted and convinced him to order Han Feizi's execution. Realizing that the ruler might change his mind, Li Si made sure that Han Feizi was not allowed to plead his case, and sent him some poison, encouraging him to kill himself before he suffered the pain and humiliation of public execution. The Qin ruler did, in fact, change his mind and decide to spare Han Feizi, but by the time news of the reprieve arrived, Han Feizi was dead. Han Feizi once wrote,

> The dragon is a creature that can be tamed and trained so that one can ride upon its back. But on the underside of its throat it has inverted scales one foot in diameter, and if any person brushes against them, the dragon will surely kill them. A ruler of men also has his "inverted scales," so if a persuader hopes to succeed, he must be careful to avoid brushing up against them. (335)

In the end, Han Feizi himself was skewered on the dragon's scales.

II. Critique of Confucianism

Han Feizi's view of human nature is similar to that of Xunzi, in that Han Feizi sees humans as primarily self-interested: "The natural aspirations of the people are such that they all move toward security and benefit and avoid danger and poverty. . . . Public-spirited people are few while private-minded individuals are numerous" (350). Also like Xunzi, Han Feizi argues that while humans do innately have some affection for others, it is too limited and capricious to rely upon. Love is inadequate to make others virtuous: "In the nature and dispositions of human beings nothing is more primary than the love of parents for their children. All children are loved by their parents, and yet children are not always well behaved" (341). Since even the love of parents is insufficient to produce good children, how can the love of rulers produce good ministers and subjects? Furthermore, even parental love has its limitations, as Han Feizi illustrates with a chilling example:

> When it comes to their children, parents who produce boys get congratulations but those who produce girls kill them. Both came from the bodies of the parents, but the boys occasion congratulations while the girls are killed. This is due to their reckoning of benefits and calculations of profit. Thus, even parents in dealing with their children use a calculating heart. How much more so those who lack the affection of parents![ii]

Because of the human fondness for private profit and the weakness of human affection, at any one time, "there are no more than ten officers in the whole world who are virtuous and honest" (346). How are we to deal with the fact that most people are not good by nature? Han Feizi uses a metaphor that seems borrowed from Xunzi:

> If people had to wait for arrow shafts that are naturally straight, then for a hundred generations there would be no arrows. If they had to wait for wood that is naturally round, then for a thousand generations there would be no chariot wheels. If in a hundred generations there is not a single arrow shaft that is naturally straight, nor a single piece of wood that is naturally round, how is it that every generation is able to ride around in chariots and shoot down birds with arrows? It is because they use the Way of straightening and bending. (357)

Despite all these points of agreement, Han Feizi disagrees with his Confucian teacher Xunzi on two fundamental issues: the effectiveness of ethical education and the usefulness of tradition as a guide to the present. In his philosophy of education, Xunzi advocates "steaming and bending" (256) humans via the effects of ritual and learning so that they become ethical. Han Feizi does not deny that it is possible to transform humans in this manner, but he suggests that it is exceedingly difficult and rarely successful:

> Kongzi was a great sage of the world. He traveled throughout the land within the four seas refining people's conduct and elucidating the Way. Everyone in the land within the four seas was pleased by his benevolence and praised him for his righteousness, but those who followed him numbered only seventy men. It seems those who value benevolence are rare while those with the ability to be righteous are difficult to find. (341)

If even Kongzi, with all his skill and Virtue, could obtain only seventy virtuous disciples, how can contemporary rulers be expected to obtain enough virtuous ministers for their state?

Didn't the sages of the past rule via Virtue and ethical transformation? Han Feizi produces three powerful arguments against using the past as a model for the present. The first two are based on skepticism about the possibility of knowing the past. Han Feizi notes that "Kongzi and Mozi both followed the Way of Yao and Shun and both claimed that they were the true transmitters of the Way of these sages, and yet the doctrines and practices that each of them accepted and rejected are not the same" (352). Furthermore, even if we were to decide, for whatever reason, to follow the Confucian or the Mohist understanding of the past,

> after Kongzi and Mozi, the Confucians split into eight factions and the Mohists split into three. The doctrines and practices that each of these factions accept and reject are divergent and conflicting, and yet each faction claims that they are the true representatives of the Way of Kongzi or Mozi. Kongzi and Mozi cannot come back to life, so who will determine which of the current schools are the right ones? (351–52)

In his third argument against following tradition, Han Feizi sketches a philosophy of history according to which great cultural heroes helped the people with innovations that solved the problems they faced. For example, "the Nester" showed the people how they could evade dangerous animals by living in tree houses, and "the Kindler" showed them how to start fires using a bow drill. This sounds like a very Confucian view of history, but Han Feizi takes it in a very un-Confucian direction. He points out that times change, and even though living in tree houses and starting fires with a bow drill *were* valuable techniques in their respective eras, if anyone proposed doing such things today they would be mocked. Similarly, the gentle and benevolent Way of governing (venerated by Confucians and Mohists alike) did work very well in the era of the ancient sages. In those times, "people were few, there was an abundance of goods, and so no one quarreled. Therefore, no rich rewards were doled out, no harsh punishments were administered, and yet the people of themselves were orderly."[iii] However, as "the number of people increases, goods grow scarce, and men have to struggle and slave for a meager living. Therefore they fall to quarreling."[iv] This is the current social and economic context, and it requires a more stern approach to governing.

> This being the case, if someone goes around praising the Way of Yao, Shun, Tang, Wu, and Yu in the present age, they will surely be laughed at by the new sages. For this reason, the sage does not expect to follow the ways of the ancients or model his behavior on an unchanging standard of what is acceptable. He examines the affairs of the age and then makes his preparations accordingly. (340)

Han Feizi uses a memorable anecdote to illustrate why we cannot simply repeat the methods that were successful in the past:

> Among the people of Song, there was a farmer who had a stump in the middle of his field. One day, a rabbit running across the field crashed into the stump, broke its neck, and died. Seeing this, the man put aside his plow and took up watch next to the stump, hoping that he would get another rabbit in the same way. . . . Now if one wants to use the government of the former kings to bring order to the people of the current age, this is all just so much stump-watching. (340)

This story survives in the modern Chinese idiom *shǒu zhū dài tù* 守株待兔, "watch a stump awaiting a rabbit," meaning to wait for good things to fall into one's lap.

If humans are not innately virtuous and it is impractical to ethically transform them, how can human society and government be successful? Han Feizi's answer is that rulers must structure government such that it is in the interest of ministers and citizens to act for the public good, not only their private good. They can do this through five techniques: the power of position, administrative methods, law, the "two handles" of government, and "the Way of the ruler."

III. The Five Elements of Han Feizi's Theory of Government

1. The Power of Position

What we render "power of position" (*shì* 勢) is a term that also occurs in military texts, where it refers to, for example, the strategic advantage that one army has over another by occupying the high ground.[v] Even if one army is somewhat smaller than another, the former will have the advantage if it fires its arrows from the high ground while its infantry and chariots advance downhill, in contrast to its opponent, which must run soldiers and vehicles uphill and shoot arrows upward. Han Feizi attributes to an earlier philosopher, Shenzi (Shen Dao), the application of the power of position to the social realm, where it refers to "the differences in power and status set up by human beings" (329).

This is a phenomenon that is simultaneously familiar yet mysterious. Suppose you are in a large lecture class. You raise your hand when you have a question and wait for the professor to call on you. If the professor says, "I don't have time for questions right now because there is some material I have to get through," you drop your hand. Why don't you just yell your question as soon as it pops into your head? And why do you put your hand down when the professor tells you that she doesn't have time for questions? You raise your hand but then put it down at her request because she's the professor. At one level, this is completely unremarkable; you don't think twice about it, but at another level it is miraculous. How is your professor invested with this power over you (and your arm)? Your professor has talents and skills (presumably), but this won't really explain the phenomenon. After all, you don't raise your hand when you have a question at a dinner party, even if you are chatting with someone who is very accomplished. Perhaps we should say that the college gives the professor that power over you because you are a student. Yes, but is it any less mysterious what the college is or how it makes you do things? Han Feizi uses the term "power of position" to refer to this phenomenon by which some people can enforce their will on others because of the social role they occupy. It seems that the metaphysics of the power of position is mysterious (e.g., What kind of thing is it? How does it fit in among

Fact: The word for "contradiction" in modern Chinese is máo dùn 矛盾, *which literally means "spear-shield." It is derived from a story that Han Feizi tells about a merchant who claimed that his shields were so strong that nothing could pierce them and his spears were so sharp that they could pierce anything. When someone asked what would happen if one of his spears were used against one of his shields, the merchant was speechless.*

the other things that exist?) but the phenomenon (its appearance to us) is familiar to the point of being banal, and this phenomenon is one of the keys to social organization.

Han Feizi makes clear that the power of position is independent of the transformative effects of Virtue. Kongzi claimed that the "Virtue of a gentleman is like the wind, and the Virtue of a petty person is like the grass—when the wind moves over the grass, the grass is sure to bend" (*Analects* 12.19). Consequently, subjects will obey a ruler with Virtue as naturally as the polestar "receives the homage of the myriad lesser stars" that revolve around it (*Analects* 2.1). Han Feizi replies that

> If Yao and Shun had relinquished the power of their positions as rulers and abandoned the law, and instead went from door to door persuading and debating with people, without any power to encourage them with veneration and rewards or coerce them with punishments and penalties, they would not have been able to bring order to even a few households. (*Han Feizi* 8; *Readings,* p. 331)

Although the power of position is metaphysically mysterious, it is clear that it does not appear out of nothing or simply because a few people will it. Your family can pronounce you king of the United States, but don't expect anyone to bow down to you. The genuine power of position can also be lost. The reigning monarch of the United Kingdom has many perks, but beheading his ex-wives is no longer among them. Han Feizi did not provide an account of how the power of position is obtained in the first place, but he had much to say about how it could be lost or maintained.

2. Administrative Methods

Many Chinese philosophers seem to be in a contest to see who can give their philosophy the most ancient pedigree: Kongzi praised the founders of the Zhou dynasty; the Mohists praised predynastic sage-kings like Yao, Shun, and Yu; then Yang Zhu said that the even earlier Emperor Shen Nong had it right. So it is a refreshing twist when Han Feizi attributes two of his key concepts to figures who lived within a couple centuries of him: Shen Buhai developed administrative methods (*shù* 術) and Gongsun Yang emphasized the importance of laws (*fǎ* 法).

Han Feizi explains that Shen Buhai, a minister to Marquis Zhao of the state of Han, developed a technique for dealing with government officials:

> Using administrative methods means to assign offices based on a person's qualifications, to heed the objectives named in a minister's

> proposal and then hold them accountable for the actual results, to manipulate the handles of life and death, and to test the abilities of the assembled ministers. (336)

Because Han Feizi saw sycophancy and favoritism as severe problems in the government of Han, it is not surprising that his philosophy of government emphasizes a meritocratic system of appointing people to government offices: "those who make genuine achievements must always be rewarded, even if they are distant and lowly, while those who make genuine errors must always be punished, even if they are close and cherished" (317).

Once the ruler has appointed someone to government office, the ruler must ensure that there is "correspondence between form and name" (324). The term rendered "name" (*míng* 名) can have various senses in early Chinese thought, but Han Feizi uses it to refer to either the appointed *duties* that go with a particular office, or a *proposal* for a government policy suggested by an official. "Form" (*xíng* 形) is (like "power of position") a term whose use may have originated in military texts, where it can refer to the "formation" of units on the battlefield.[vi] In the thought of Han Feizi, "form" is either the *actions* that a minister undertakes, or the *achievements* that result from his actions. Han Feizi explains that the ruler enforces correspondence between these two pairs

> to see how what is said differs from what is done. When those who serve as ministers lay out proposals, the ruler assigns them tasks based on their proposals, and then uses their tasks to hold them accountable for their achievements. If the achievements accord with the task and the task accords with the proposal, then the minister is rewarded. If the achievements do not accord with the task or the task does not accord with the proposal, then the minister is penalized. (324)

The importance of ensuring that officials actually achieve what they are responsible for and what they propose is obvious ("name" cannot exceed "form"). Consequently, "[i]f someone's proposals are not matched by actual achievements, he should be faulted" (325). However, Han Feizi also stresses that it is dangerous if officials are allowed to achieve *more* than what they are responsible for or propose ("form" cannot exceed "name"). Han Feizi illustrates this point with another of his memorable anecdotes:

> Marquis Zhao of Han once became drunk and fell asleep. The Steward of Caps, seeing that his ruler was cold, placed the Marquis' cloak over him. When Marquis Zhao awoke he was pleased by this, and

asked his attendants, "Who covered me with my cloak?" His attendants replied, "It was the Steward of Caps." Consequently, the ruler punished both the Steward of Caps and the Steward of Cloaks. He punished the Steward of Cloaks because he felt the man had failed to fulfill his appointed task, and he punished the Steward of Caps because he felt the man had overstepped the bounds of his position. It was not that the Marquis did not dislike the cold, but rather that he felt that the harm that comes from ministers encroaching on each other's office is even greater than the harm that comes from being cold. (325)

The danger is that officials allowed to exceed their appointed assignments will be able to accumulate power and "form cliques and factions to assist each other" (325) in pursuing their private benefit, until eventually they threaten the authority of the ruler. Without a strong ruler, the state will be reduced to chaos. Consequently, "[i]f someone oversteps the boundaries of his office, he should die" (325).

What we find encapsulated in a handful of phrases by Han Feizi is the basic theory of one of the most momentous and crucial inventions of the human species: bureaucracy. Whether in China or the West, most people love to hate bureaucracy, and to many, to be called a "bureaucrat" is almost an insult. However, bureaucracy is necessary for all large-scale human institutions, and when it functions even moderately well it is tremendously effective in achieving organizational goals that would otherwise be impossible. Of course, bureaucrats who overstep the bounds of their office aren't punished with death nowadays, but the dangers facing society today are not as dire as they were in Han Feizi's era.

3. Laws

Administrative technique is a tool limited to the management of government officials. In contrast, laws apply to everyone, from the highest ministers, to the relatives and favorites of the king, to the lowliest peasant. Han Feizi attributes the emphasis upon laws to Gongsun Yang (also called Lord Shang), a minister to the ruler of the state of Qin:

> Government through law exists when the ruler's edicts and decrees are promulgated among the various departments and bureaus, when the certitude of punishments and penalties is understood in the hearts of the people, when rewards are given to those who respect the law, and when penalties are imposed on those who violate the ruler's decrees. (336)

Han Feizi particularly emphasizes three aspects of the law. First, the laws must be easy to understand: "if when making laws for the masses, you use language that even the wisest people find difficult to understand, then no one will comprehend or follow your laws" (345). Second, the laws must be consistent. Han Feizi points out that, because the laws of his own state are an inconsistent amalgam or older and more recent laws,

> if there was something beneficial [to themselves] in the old laws and the former decrees the ministers would follow these, but if there was something beneficial in the new laws and the later decrees they would follow those. Since the old and the new laws were mutually contradicting, and the former and later decrees were mutually conflicting . . . the corrupt ministers still had the means to deceive [their ruler] with their words. (337)

Third, the laws must be backed up with substantial rewards for obedience and heavy punishments for violation.

4. The Two Handles of Government

Han Feizi refers to rewards and punishments as the "two handles" of government (323) and stresses that it is crucial for a ruler to "take hold of the handles of punishment and reward and maintain firm control of them" himself (315). To illustrate this point, Han Feizi tells the story of the Lord of Song, whose minister Zi Han made the following, seemingly helpful, proposal: "Veneration, rewards, boons, and gifts—these are things that the people all enjoy. Let you, my Lord, take care of these things yourself. Death, mutilation, punishments, and penalties—these are things that the people all hate. Let me, your servant, take care of these" (324). The Lord of Song agreed, and as a result Zi Han was able to usurp all authority in the state, because people realized that *he* was the one who chose whom to punish and the severity of the punishment. Han Feizi believed that the ruler must not only control these handles but also endow them with sufficient weight to have an effect: "when handing out rewards, it is best to make them substantial and dependable, so that the people will prize them; when assigning penalties, it is best to make them heavy and inescapable, so that the people will fear them" (343).

Han Feizi acknowledges that even if one puts into effect all of the practices that he recommends, a sufficiently bad ruler will produce chaos: "if a Jie or Tyrant Zhou is born into a superior position, then even if there are ten Yaos or ten Shuns they cannot bring about good order" (330). However, Han Feizi claims that his system of government accommodates the fact that most rulers are neither exceptionally good nor exceptionally bad, but simply mediocre:

> even if a Yao, Shun, Jie, or Tyrant Zhou only emerged once in every thousand generations, it would still seem like they were born bumping shoulders and treading on each other's heels. But those who actually govern each age are typically somewhere in the middle between these two extremes. . . . If they hold to the law and depend on the power of their position, there will be order; but if they abandon the power of their position and turn their backs on the law, there will be disorder. (*Han Feizi* 8; *Readings*, 330–31)

Once instituted, a well-structured government will tend to be self-sustaining, assuming only minimal competence in its rulers. Nonetheless, there is a subtle "Way of the ruler," which lies beyond laws, administrative methods, and the other more obvious and almost mechanical techniques of government.

5. The Way of the Ruler

The Way of the ruler is described in language very reminiscent of the *Daodejing*. In fact, Han Feizi wrote the first commentary on this classic. However, he uses the concepts of the *Daodejing* in ways that may seem surprising to us.[1] For example, the ruler should be "empty and still." This is not a spiritual discipline to achieve Virtue; it is a tactic. To be "empty" is for a ruler to "never reveal what he desires. For if he reveals what he desires, the ministers will cut and polish themselves accordingly" (314). To be "still," a "ruler should never reveal what he intends. For if he reveals what he intends, the ministers will try to make themselves look distinctive" (314). In other words, if ministers fully understand the desires and intentions of their ruler, they can take advantage of this knowledge to manipulate the ruler for their own interest. As Han Feizi explains when giving advice about the other side of this equation, ministers addressing rulers: "the true difficulty of persuasion lies in knowing what is in the heart of the person being persuaded, so that I can use my persuasion to match it" (332).

Han Feizi also invokes the Daoist term "nonaction," but as a conscious technique by which a ruler makes the best use of his ministers:

---

1. Of course, it is possible that Han Feizi's interpretation is more accurate than the one I presented in Chapter 8.

He makes it so that the worthy refine their natural talents, while he makes use of those talents and employs them. Thus, he is never lacking in ability. He makes it so that when there are achievements he gets the credit for their worthiness, and when there are errors the ministers take the blame. Thus, he is never lacking in reputation. . . . The ministers perform the work, and the ruler enjoys the final achievement. (*Han Feizi* 5; *Readings,* 315)

Thus, "When an enlightened ruler practices nonaction above, the assembled ministers will be anxious and fearful below" (315). According to the *Daodejing,* the best ruler transforms people without manipulation, through the gentle power of selfless Virtue. But Han Feizi reads the *Daodejing* through his underlying assumption that humans are overwhelmingly self-interested. The wise ruler understands that humans are self-centered, so he never lets down his guard: "See others but do not allow yourself to be seen; hear others but do not allow yourself to be heard; know others but do not allow yourself to be known" (315).

IV. The Question of Amoralism

One of the major issues that divides interpreters of Han Feizi is whether it is accurate to describe his philosophy of power as "amoral." In other words, does Han Feizi teach how to accumulate power without regard for the goals or purposes to which that power is put? One of the considerations favoring an amoral reading is that, as we have seen, Han Feizi's philosophy does not rely upon the Virtue of rulers or ministers, nor does it deem effective the cultivation of human compassion and integrity. One can also note that Han Feizi gives advice both to rulers who want to avoid being manipulated by their ministers and to officials who want to manipulate their rulers.[2]

However, I would argue that there *is* an ethical vision in Han Feizi's work, albeit of a very narrow kind. Han Feizi stresses that

When the sage brings order to the people, he measures by the most basic; he does not indulge their desires, he simply looks ahead for what will benefit the people. Therefore when he imposes punishments on them, it is not out of hatred of the people, it is basic to his concern for them.[vii]

---

2. See, respectively, "The Way of the Ruler" (314–17) and "The Difficulties of Persuasion" (332–35).

Fundamental to Han Feizi's thought is the distinction between private inter-ests (those of an individual, his family, his clique) and public interests (that of the state). The two kinds of interest are innately opposed.[3] Left to their own devices, humans will naturally serve their private interests:

> They will deliberate a hundred times about the welfare of their pri-vate households, but never once make plans for their ruler's state. . . . [T]he noble houses work to make each other flourish and do not strive to enrich the state; the great ministers work to make each oth-er respected and do not strive to bring respect to the ruler; and the minor ministers look for promotions and stipends by cultivating advantageous relationships and do not attend to the duties of their office. (*Han Feizi* 6; *Readings,* 319)

Thus, Han Feizi advocates a system of government in which—due to the power of the ruler's position, laws, bureaucratic techniques, rewards, and punishments—no one can achieve their private interests without acting in the public interest: "When a sage governs a state, he does not wait for people to be good in deference to him. Instead, he creates a situation in which people find it impossible to do wrong" (357).

What *is* the public interest? Han Feizi explains, "if a ruler can get rid of private crookedness and promote the public law, his people will become se-cure and his state will become well ordered" (318). Recall that Han Feizi lived during what is perhaps the low point of the Warring States Period, one of the worst times of chaos and conflict in world history. Han Feizi recognized something that many of us tend to forget: it is not an insignificant achieve-ment of a government if it keeps its people well fed and secure from criminals, foreign invaders, and corrupt officials. Han Feizi believed that the only way for a society to achieve this goal was to have a strong ruler who used the "power of his position," prevented his officials from usurping his authority with "administrative methods," kept his people in line with "laws," and wielded the "two handles" of rewards and punishments firmly, but not arbitrarily. If the ruler was too feckless and foolish to do this, it was up to the most able of the ministers to find a way to persuade the ruler to do what was most

---

3. Han Feizi suggests that this is built into the very structure of the characters, where "public," *gōng* 公, is formed from the characters for "separation," *bā* 八, and "private," *sī* 厶. Han Feizi's etymology, which may not be accurate, is based on the ancient form of the character for "private"; the modern form is 私. In addition, the character he identifies as meaning "separation" is now used exclusively as a "phonetic loan" (see Appendix B) for the word "eight."

expedient. Most people in the Warring States Period (perhaps most people in world history) would gladly have traded their social context for the sort of society Han Feizi's political philosophy was designed to achieve.[viii]

V. Historical Significance

One translator of the eponymous *Han Feizi* neatly summed up its ambivalent later reception: "Generations of Chinese scholars have professed to be shocked by its contents . . . and have taken up their brushes to denounce it. But there has never been an age when the book was unread."[ix] Han Feizi will always be read because of the elegance of his writing and his unforgettable anecdotes, but there are deeper reasons for his continuing appeal. Power is an inescapable aspect of all human society. Furthermore, whether we are in imperial China or the contemporary United States, all large-scale organizations ultimately have to be bureaucratic. Consequently, from intra-office politics to international relations, we ignore at our peril Han Feizi's lessons on law, administrative methods, and the more subtle strategies of power.

Today, it is often said that Han Feizi seems the most modern of the ancient Chinese philosophers. In terms of content, his frank discussions of the importance of political power are reminiscent of Niccolò Machiavelli (1469–1527), whose book *The Prince* is a major influence on modern political theory. Han Feizi's views also have intriguing similarities with more recent philosophers. For example, the power of position can be thought of as a manifestation of what French philosopher Michel Foucault (1926–1984) referred to as "surveillance."

Han Feizi seems modern in his philosophical methodology as well. Rather than claiming to be following some ideal sage or practices of the past, Han Feizi synthesizes the work of earlier philosophers. To be sure, all the philosophers we have studied in this book were influenced by their predecessors, and Han Feizi's teacher Xunzi had presented Confucianism as the most comprehensive of the various Ways advocated during his era, but even Xunzi did not acknowledge that his formulation of Confucianism is itself a synthesis of these other positions. Han Feizi is distinctive for his conscious and explicit synthesis of earlier thinkers and in his willingness to criticize even the thinkers whom he most admires.

When he drank poison in the dark dungeon of the state of Qin, Han Feizi must have felt hopeless. His home state, with its foolish king, would obviously soon be conquered. He must have expected that his own writings, too, would be consigned to the dustbin of history. Little could he have imagined that he would be read attentively by intellectuals and government officials in every

Chinese dynasty for thousands of years, that expressions from his writings would become part of Chinese language, and that even "barbarians" like professors from the other side of "the four seas" would study and teach his works.

But whatever happened to Li Si, who envied and feared his classmate's abilities so much that he engineered his death? Read the next chapter to find out.

Review Questions

1. What personal difficulty made it hard for Han Feizi to achieve success in the public career his noble family expected him to follow?

2. What story is the origin of the contemporary Chinese idiom, "to watch a stump waiting for a rabbit"? What point does Han Feizi use this story to illustrate? What is the contemporary meaning of this idiom?

3. What is one important respect in which Han Feizi agrees with his teacher Xunzi and one major point on which he disagrees with him?

4. What are Han Feizi's three arguments against following tradition?

5. What is the "power of position"? In what respect is it very familiar, and in what respect is it mysterious?

6. What are the roles of "name" and "form" in administrative methods?

7. What are the "two handles" of government? Why does Han Feizi believe that it is crucial for the ruler to control them himself?

8. According to Han Feizi, what does it mean for a ruler to be "empty and still"? Why is this important for a ruler?

9. What is the meaning, for Han Feizi, of "nonaction"? What benefits does a ruler obtain through it?

10. How could we see Han Feizi's emphasis on power as being not amoral but as reflecting certain ethical values?

11. Name at least one Western thinker to whom Han Feizi could be compared.

■ 12 ■

LATER CHINESE THOUGHT

The empire, long divided, must unite; long united, must divide.
—Romance of the Three Kingdoms

The original Great Wall was a redoubt of stamped earth; the crenellated brick wall with regular guardhouses we know of today was only made in the much later Ming dynasty.

All the philosophers we have studied so far in this book lived during the Zhou dynasty (c.1040–221 BCE). This period came to an end in 221 BCE, when the ruler of the state of Qin, having defeated every other state, proclaimed himself the "First Emperor" of a new dynasty. With the unification of China under the Qin, the intellectual and political climate changed drastically. Chinese history after the Qin runs more than two millennia and is as complex as that of any major civilization. Consequently, it would be wise to end our account at this natural stopping point. However, even a cursory overview of later Chinese history will help to explain the long-term significance of ancient philosophy up to the present day. Therefore, I shall attempt to sketch two thousand years of Chinese history in one chapter. Buckle up.

I. Qin Dynasty

The First Emperor of Qin bragged that his dynasty would last through ten thousand future kings. In reality, it lasted only from 221–207 BCE.

The significance of the Qin conquest has always been controversial. One traditional account portrays the First Emperor as simply a violent megalomaniac who ruthlessly killed everyone in his way. After founding the dynasty, he banned all "private discussions" of government affairs and burned all private copies of books of philosophy and literature.[1] He ordered the building of the Great Wall (true), and worked people to death on it, grinding up the bones of the dead to make more mortar (not true). Confucian scholars objected to the cruelty of his laws (true), so he had them buried alive (not true). Paranoid and superstitious, the First Emperor made a lavish tomb with an army of life-sized warrior statues to guard him in the afterlife and died while on a trip to find an elixir of immortality (true, but misleading).

Here is alternative view that many contemporary historians find more compelling. The Qin defeated the other states because they were better organized and more efficient than their rivals. Under the Zhou system of government, every duke had his own army, made his own laws, and collected his own taxes. This decentralization of power was inefficient and led almost inevitably to disintregration. In the Qin state, authority was centralized and laws were standardized, so everyone knew what they were supposed to do,

---

1. The Qin ruler thus followed the same practice as totalitarian rulers in every society, who immediately silence philosophers and other intellectuals who might question their actions. Keep this in mind the next time someone claims that philosophy is of merely academic importance.

understood the consequences of violating the rules, and realized that they were ultimately answerable only to the Qin sovereign. This bureaucratic efficiency at every level of society no doubt helped the Qin defeat their rivals. In addition, the Qin army had better training and discipline than those of the other states.

After the conquest, it was easier to buy and sell goods because the First Emperor standardized weights and measures. If someone bought five *chi* of fine cloth for one *tael* of silver, he knew exactly what he was getting. Communication became more efficient because the First Emperor standardized the writing system, eliminating variant forms of characters. He started several major public works projects, including canals for the transportation of goods, and the Great Wall, to protect the people against the "barbarians" who raided the northern frontier.

There were several assasination attempts against the First Emperor while he was alive, so his concern for his life was not due to paranoia. The immortality elixir he sought would have been taken seriously as medicine by his contemporaries. And his tomb with its terra-cotta warriors was no more excessive for the ruler of so many people than the Great Pyramid at Giza or the Taj Mahal.

However we evaluate it, the Qin dynasty was short-lived. A traditional account would attribute this to the Draconian laws of the state, which made even small violations capital offenses, thereby alienating the populace. However, the lack of an able successor to the First Emperor was at least as significant a factor. After the First Emperor died, two of his closest advisors forged his will so that his successor would be one of the least able and most weak-willed of his sons. The advisors thought that this would give them a ruler easy to manipulate to their advantage. But any new dynasty needs at least a few able rulers at the start to firmly establish itself, and the Second Emperor's incompetent rule led to rebellions, eventually resulting in the destruction of the dynasty in 207 BCE. One of the advisors who put the Second Emperor on the throne was Li Si, who had proposed the burning of books and orchestrated the death of his fellow student Han Feizi. In one of the few pleasant ironies of history, Li Si fell out of favor and was himself executed before the fall of the Qin.

II. Han through Six Dynasties

The next dynasty, the Han (202 BCE–220 CE), presented itself as opposed to the excesses of the Qin state. (The traditional image of the First Emperor as unnecessarily cruel owes much to this ideology.) However, the Han learned much from the example of Qin government. Although there were many variations and changes over time, successful Chinese government from the Qin on would always be centralized and bureaucratic, a neccessity in governing such vast territories prior to the advent of modern transportation and communication.

The Han dynasty was also noteworthy for its preservation and study of classic texts. What we now consider the standard versions of the ancient classics date from this era, as do almost all of the earliest surviving commentaries. For example, the *Analects* and *Daodejing* may have been radically different prior to the Han. In addition, Confucianism identified a specific set of canonical texts, the *Five Classics:*

1. The *Odes* (also known in English as the *Songs, Book of Poetry,* or *Classic of Poetry*): This anthology of poetry was already revered by the time of Kongzi, and we saw that he used it in teaching his disciples. Han Confucians followed what seemed to be Kongzi's practice of finding hidden meanings in the odes.

2. The *History* (also referred to as the *Documents, Book of History,* or *Classic of History*): This is a collection of historical documents (generally speeches or proclamations). A version of it existed in the Warring States Period (Mengzi refers to it often), but the work that came out of the Han dynasty includes some sections that are genuinely ancient and others that are much later forgeries.

3. The *Spring and Autumn Annals:* This is a cryptically terse historical chronicle of dates and events from 722–481 BCE, lacking narrative flow or context. Han Confucians believed that Kongzi had encoded esoteric teachings in the *Annals* via subtle use of language. Kongzi's use of one word as opposed to another, or his decision to leave out one particular historical detail, provoked pages of commentary explaining how this indicated his approval or disapproval of the actions referred to by the text.[i]

4. The *Changes* (also called the *Book of Changes, Classic of Changes,* or *I Ching*): Most of this book is a guide to divining the future and the will of the spirits, and this is how it was treated during the Warring States Period. In fact, it was exempted from the Qin dynasty burning of books because it was not considered a work of philosophy. However, during the Han dynasty, the appendices to the *Changes* became philosophically influential. The Great Appendix in particular sketches a philosophical view according to which complementary oppositions (*yin* and *yang*) are the fundamental organizing principle of Heaven and earth. *Yin* is what is dark, moist, falling, and so on, while *yang* is what is light, dry, rising, and so forth. Human ethics is grounded in this complementary structure of Heaven and earth.

5. The *Rites* (also known in English as the *Record of Rites*): This is largely a collection of detailed rules for performing various rituals. However, mixed in are a few chapters on philosophical topics. In particular, two brief chapters from the *Rites* would be singled out later in the Tang and Song dynasties as especially important: the *Greater Learning* and the *Mean*.

Under the Han dynasty, there were government specialists in each of these texts, *bóshì* 博士, meaning "broadly learned scholar." In addition, Emperor Wu (r. 141–87 BCE) created the Imperial University focused on Confucian teachings, and government officials were expected to study in this university and pass its examination.

Confucianism was now the orthodox philosophy of the state; however, this simple statement belies the complexity of the situation. To begin with, the version of Confucianism endorsed by Emperor Wu would not seem very familiar to you after reading the chapters on Kongzi, Mengzi, and Xunzi in this book. Dong Zhongshu, the scholar who convinced the emperor to patronize Confucianism, had combined it with a cosmology based on the reciprocal influences of the human and natural worlds. According to this cosmology, the virtues and vices of the ruler would be reflected in the natural realm. Unusually abundant harvests or positive signs from the Heavens show endorsement of the emperor's actions. An earthquake, drought, or freakish prodigy indicates Heaven's displeasure with the emperor. Positive omens validate the emperor's decisions, but he must respond to negative signs by reforming his actions and even doing penance. Of course, these signs must be interpreted (e.g., "A double rainbow! What does it mean?"). Dong Zhongshu sold the emperor on the idea that the Confucians, with their detailed understanding of the hidden meanings of the classics, were best equipped to do this interpreting. (Imagine how strongly Xunzi would have objected to this understanding of Heaven.)

Dong Zhongshu's correlative Confucianism was immensely influential. In fact, as late as the nineteenth century Chinese emperors were issuing public apologies for natural disasters like floods and droughts.[ii] However, it would be an oversimplification to say that the Han established a monolithic Confucian ideology. Indeed, one scholar aptly described the Han as having "content-free Confucianism."[iii] To be a Confucian, one needed only be committed to the sagacity of Kongzi and the importance of the *Five Classics*. However, Confucians disagreed heatedly about what these commitments implied for ethics, government policy, and cosmology.

Furthermore, not everyone in the Han dynasty was a Confucian. For example, Sima Qian was the author of the first official dynastic history, *Records of the Historian*. He was not inclined to be fond of Confucianism, though, because Emperor Wu, the patron of Confucianism, had him castrated for a perceived slight of the emperor's brother-in-law. Scholars have long recognized that the *Records of the Historian* implies criticisms of Confucianism that are sufficiently subtle to escape the notice of a careless reader (such as Emperor Wu). In addition, Sima Qian's father, Sima Tan, was an avowed Daoist, and the *Records of the Historian* includes his essay, "On the Six Schools of Thought," which argues that Confucianism, Mohism, Legalism, the "School of Names," and the Yin-yang School each have their strong and weak points, but Daoism is the school of thought that is most all encompassing and best.

It was also under the Han that Vietnam came under Chinese control and remained so for a millennium. The name "Vietnam" derives from its Chinese name, *Yuenan,* literally "South of (the state of) Yue." As a result, Confucianism, Daoism, the Chinese written language, and Mahayana Buddhism (discussed below) had an influence on Vietnam unlike that in the rest of Southeast Asia.

After the Han dynasty fell, there was a long period of chaos in which no one dynasty controlled China. Although Buddhism had come to China in the first century CE (during the Han), it was during this Six Dynasties Period (220–589 CE) that it came to intellectual maturity and became popular among both the beleagured general populace and disillusioned intellectuals. Central to Buddhism is the notion that the primary cause of human suffering and wrongdoing is a craving for permanence that can never be satisfied. Craving results from selfishness, the mistaken commitment to persistent, independent selves. Because I suffer from the illusion that you, I, and an expensive car are three distinct things, I will compete with you so that I obtain the car instead of you. Even if I get the car, I will cling to it as if it were eternal. So I will be disappointed once it loses its new car smell, and I will be saddened when it gets its first scratch. In contrast, if I am enlightened and come to understand selflessness, I will recognize that individuality is a metaphysical illusion and that we are all interconnected. I can no more begrudge you the car than I can begrudge the me of this morning breakfast. Similarly, I can't have an unscratched car now unless I have a scratched car later, so how can I be fond of one but not the other?

There are two major forms of Buddhism, Theravada and Mahayana. Theravada Buddhism, which some would argue represents its earliest philosophical formulation, emphasizes the absence of individual selves. Typical is the *Questions of King Milinda,* an extended dialogue between the monk Nagasena and a philosophically astute monarch. The monk argues that "Nagasena" is merely a name, used by convention because it is convenient rather than because it refers to some distinct, independent entity. When King Milinda challenges Nagasena to explain how this could be possible, Nagasena replies with the famous "simile of the chariot." Just as we can talk about "a chariot" even though there is nothing we can identify that *is* the chariot (it is not its wheels, its axle, its yoke, etc.), so we can talk about "Nagasena" even though there is nothing we can refer to that *is* him (he is not his flesh, blood, thoughts, desires, etc.).[iv]

The version of Mahayana Buddhism that became popular in China would not deny Nagasena's claim but would place more emphasis on the interdependence of things, as illustrated by the metaphor of "Indra's Net." Supposedly, the Indian god Lord Indra had a net with a jewel at the intersection of every two strands. The jewels were so bright that one could see reflected in any one jewel every other jewel in the net. Now, think of each jewel as being a "dharma"—a momentarily existing configuration of matter or mental state—and think of each strand as a causal connection between two dharmas. Every dharma exists only as a part of a larger causal web. My current feeling of hunger is caused by the hypoglycemia of my blood, and that same hunger causes a desire to eat, which causes my limbs to move me toward the refrigerator. Ultimately, every dharma is connected to every other even though the connections are in some cases very indirect. This might seem fanciful, but just try to reconstruct some of the causal strands responsible for a man of Polish and Dutch descent, employed by a college founded one hundred fifty years ago by a New York brewer, drinking coffee harvested in Colombia, and writing about philosophers who lived two millennia ago and on the other side of the world. It can't be much harder to sketch the causal chain connecting your left foot to the dying words of an unremembered Arabian herder from 1000 CE. So just as every jewel in Indra's Net reflects every other, so are my cup of coffee and your left foot intrinsically interconnected with each other and with everything else.

III. Sui through the Ming

The Sui dynasty (581–618 CE) reunified China for the first time in centuries, and its first emperor and empress were strong supporters of Buddhism. Although short-lived, the Sui laid the foundation for the long period of comparative peace and prosperity under the Tang dynasty. Official patronage of Buddhism reached perhaps its greatest height under Tang Empress Wu Zetian, who invited the Buddhist monk Fazang to the palace to teach her. Fazang was the greatest exponent of Huayan Buddhism, whose motto is "one is all; all is one." Fazang explained the metaphor of Indra's Net to the empress in a talk that became the influential "Essay on the Golden Lion."

Chan Buddhism (better known in the West by its Japanese name, "Zen") also developed during the Tang. Like Huayan, Chan stresses the interconnectedness of things, but it is perhaps most distinctive for its emphasis on techniques to assist people in achieving the mystical insight that is enlightenment. Among these techniques are *zazen* (seated meditation), koans (apparently nonsensical riddles, like "What is the sound of one hand clapping?" designed to short-circuit rational thinking and shock a person into enlightenment), and practical activities performed with selfless focus, ranging from cooking and cleaning to calligraphy, flower arrangement, and archery.[2]

Although Huayan, Chan, and other forms of Buddhism have fascinating metaphysics and theories of cultivation, they all insist that everything else is secondary to achieving enlightenment and the ethical transformation that accompanies it. Recognizing that there is no fundamental distinction between oneself and others, the enlightened person will have universal compassion for the suffering of all people. Furthermore, since there are no selves, it would be wrong for me to be particulary attached to *my* father or *my* wife.

Buddhist universal compassion is reminiscent of the impartial caring advocated by the Mohists. However, the Buddhists took it even further, arguing that familial, romantic, and sexual attachments are almost intrinsically forms of selfish craving. Consequently, Buddhist monks and nuns (in most cultures) leave their families behind and maintain celibacy, shaving their heads and donning robes to indicate their separation from ordinary society.

Buddhism was introduced to Japan in 538 (via Korea), and during the Sui and Tang dynasties, China and Japan exchanged many diplomatic missions. Japan adopted Chinese characters (which they called "kanji") as their primary writing system, and Japanese government, art, literature, and religion were deeply influenced by Chinese precedents. However, Japan has never been a culture that simply imitates. Particularly during the Heian Period (794–1185 CE), Japan added its own distinctive style to the cultural elements it had imported from China. For example, the *Tale of Genji* was written by Lady Murasaki Shikibu during this era. It is a masterpiece of world literature, noteworthy for the psychological realism of its characters and its refined appreciation of transient beauty.

Just a few decades after the Buddhist monk Fazang was feted by the empress, Han Yu (768–824 CE) began the Confucian revival known in English as "Neo-Confucianism." When the emperor called for national veneration of a Buddhist holy relic, a bone supposedly from the Buddha himself, Han Yu sent the emperor "A Memorandum on the Bone of the Buddha." In this inflamatory essay, Han Yu suggested that the emperor was just pretending to honor the Buddha to humor the ignorant populace. However, Han Yu urged,

---

2. We see in this last technique the clear influence of Zhuangzi's image of the butcher who follows the Way in the mundane activity of carving an ox (see Chapter 9).

this policy was shortsighted. Buddhism, he argued, is a barbarian teaching that had brought no benefit to China and had led many naive people to mortify their own flesh and leave their social and familial duties behind to become monks and nuns. The emperor was so outraged by Han Yu's suggestions that he wanted to have him executed, but Han Yu's suporters got the sentence commuted to banishment. Many intellectuals were receptive to Han Yu's message that China should rediscover Confucianism, and he was soon recalled from exile. In addition, his suggestion that Mengzi was the most pure of the later followers of Kongzi, and his frequent appeal to two chapters from the *Rites* (the *Greater Learning* and the *Mean*), had considerable influence.

Han Yu was not a deep thinker, though, and Neo-Confucianism only came to philosophical maturity during the Song dynasty (960–1279). The Song Confucians conceived of themselves as simply explicating the same Way as the ancient sages, but like anyone else they interpreted the texts they read using the concepts they had at their disposal. In particular, their two primary metaphysical concepts—*qi* 氣 and *li* 理—meant something very different for them than they had for Kongzi, Mengzi, and Xunzi.

In the Warring States Period, *qi* was conceived of as just one entity among others in the world: a fluid that flows through the human body and its environment, and is responsible (among other things) for human emotional states. As A. C. Graham explained, *qi* "is like such words in other cultures as Greek *pneuma* 'wind, air, breath.' It is the energetic fluid which vitalises the body, in particular as the breath, and which circulates outside us as the air."[v] These senses are suggested by the expressions "clouds and *qi*" and "blood and *qi*." However, around the beginning of the Han dynasty, Chinese philosophers began to think of *qi* as the underlying "stuff" out of which everything else condenses, analogous to the manner in which water condenses as dew or crystalizes into ice. Benjamin Schwartz has observed that, when used in this later sense, we should *not* think of *qi* as being like "matter in terms reducible to minimal, physical properties, such as can be assigned to water and air or the properties of 'mass' and 'movement' which we find in modern physics." If *qi* is like anything in Western thought, it is "the boundless" postulated by the pre-Socratic philosopher Anaximander: an "indescribable encompassing reality from which all limited things 'emerge.'"[vi] The notion that everything condenses out of this originally amorphous *qi* became one of the central ideas of Neo-Confucianism.

Li originally referred to any pattern that distinguishes one thing from another. For example, in the *Mengzi, li* describes the "harmonious patterns" with which an orchestral performance begins and ends (5B1), the "order" that is pleasing to one's mind (6A7), and whether or not someone's speech is "articulate" (7B19). Similarly, Zhuangzi's butcher refers to the "Heavenly pattern" of the bones, muscles, and joints that he follows as he carves up the ox, and Xunzi describes how the sages invent ritual and standards of righteousness in accordance with the "patterns" of the world. None of these uses entails any elaborate metaphysical commitments. However, the Huayan and Chan Buddhists adopted this same term to refer to the cosmic web of interrelationships symbolized by Indra's Net.[3] After hundreds of years in which Buddhism was the dominant mode of thought, it was almost inevitable that Song dynasty Confucians would see a cosmic "Pattern" as central to any plausible metaphysics.

The Neo-Confucians adopted the term "Pattern" to refer to the structure of the universe, fully present in everything that exists, from a mote of dust, to a cat, to Tyrant Jie, to Kongzi himself. This Pattern is simultaneously descriptive and prescriptive. Because of the Pattern, it *is* the case that everyone will feel alarm and compassion at the sight of a child about to fall into a well. However, the Pattern also dictates that we *ought* to extend this compassion to everyone. Although the Pattern is the same in everything, entities are made into separate kinds and individuals by having distinct allotments of *qi*. Thus, rocks differ from plants because the *qi* of the former is more turbid than the clear *qi* of the latter, resulting in a more full manifestation of the Pattern (as shown in the greater responsiveness of plants to their environment). Furthermore, I am different from Kongzi not only because his *qi* occupies a different time and place from mine, but also (and more importantly) because his clear *qi* manifests the Pattern fully, while my turbid *qi* does not. This view is moderately monistic in that the shared Pattern makes everything part of a potentially harmonious whole. However, because allotments of *qi* differ (spatially, temporally, and qualitatively), there genuinely are distinct individuals, such as *this* son who owes filial piety to *his* father, and *this* mother who loves *her* children more than those of her neighbor. This prevents the Neo-Confucian position from completely collapsing into the Buddhist one, and justifies the differentiated care so central to Confucianism.

Nonetheless, the Neo-Confucian position frequently betrays its Buddhist roots. The term "selfishness" (*sī* 私) is rare in the ancient texts (and more typically means "private" as opposed to "public"), and "enlightenment" (*wù* 悟) is never found in the Confucian classics, but both words play central roles in Neo-Confucianism. The term "Pattern" occurs precisely zero times in the *Analects* of Confucius, but Neo-Confucian commentaries on the *Analects* invoke this concept repeatedly. We might thus say that Neo-Confucianism is Confucianism seen through Buddhist lenses.

Ths most influential of the Neo-Confucian philosophers was Zhu Xi (1130–1200 CE). Zhu Xi was concerned that people were studying in the

---

3. We will capitalize it as "Pattern" in English from here on, to reflect the new understanding. You will find the same term rendered "Principle" in some translations.

wrong way and for the wrong reason. They were reading many things but in a superficial manner, because doing so was good enough to impress others and obtain government positions for prestige, power, and pelf. Zhu Xi wanted people to read less but more carefully and with a greater depth of understanding, so that their reading could ethically transform them. In order to achieve this goal, Zhu Xi effected a revolution in Chinese education by shifting the focus from the *Five Classics* to the *Four Books:* the *Analects,* the *Mengzi,* the *Mean,* and the *Greater Learning.* The *Four Books* were better for students to focus on, Zhu Xi argued, because they expressed the essence of Confucianism in a more concise and direct manner than the *Five Classics.* In addition, Zhu Xi wrote brief, clear, elegant commentaries to aid students in appreciating these texts. The *Four Books,* accompanied by Zhu Xi's commentaries, became the basis of the Chinese civil service examinations in 1313, guaranteeing that generations of scholars literally committed the texts-with-commentaries to memory.

The influence of Zhu Xi and other Neo-Confucians has not been limited to China. Neo-Confucianism deeply affected education, philosophy, and culture in Korea during its Joseon dynasty (1392–1897 CE), and in Japan during its Tokugawa Shogunate (1603–1868 CE).

Even today, many scholars (both in East Asia and the West) take Zhu Xi's interpretations of the classics for granted. For example, we often see attributed to Mengzi the claim that "human nature is originally good." However, Mengzi does not say that human nature is *originally* good; he says that it is *good,* without qualification. Where has this "originally" crept in from? The source is Zhu Xi's commentary. Zhu Xi was committed to the principle that the *Four Books* express different aspects of one consistent philosophical vision. Mengzi's claim that human nature is the same in everyone (*Mengzi* 6A6) seems to be in tension with Kongzi's claim that human natures are merely "similar" to one another (*Analects* 17.2). Consequently, Zhu Xi explains that Mengzi is talking about what human nature is like originally or fundamentally (the Pattern in itself), while Kongzi is talking about human nature as manifested (the Pattern as expressed through particular endowments of *qi*). While I often disagree with Zhu Xi, I have unbounded admiration for his genius. His interpretations are brilliant, and we can pay him the highest compliment a scholar can earn: even when he is wrong, he has a good reason for his opinion.

IV. Qing through Mao Zedong

After the Song came the Yuan and Ming dynasties, whose adventures we must pass over in silence. But the Qing dynasty (1644–1911 CE) cries for our attention. The last imperial dynasty, the Qing was founded by a non-Chinese ethnic group, the Manchus, who invaded China from a region northeast of the Yellow River Valley (the center of classical Chinese civilization). The Manchus had their own way of life, but they became sinicized during their long reign, adopting Chinese language and culture. This has reached such an extreme that today the Manchu language is almost extinct, even though millions of Chinese have some Manchu ancestry.

The Qing dynasty included what is recognized as one of the high points of Chinese civilization, the reign of the Kang Xi emperor (1661–1722), a great statesman, military leader, and patron of culture and scholarship. It was under his rule that Tibet first came under Chinese control and that Taiwan, an island important to China's later history, was incorporated into China. However, within a century after Kang Xi's rule, the Qing dynasty was in serious decline, and less than century after that the Qing, and the imperial system of government, were gone forever.

One of the turning points for the Qing dynasty was the First Opium War of 1839–1842. The West had been importing products from China for years, particularly tea, silk, and porcelain. However, the Chinese had little use for Western products, so a severe trade imbalance developed, in which silver was being drained from the West to pay for Chinese goods. Inventive British traders developed a solution to the problem by exporting opium from India into China. Although the importation of this highly addictive narcotic was quickly outlawed in China, the British East India Company developed elaborate schemes to keep the drug flowing. Finally, in 1839, Confucian official Lin Zexu received imperial approval to use the military to seize and destroy British opium shipments. Lin also wrote an impassioned letter to Queen Victoria, appealing to her conscience and asking her to stop the opium trade. The British took the moral high ground by sending ships and troops to coerce China to allow opium importation. The British force was far more advanced technologically than the Qing military and included the *Nemesis*—the world's first oceangoing ironclad steam-and-sail warship—which made easy work of the Chinese war junks. The Qing government was decisively defeated, and China was forced to accept humiliating terms in the Treaty of Nanjing, including paying an indemnity and ceding control of Hong Kong to Britain. Later treaties gave British citizens extraterritorial rights while in port, meaning that they could not be charged by Chinese courts for crimes, and specified that Hong Kong would belong to Britain until 1997.[4]

---

4. What is now the largest bank in the world, the Hongkong and Shanghai Banking Corporation—better known as HSBC—was established to meet the needs of British merchants working in Hong Kong trading opium and other goods.

The next major disaster for China was the Taiping Rebellion of 1850–1864. The Taiping were militant, unorthodox Chinese Christians, led by a man who claimed that he was Jesus' younger brother. They attracted millions of fanatical adherents and revolted against the government, seeking to establish a new dynasty. The government eventually won, but during this fourteen-year conflict approximately twenty million people died. (For perspective, know that twenty million people is the approximate current population of the state of New York.)

As if things could not get any worse, the Second Opium War (1856–1860) broke out during the Taiping Rebellion. This war went as badly for China as the First Opium War and led to more indemnities and more concessions from the Qing government. The difficulty the Qing had in suppressing the Taiping and its failure to defend itself from the Western powers illustrated the weakness of the government and decreased support for it among both intellectuals and commoners.

By the end of the nineteenth century, foreign powers had begun to talk openly about "carving the Chinese melon," meaning dividing up China into spheres of influence that each state could economically exploit. Because of these experiences, China remains, even today, very sensitive about anything it perceives to be foreign interference in Chinese affairs or efforts to separate anything it regards as part of China. This is true whether we are talking about Tibet, Taiwan, or the Spratly Islands.

During this time, Japan was in the Tokugawa Shogunate (1603–1868), in which the Shogun (a hereditary military dictator) ruled in the name of the figurehead emperor. During this long era of peace, prosperity, and stability, high culture flourished, including the distinctively Japanese poetic form haiku. The highest social class was the samurai. The ideal samurai was a scholar-warrior, steeped in traditional culture but also skilled in *kenjutsu,* the art of sword fighting. However, during the long period of peace under the Tokugawa, the samurai had little use for their martial skills. In addition, the merchant class became increasingly wealthy and influential.

In order to maintain the status quo, the Shogunate closed Japan almost completely to foreign influences. Christianity was banned under penalty of torture or death, although a handful of Japanese Christians maintained their faith in secret for centuries. Foreign trade was also outlawed except for occasional visits from Dutch ships permitted to trade in Nagasaki. However, in 1853, the "Black Ships" of U.S. Commodore Matthew Perry arrived in Tokyo Bay with a demand that the Japanese government sign a trade treaty. When Japanese officials demurred, Perry "persuaded" them by opening fire on buildings in the harbor until they allowed him to land and present a letter from President Millard Fillmore. Perry said that he would return in one year for their answer. As was the case in China, the Japanese government recognized that "resistance is futile" in the face of a technologically superior power and agreed to all U.S. terms when Perry returned. Perry received a hero's welcome back in the United States, where he retired, wrote his memoirs, and finally drank himself to death (dying by cirrhosis of the liver) a scant four years after he left Tokyo Bay for the last time.

Having shown itself feckless in the face of Western power, the Shogunate was overthrown in the Meiji Restoration of 1868, and the age of the samurai came abruptly to an end. There were a handful of battles to wipe out the last holdouts who refused to give up the old way of life, but within a few decades upper-class Japanese had traded swords for briefcases. During this Meiji Period (1868–1912) Japan sent students to the West to learn everthing they could about Western science and technology, including railroads, telegraphs, newspapers, rifles, canons, warships, and medicine. The process was so effective that Japan was soon able to force its will on its neighbors as easily as had the Western powers, as is evident from the following events:

- 1875, Ganghwa Island Incident: A Western-style Japanese battleship provoked a confrontation with Korean forces and won an easy victory. In the resulting Treaty of Ganghwa, Korea was forced to give extraterritorial rights to Japanese in Korea, open Korean ports to trade with Japan, and specify that Korea was no longer a tributary state of China. Japan would go on to formally annex Korea in 1910.

- 1894–1895, First Sino-Japanese War: Chinese forces were decisively defeated by the Japanese in a war over dominance of Korea. China's loss shattered its vision of itself as the preeminent cultural and military force in East Asia. As a result of the war, Taiwan was ceded to Japan and remained under Japanese control until the end of World War II.

- 1904–1905, Russo-Japanese War: Fighting for control of Manchuria and Korea, Japan scored a clear victory, thereby showing that it was on par militarily with the European powers.

The success of Japan in modernizing during the Meiji Period invites a question. Why didn't China Westernize in the same way after the painful lessons of the Opium Wars? China's situation was different from Japan's in at least two important respects. First, the Tokugawa Shogunate bequeathed to the Meiji Period a stable society with centuries of successful centralized government. As the Taiping Rebellions showed, Chinese society was not stable, and the Qing government could not exercise effective control over the country.

A second factor impeding China's modernization was that the Qing was a Manchu dynasty, not a natively Chinese one. Although the Manchu had initially conquered China by brute military force, part of the ideology by which they maintained power was their claim to be faithful adherents of the Confucian Way. So any fundamental change in Chinese culture would undermine the legitimacy of the Qing dynasty itself. In contrast, the Meiji reformers presented themselves as restoring the rightful place of the emperor as leader of Japan. Of course, the emperor was as much of a figurehead during the Meiji Period as he had been under the Shogunate. What is crucial, though, is that the Meiji ideology made it possible to present change and modernization as loyal and patriotic.

The Qing court eventually made a few reforms (such as establishing what would become Peking University in 1898 and eliminating the Confucian civil service examinations in 1905). However, it was too little too late. The penultimate Chinese emperor died in 1908, leaving his infant son on the throne. It is doubtful that Sage-King Shun could have saved the Qing, let alone the two-year-old Puyi. The Qing dynasty sputtered and gasped its way to its conclusion in 1911, when Sun Yat-sen founded the Republic of China.[5]

China's suffering and exploitation were not over, though, because the Republic of China did not have the power to unify China any more than had the Qing government. China quickly sank into a period of chaos in which many areas were dominated by local warlords. China was also still subject to foreign imperialism, as was illustrated by the events that led to the May Fourth Movement, to which we now turn.

As part of "carving the Chinese melon," Germany had been granted special economic and legal rights in Shandong Province. (The brewery that produces the popular Chinese beer, Tsingtao, is a pleasant aspect of the German legacy.) When World War I broke out, China fought on the Allied side, in exchange for a promise that Shandong would be returned to their rule. Unfortunately, among the many imprudent and unjust aspects of the 1919 Treaty of Versailles was that it simply transferred the German concessions in Shandong to Japan. This sparked widespread protests in China against imperialism and in favor of political reform and modernization. This May Fourth Movement was the most visible event in the broader New Culture Movement that traced its origins to scholars at Peking University and the founding of the seminal journal *New Youth* in 1915. The slogan of the New Culture Movement was that China must "overturn the shop of Kongzi," meaning eliminate the legacy of Confucianism and replace it with Western freedom, democracy, science, women's liberation, and technology.

---

5. The Republic of China is not the same as the later People's Republic of China (discussed below).

Among the lasting achievements of the New Culture Movement was the beginning of contemporary Chinese literature. After millennia of writing in Literary Chinese, authors began to write in the vernacular.[6] Lu Xun was perhaps the greatest of these early vernacular writers. His works are noteworthy for their incisive criticisms of traditional Chinese culture and society. For example, the main character of his short story "Kong Yiji" is a pedantic, alcoholic scholar near the end of the Qing dynasty, who frequents a bar in the village of Lu. Wearing shabby, tattered clothes, Kong Yiji is openly mocked by the lower-class patrons in the bar and ignored by the wealthy. Kong Yiji (who shares the same surname as Kongzi and whose home town is named after Kongzi's home state) symbolizes what Lu Xun takes to be the pathetic state of Confucianism in his era and its utter uselessness in the face of China's problems.

In 1926, the Republic of China (now dominated by the Chinese Nationalist Party) launched the Northern Expedition, a military campaign to end the period of warlordism and unify China. The campaign ultimately succeeded, but during the conflict the Chinese Civil War broke out between the Nationalists and the Chinese Communists.[7] The Nationalists had the upper hand at first, and the Communists were forced to retreat in the infamous Long March (1934), during which Communist military units and political leaders marched with their families and supplies through some of the most difficult terrain in China. In a little over a year, they traveled at least three thousand miles (with some estimates running as high as eight thousand miles). Of those who began the Long March, 90 percent died or gave up along the way. By the end, Mao Zedong (Mao Tse-tung) had emerged as the undisputed leader of the Chinese Communists.

Meanwhile, Japan continued its aggressive stance toward China, invading Manchuria in 1931 and setting up a puppet kingdom, with the last Chinese emperor, Puyi, as its nominal monarch. Full-scale war between China and Japan broke out in 1937.[8] The Nationalists and Communists agreed to suspend hostilities to fight the Japanese invasion, but the Civil War resumed soon after the Japanese defeat in 1945. In what would become typical of Cold War superpower foreign policy, the Soviet Union supported the Communists and the United States supplied the Nationalists. The decisive factor in the war, though, was that the Communists had the support of peasant farmers, a huge portion

---

6. Vernacular Chinese is related to Literary Chinese the way Italian is related to Latin.

7. The Chinese Communist Party had been founded soon after the May Fourth protests and had gained considerable support, especially in rural areas.

8. The start of this Second Sino-Japanese War effectively began World War II, although Hitler did not invade Poland until 1939 and Pearl Harbor was not bombed until 1941.

of the population, who were promised better lives through land reform. This time it was the Nationalists who made a desperate retreat, to the island of Taiwan. On the mainland, Mao stood atop the Gate of Heavenly Peace, looking out onto a mass of cheering supporters in Tiananmen Square, and announced the foundation of the People's Republic of China (PRC) in 1949.

Mao's legacy is extremely controversial, both within China and beyond it. On the one hand, it was a great accomplishment to finally unify mainland China. The chaos of the early twentieth century (so much like the earlier periods of disunity in Chinese history) was now gone. In addition, it soon became evident that China could finally stand up to the Western powers. In 1950, the United States (with UN approval) intervened in the Korean War, after North Korea launched a surprise invasion of South Korea. The United States was able to push the North Koreans back until they were almost at the border between North Korea and China.

The PRC supported North Korea for ideological reasons (it was a fellow Communist state) as well as military ones. It seemed the United States was going to completely eliminate the North Korean military, allowing South Korea to control the entire Korean peninsula. This would put a U.S. ally directly on China's border.[9] In addition, the PRC was aware that there were serious discussions among pundits in the U.S. media about whether it might be a good idea to simply go on to invade China after finishing off North Korea. The PRC decided not to wait to find out what the United States had in mind, so a massive Chinese army roared across the Yalu River and pushed the U.S.-led UN forces back to the middle of the Korean peninsula. When open hostilities ended in 1953, the PRC, led by Mao, had shown that it could battle the West's greatest superpower to a draw.

Mao was also responsible, though, for terrible suffering among his own people. He brutally supressed anyone who dared to question him, including some people who had loyally served with him since the Long March. Fear of telling Mao anything he did not want to hear exacerbated the problems caused by the Great Leap Forward of 1958–1961. The Great Leap Forward was an effort to rapidly modernize China's agriculture and industry. However, its methods were unrealistic, such as trying to produce steel in backyard furnaces. Under Mao's directions, peasants stripped all the iron they could find (including functional tools), tossed it into crude furnaces, and produced nothing but lumps of almost worthless pig iron.[10]

---

9. Similar considerations led China to send military supplies to the Viet Cong during the Vietnam War.

10. Steel production requires extremely high temperatures and a method of blowing oxygen into the iron.

Changes in agricultural practices during the Great Leap Forward were equally impractical. Over the centuries, peasant farmers had developed economic practices and social traditions that allowed them to scrape by even during bad harvests. By collectivizing the farms and destroying the earlier practices, the Great Leap Forward made peasants especially vulnerable to droughts and floods. The effect of the Great Leap Forward was to kill off at least fourteen million peasants (and perhaps many more, we may never know) from starvation and illness. (Allow a moment for the enormity of the deaths of fourteen million people to sink in.) Despite these disasters, officials in the provinces initially reported to Mao that everything was going even better than expected, rather than risk their lives by bearing bad news.

Mao and the other Chinese Communists were officially dismissive of traditional Chinese philosophy; however, the situation is complex. Some of Mao's own thought betrays traditional influences. For example, as noted in Chapter 8, his guerilla strategy of warfare may have been inspired by the *Daodejing.* Furthermore, one of his major philosophical works, the essay "On Contradiction," can be seen as reflecting the theory of complementary opposites, *yin* and *yang,* outlined by the *Changes.*[11]

A much more explicit influence of traditional philosophy can be seen in the thought of Liu Shaoqi. Liu was initially a trusted colleague of Mao's, who suffered with him on the Long March, and later went on to become the second president of the PRC. One of his books has been translated into English under the quaint title *How to Be a Good Communist,* but it is much more interesting and sophisticated than this makes it sound. A more accurate translation of the title would be *The Cultivation of Communist Party Members.* Liu's work deals with a theoretical problem that has long bothered Chinese Communists. According to Marx, the beliefs of an individual are determined by his socioeconomic context. Because most Chinese were not born into a communist society, how could they learn to think and act like Communists? Liu's ingenious solution was to develop a communist theory of ethical self-cultivation. This was not only inspired by traditional accounts of self-cultivation, but it even cites Confucian classics in order to make its points! Liu brilliantly synthesized Chinese Communism and Confucianism.

However, when Liu was president, he reversed Mao's policies from the Great Leap Forward, so Mao turned on him during the Great Proletarian Cultural Revolution (1966–1976). This movement was instigated by Mao, supposedly to eliminate bourgeoise elements, capitalist roaders, and the last races of feudalism in the Party and society at large. Traditional Chinese

---

11. However, Mao suggests that he is following the dialectical materialism of Lenin, and this was certainly an important source of his ideas.

philosophy was part of the feudal past that this movement aimed to overturn. Young people were called upon to drop out of school, join the civilian mass movement known as the Red Guards, and follow Mao's directive:

> Concentrate all forces to strike at the handful of ultra-reactionary bourgeois Rightists and counter-revolutionary revisionists, and expose and criticize to the full their crimes against the Party, against socialism and against Mao Tse-tung's thought so as to isolate them to the maximum.[vii]

Fueled by this extremist rhetoric and operating largely outside the law and external control, the vigilante Red Guards ran amok. With all the kindness of the Inquisition and objectivity of the Salem witch hunt, the Red Guards hunted down suspected counterrevolutionaries, publicly humiliating them, beating them, and in some cases simply murdering them. Cultural treasures were also destroyed or vandalized.[12]

Liu Shaoqi was one of the victims of the Cultural Revolution. He was removed as president and forced to issue a series of "self-criticisms" in which he publicly confessed his "errors," which seemed to largely consist of having the temerity to disagree with Mao:

> Most important was the fact that I did not make a good study and grasp Mao Tse-tung's thought, [and I was] unable to apply Mao Tse-tung's thought correctly in work and struggle. I did not learn from the masses in practice, nor did I seek sufficient instructions from and make enough reports to Chairman Mao. Sometimes, I acted contrary to Mao Tse-tung's thought.[viii]

Liu was arrested and disappeared from public view, dying a few years later in prison.

During this period, interest in and study of traditional Chinese thought continued outside of mainland China (particularly in Hong Kong and Taiwan). One of the most significant intellectual events was the development of "New Confucianism." New Confucianism should not be conflated with Neo-Confucianism; however, the two movements are closely related. This is illustrated by "A Manifesto on the Reappraisal of Chinese Culture," a seminal essay published in 1958 by five leading New Confucian scholars. The

---

12. For example, I have seen the remains of a centuries-old monument that still bears the graffiti "There are no crimes in a revolution!" that the Red Guards scrawled on it after tearing it down.

Manifesto claims that "Chinese culture has enjoyed from its origin a unitary orthodoxy," in contrast with the West, which is more fragmentary, due to its multiple cultural sources, including Greek, Hebrew, Roman, and others.[ix] This unitary orthodoxy consists of "the Chinese teachings of Hsin-Hsing [heart and nature] handed down from Confucius and Mencius to the Sung-Ming savants."[x] The New Confucians follow the Neo-Confucian understanding of Chinese intellectual history: there is really only one Chinese Way; it has been preserved throughout Chinese history; Kongzi passed it on to Mengzi; and it was recovered and explicated by the Neo-Confucians of the Song and Ming dynasties, such as Zhu Xi. The New Confucians also use Neo-Confucian language in describing the content of this Way:

> all Chinese virtues in the Confucian conception have their roots in human nature or in the mind in its transcendental sense. This nature is identical with the highest universal reason, the Heavenly ordained principle [Pattern], and this mind, is also communicated with Heaven's mind, cosmic mind.[xi]

The Manifesto is critical of both the May Fourth Movement and the Chinese Communists for dismissing the value of China's "unitary orthodoxy." However, it acknowledges that "historical Chinese culture lacked the modern Western democratic system, Western scientific study, and the current practical skills in technology. As a result, China has been unable to attain real modernization and industrialization."[xii] Nonetheless, the Manifesto suggests that democracy, science, and technology are not only consistent with Confucianism but will allow a more complete expression of its tenets.

One of the themes of this book has been the diversity of Chinese philosophy in classical times, and in this chapter we have seen the many ways that Confucianism has been understood in different periods of Chinese history. Consequently, the monolithic and ahistorical picture of Chinese culture that the New Confucians present seems implausible. However, while New Confucianism is sometimes bad history, it is often very interesting philosophy in its own right. In particular, it is very unfortunate that most of the works of T'ang Chun-i and Mou Tsung-san, perhaps the two greatest New Confucian philosophers, have never been translated into English.

V. China Today and Tomorrow

In Taiwan, the Republic of China (ROC) still exists. The Nationalists, who once had a rather authoritarian grip on power, are now just one party in a flourishing, multiparty, democratic government. The ROC in Taiwan and the People's Republic of China (PRC) in mainland China each officially claim that they are the sole, legitimate government of China. However, there is a growing movement in Taiwan to declare independence as a separate country. The PRC regards Taiwan as one of the last pieces of the "Chinese melon," so it has no intention of allowing it to permanently separate from the rest of China. Hence, the PRC has made clear that it will invade Taiwan if it declares independence. The United States recognizes the PRC as China's rightful government; however, the United States has a pact with Taiwan that commits it to defending Taiwan in the event that it is attacked. Consequently, if Taiwan ever declares independence it will set in motion a chain of dominoes that will lead to war between the United States and the PRC. Given that the PRC has one of the largest and best-equipped militaries in the world, including nuclear-tipped intercontinental ballistic missiles (ICBMs), this would be a very unpleasant eventuality.

On the mainland, the Cultural Revolution ended and most of Mao's policies were reversed after his death in 1976. China quickly opened up again to foreign trade (on its own terms, this time), and the economy raced forward once the communist shackles were removed. Marxism-Leninism-Maozedong Thought is still the nominal ideology of the PRC, but in reality mainland China is a prosperous capitalist state, albeit a nondemocratic one. Though there is not complete freedom of expression, people enjoy much more liberty overall than they had under Mao. During my visits to China, I have found that everyone from cab drivers to college professors is happy to talk openly about anything (as long as their words are not in print or broadcast on the airwaves). In particular, Confucianism, Daoism, and Buddhism are widely discussed and promoted. New Confucianism (which would have been anathema to Mao) is just one of the positions that is now popular.

The continuing relevance of Chinese history to the present is evident in the controversy over the film *Hero* by Zhang Yimou. Zhang initially achieved international acclaim for *To Live,* a deeply moving story of one family, from the last years of the Qing dynasty through the Cultural Revolution. The suffering that the family undergoes, particularly during the Great Leap Forward and the Cultural Revolution, was perceived as an indictment of the Chinese Communists. Zhang's more recent *Hero,* in contrast, is a historical drama about an assassination attempt against the First Emperor of the Qin dynasty. In the United States, *Hero* was enjoyed for its action, its *Rashomon*-like plot, its stunning cinematography, and the moving relationships among the characters. Chinese audiences are also aware, though, that Mao Zedong explicitly compared himself to the First Emperor. In this film, the First Emperor is depicted as ruthless, but as someone whom China needs in order to bring it order and unity. *Hero* thus seems to have a strong political message about China's more recent history: Mao did much wrong, but China needed him, and his vision of unifying *all* of China should be an inspiration.

My impression is that the vast majority of Chinese people are very proud of their philosophical and literary traditions, and they hunger for deeper understanding. An indication of this is the fact that a book about Kongzi was a surprise best seller in 2007: Yu Dan's *Insights into the* Analects.[xiii] In my opinion, Yu's book (not yet available in translation) presents the *Analects* as a simple self-help book of the sort one might find in any popular bookstore, and she sidesteps the challenging aspects of Kongzi's political views. However, anything that gets people reading and discussing the *Analects* is to the better.

Opinions about Chinese philosophy are not uniform today (any more than they were in the Warring States Period). Consider two extremes. I know of one leading Chinese professor who advocates (in all seriousness) re-creating a handful of functional Confucian communities modeled on premodern culture, including its styles of dress, its rituals, and the practice of men having concubines. Another colleague assured me that the American National Basketball Association (NBA) is more culturally relevant to contemporary Chinese than the *Analects*. The only thing that is clear is that the future is not clear.

■ APPENDIX A ■

HERMENEUTICS, OR
HOW TO READ A TEXT

Here's what is necessary: one blow with a club, one scar; one slap on the face, a handful of blood. Your reading of what other people write should be like this. Don't be lax!

—Zhu Xi

This image shows the text of the *Analects* of Kongzi (in large, boldface characters) with the orthodox commentary of Zhu Xi (written in double columns beneath each section of the original classic). Textual commentaries like that of Zhu Xi are needed because of the "hermeneutic circle" between the reader and the text.

I. Faith and Suspicion

Hermeneutics is the theory of how to understand texts. Hermeneutics is necessary and important because the relationship between readers and texts depends on complex cultural factors. For example, prior to the invention of printing with movable type (which came about in China in the eleventh-century CE, and then in fifteenth-century Europe), written works had to be copied by hand. This was extremely labor intensive, so books were rare and expensive. However, with the invention of the printing press, books could be mass-produced, so they were cheaper and more readily available. This changed many things in society, including how we read. Prior to mass-production, people read *intensively:* they read a few books that really mattered to them and they read those books slowly, carefully, and repeatedly. Nowadays, we are expected to read more *extensively,* but as a result we read once, or perhaps just skim, a lot of different books. In many ways, this is a good thing. The profusion of books led to increased knowledge and literacy. And, frankly, most books are worth only one reading, at most. As Renaissance philosopher Francis Bacon put it:

> Some books are to be tasted, others to be swallowed, and some few to be chewed and digested; that is, some books are to be read only in parts; others to be read, but not curiously; and some few to be read wholly, and with diligence and attention.[i]

There is a downside to extensive reading: we can become so used to skimming books casually that we forget to slow down when we need to. The thinkers we are examining in this book are among the greatest philosophers of world history. The depth of what they have to say can only be appreciated if we read them carefully and repeatedly. So the first lesson that hermeneutics can teach us is that we should read and reread classic texts "wholly, and with diligence and attention."

There are two broad hermeneutic approaches: a *hermeneutic of suspicion* and a *hermeneutic of faith.* The distinction is easiest to grasp with an example. Sir Arthur Conan Doyle was a medical doctor and author of one of the greatest literary paradigms of rationality, Sherlock Holmes. However, he was also an enthusiastic advocate of Spiritualism. How should we interpret Doyle's claim that one can communicate with the dead through Spiritualist practices such as Ouija boards, séances, and mediums?

Doyle became friends with the famed American escape artist and magician Harry Houdini. Houdini examined the evidence that Doyle presented to justify his belief in spiritualism. Mediums had reported to Doyle many facts about his deceased relatives. In addition, objects had levitated during séances Doyle had attended. Doyle argued that these things would be impossible without the assistance of spirits. Houdini replied that people claiming to communicate with the dead might use a stage magician's technique called "cold reading" that appears to report new information, when it is actually just the medium eliciting information from the audience. Similarly, the movement of objects during séances (during which participants are asked to sit very still, in darkness) is easily explained by wires or the assistance of the medium's accomplices. Doyle was never convinced by Houdini's explanations and died a committed Spiritualist.

Although he disagreed with Doyle, Houdini was using a hermeneutic of faith in interpreting what Doyle claimed. In a hermeneutic of faith (also called a hermeneutic of restoration), one examines the rational justification for someone's claims. What evidence does someone give for the claims? Why might we think that the claims are plausible? What are the arguments given in favor of the claims? In general, a hermeneutic of faith asks, "Why might we think that what someone is claiming is *true?*" As the case of Doyle and Houdini illustrates, using a hermeneutic of faith does *not* require that we agree with the person or text we are interpreting—it's not a hermeneutic of *blind* faith. However, a hermeneutic of faith takes a text seriously as a candidate for *truth*.

There is more to the story of Doyle's Spiritualism. Doyle had fallen into a severe depression after his own son, his brother, his two brothers-in-law, and two of his nephews were killed during World War I. His interest in Spiritualism grew after the war. His belief that séances offer evidence of an afterlife and allow the living to communicate with the dead helped bring him out of his depression. Consequently, it seems likely that Doyle believed in Spiritualism so firmly (even in the face of strong evidence against it) because it offered him psychological comfort over the death of his family members.

The explanation I have just given for Doyle's belief employs a hermeneutic of suspicion. When using a hermeneutic of suspicion, one looks for explanations for why someone makes certain claims that sever the connection between those claims and truth. Among the most famous practitioners of hermeneutics of suspicion are Karl Marx, Friedrich Nietzsche, Sigmund Freud, and Michel Foucault. Marx claimed that (for example) philosophers argue in favor of the existence of a right to private property not because it is *true* that there is such a right or because there is good *evidence* in favor of it but because the belief in such a right serves the economic interests of the capitalist class. Nietzsche and Foucault both attempt to explain individual actions, theories, and social institutions in terms of expressions of human power. So philosophers like Plato claim to be engaged in a disinterested search for objective truth, but (Nietzsche suggests) they actually use philosophical argument as a tool to control and silence others. Words are the weapons that philosophers use instead of fists. If you think of how arguments are often used in courtrooms or political debates today, you'll understand Nietzsche's point. In general, to use a hermeneutic of suspicion, ask how making a claim and convincing someone of it serves someone's ulterior interests (such as for wealth, power, or just psychological comfort).

A hermeneutic of faith considers whether a text might be true or rationally justified, while a hermeneutic of suspicion examines the hidden motivations for composing a text that are not connected to its being true or justified. Most people have a preference for one hermeneutic style over the other. When the president gives a speech in favor of a new law or policy, what do you focus on? Are you primarily interested in whether his proposals are *justified?* Do you examine whether there is evidence to back up what he is saying? Are you concerned with the ethical values that he is promoting and whether you share them? If so, you probably prefer a hermeneutic of faith. Or do you focus on the likely political *motives* of the president's speech? Is he giving this speech in order to firm up support among the voters and politicians of his own party, because he'll need it to get his legislation passed? Or is the president reaching out to swing voters, because he is coming up for reelection himself or wants to help his party's Congressional candidates in the upcoming midterm election? These are the questions that a hermeneutic of suspicion asks.

Whichever hermeneutic you prefer or are accustomed to, we really need both. It is naive to deny that people often pass laws, write books, and even create works of art out of hidden needs for power, wealth, and psychological comfort. However, it is impossible to avoid using a hermeneutic of faith. In fact, every time we use a hermeneutic of suspicion, we are assuming a hermeneutic of faith. For example, when Nietzsche says that philosophical argument is really motivated by the desire to exercise power over others, he wants us to agree that what he is saying is true, and he wants us to take seriously the justification he offers for the truth of his claim. In other words, Nietzsche wants us to interpret him using a hermeneutic of faith. This is not an accidental feature of Nietzsche's philosophy. Every philosophical view assumes the need for a hermeneutic of faith—even those positions that are themselves hermeneutics of suspicion.

In philosophy as an academic discipline, hermeneutics of faith are more commonly employed than hermeneutics of suspicion. In other humanities disciplines and in the social sciences, it is more common to use hermeneutics of suspicion in interpreting others. In this book I mainly employ a hermeneutic of faith.

One of the basic principles of a hermeneutic of faith is the "hermeneutic circle." There are actually two kinds of hermeneutic circle. The first kind is inside the text, and the second kind is between the text and the reader. In order to understand the hermeneutic circle inside a text, let's look at an example involving the very first passage in the *Analects,* the collection of sayings attributed to Kongzi (Confucius) and his disciples. Book 1, Chapter 1 (i.e., 1.1) of the *Analects* begins, "The Master said, 'To learn, and then have occasion to practice what you have learned—is this not satisfying?'" ("The Master" refers to Kongzi himself.) So what does this passage mean? At first glance, the message seems to be this: learning is fun.

Kongzi is supposed to be an inspiring and important thinker. Having him tell you something as banal as "learning is fun" is probably a bit of a letdown. But if a text has been considered a profound, inspiring work for centuries, there probably is a good reason for its appeal. Keep reading and keep asking questions until you see what's at stake.

The key to appreciating 1.1 is understanding what Kongzi means by "learning" and "practice." Consider what he says in 1.14*: "The gentleman is not motivated by the desire for a full belly or a comfortable abode. He is simply scrupulous in behavior and careful in speech, drawing near to those who possess the Way (of virtue) in order to be set straight by them. Surely this and nothing else is what it means to love learning." When we read 1.1 in the context of 1.14*, we realize that learning, for Kongzi, is not something purely theoretical (like pure mathematics), nor is it something technical but amoral (like engineering). Learning means learning to be a better person.[1]

In light of reading it in context, 1.1 may look a little more interesting. We may now see Kongzi as more than a bookworm or trivia buff. Instead, he wants to be a better person and wants to encourage others to do the same. We can learn even more about 1.1 when we compare it with 17.2, where the Master says, "By nature people are similar; they diverge as the result of practice." *Analects* 1.1 tells us that to become a better person, first you "learn," and then you "practice" what you have learned, while 17.2 suggests that this practice alters (or at least supplements) human nature. What is human nature like? Unfortunately, Kongzi says nothing explicit about this topic outside of 17.2. (Indeed, one of his disciples sighed that "one does not get to hear the Master expounding upon the subjects of human nature or the Way of Heaven" [5.13].) However, he does say things that seem to imply a view of human

---

1. On learning as having an ethical purpose, see also 1.7*, 6.3, 7.3, and 7.17; and 13.4, 13.5, and 15.3.

nature. For example, Kongzi heartily agrees when a disciple compares becoming a better person to the laborious process of cutting and carving raw jade to make it into a beautiful work of art (1.15). Passages like this suggest that Kongzi believes human nature is initially fairly resistant to virtue, so it takes long practice to become a better person.

This learning and practice does not consist of rote memorization or blind obedience. Kongzi makes clear that he has no interest in disciples who are not ready to think hard: "I will not open the door for a mind that is not already striving to understand, nor will I provide words to a tongue that is not already struggling to speak" (7.8). Although this "striving" and "struggling" is extremely challenging, 1.1 reminds us that humans will find this learning and practice ultimately "satisfying."

What does all this have to do with hermeneutics? At first glance, 1.1 looked like the sort of smarmy moral that comes at the end of an educational cartoon for children. But once we came to understand what role it plays in Kongzi's thought as a whole, we saw that it is actually a complex and challenging statement that involves ethics, human nature, and educational psychology. You might disagree with it, but you cannot dismiss it as trivial.

This process, by which we came to understand *Analects* 1.1 better by reading it in the light of other passages in the text, illustrates the kind of hermeneutic circle that operates inside a text. In order to understand any one sentence in a text, you have to understand how it relates to other sentences in the same text. This is as true of each of those other sentences as it is of the sentence you began with. In other words, I start with a sentence S_1 that I want to understand. I can only do this by seeing how it is related to other sentences, like S_2. But I understand S_2 only in terms of S_3 and I understand S_3 only in terms of S_4. And . . . the process goes on until eventually I understand S_x in terms of S_1. The same is true of the words in a text. But we learn what words mean through the sentences they occur in.

Because of the hermeneutic circle, there is no absolutely certain foundation in interpreting a text. Everything is open to question. There is also no method that will guarantee *the* right interpretation. However, this does not imply that a text means whatever you want it to mean or that any interpretation is as good as another. There is no one best interpretation, but there are very few good interpretations and lots of shallow, implausible ones.

II. "Our" Worldview and "Theirs"

The second hermeneutic circle is the one between the text and the reader. We have already encountered this circle in thinking about what Kongzi means by learning. If you are like most contemporary readers of this book, you probably have one of two views about the purpose of education. One of these views has its roots in the thought of Plato, the other in that of Francis Bacon. Plato thought that the best kind of life was the life of theoretical inquiry and understanding. On this view, learning about things like mathematics and pure science is worth doing for its own sake. When poet Edna St. Vincent Millay declared "Euclid alone has looked on beauty bare," she was expressing a Platonistic sentiment.[2] Plato thought that theoretical understanding would also make you a better person. He believed that intellectual speculation would help people learn to transcend the temptations and petty concerns of the everyday world. But this is not necessary to make knowledge valuable: knowledge is for the sake of knowledge.

In contrast to Plato, Francis Bacon is famous for the claim that knowledge is power, or as he put it, "Human knowledge and human power meet in one."[ii] Bacon lived during the beginning of the scientific revolution. He encouraged people to not just theorize but also experiment and learn how to control the world.

Think about what side of this debate you come down on. Do you enjoy learning for the sake of learning? Is knowledge exciting and interesting to you whether you can apply it or not? Do you think that being intellectually active and curious makes someone a better person (at least to some extent)? If so, you are a Platonist. Or, is it very important to you that you be able to *use* what you have learned? Do you tend to scoff at knowledge that is "only theoretical" or "not practical"? Do you most admire people who can make things work "in the real world"? If so, you are a Baconian.

The point of these comparisons is that whether you are a Platonist or a Baconian concerning the value of learning, you may have misread what Kongzi meant when he said, "To learn, and then have occasion to practice what you have learned—is this not satisfying?" If you are a Platonist, you will think, "Yes. Learning is satisfying for its own sake, whether it has any practical application or not." If you are a Baconian, you might agree with Kongzi's saying, but only because you assume that what Kongzi has in mind is amoral, technical learning. Or you might disagree with Kongzi because you assume he is talking about what the Platonist means by learning. Either way, your assumptions (based on what learning means in your social context) would lead you to misread the text. Learning for Kongzi is not knowledge for the sake of knowledge, nor is it technical knowledge without moral focus.

---

2. Ironically, Plato didn't have much respect for poetry or for fine arts like painting, sculpture, and plays, but later philosophers influenced by him, such as Iris Murdoch, argued that the appreciation of artistic beauty for its own sake is also valuable.

This kind of misunderstanding, and overcoming it to reach a better understanding, illustrates the hermeneutic circle between the reader and the text. We always approach a text with assumptions about what it means. We have to. How could you even read the first sentence of the *Analects* without at least *some* assumptions about what "learning" and "practice" are? However, we may find that our assumptions don't do a very good job of making sense of the text. If we bring to the *Analects* a Platonic conception of learning, we will have trouble making sense of the fact that Kongzi condemns people who know a lot of poetry but cannot apply it successfully "when delegated a governmental task" or "when sent abroad as an envoy" (13.5). If we have a Baconian view, we will be puzzled by the fact that Kongzi dismisses as a "common fellow" a disciple who asks to learn about agriculture from him (13.4).

When a text fails to make sense to us, it should lead us to question whether our assumptions about the topic are obscuring the text's meaning. For example, if we do not understand what Kongzi says about learning, perhaps it is because he has a conception of the goal of learning that is different from our own. Once we understand better what the text is claiming, we should question whether our own assumptions are correct. Maybe Kongzi is right and it is possible to learn to be a better person. Maybe knowledge is neither pure theory nor amoral technique. In the hermeneutic circle, we read the text in the light of the worldview that we bring with us. If we are open-minded, we notice when the text surprises us or doesn't match our preconceptions. This leads us to reformulate our assumptions about what the text means, and it may also lead us to question the truth of our own beliefs. Hans-Georg Gadamer, a great hermeneutic theorist of the twentieth century, said that our goal in interpreting is to achieve a partial "fusion of horizons," meaning a fusion of our perspective on the world (our "horizon") with that of the text.

Because a large part of understanding a text is seeing where and how one's preconceptions do or do not fit, I will close this introduction to hermeneutics by discussing four common assumptions of twenty-first century Westerners. Of course, not all readers of this text will be comfortable identifying themselves as Westerners. For many, an important part of their own identity is their origin or ancestry in other parts of the world (including Africa and Asia). Even those who may comfortably describe themselves as Western, may not share these assumptions. (I don't agree with all of them myself.) However, the assumptions below are, in fact, characteristically Western, and I have found that most contemporary college-educated people in the English-speaking world share them. Consequently, these assumptions need to be made explicit, because is hard to understand Chinese philosophy without being aware that there are legitimate alternatives to these Western assumptions.

The first assumption is relativism as opposed to objectivism. A relativist is someone who says that truth and falsity depend upon one's point of view. For

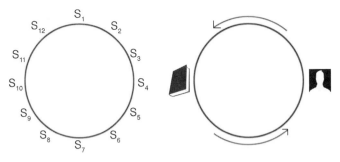

The diagram on the left illustrates the hermeneutic circle inside the text: sentence S_1 is understood in terms of S_2, which is understood in terms of S_3 . . . until we come to S_x, which is understood in terms of S_1 again. The diagram on the right illustrates the hermeneutic circle between the text and the reader: the reader brings preconceptions to the text, but when these fail to make sense of the text the reader is led to question her preconceptions (both about the meaning of the text and about the world in general).

example, is it true or false that "pornography is immoral"? A relativist will say that this statement might be true relative to your viewpoint (or the viewpoint of your culture), but false relative to my viewpoint (or the viewpoint of my culture). An objectivist, in contrast, says that the statement "pornography is immoral" is either true or false, independently of any individual's or culture's point of view.[3] Historically speaking, most people in the West (and most people in the world today) have not been relativists. However, relativism has become so widely accepted on college campuses today that it is often a dogma. One Chinese thinker we examine in this book, Zhuangzi, might be a relativist. However, the vast majority of Chinese philosophers are objectivists: they think there are objective facts about the way the world is and about right and wrong. Because relativism is the new dogma in the West, be open-minded about the possibility that the Chinese sages might be right in favoring objectivism.

A second common assumption among contemporary Westerners is skepticism, as opposed to epistemological optimism. A skeptic is someone who thinks that it is impossible to obtain knowledge. Consider an example: was there a dinosaur standing on the ground beneath you precisely seventy million years ago? Either there was or there was not, but we have absolutely no way of knowing the answer to this question. We have to remain skeptics about it. A radical philosophical skeptic thinks that every issue is like this. We cannot know that the sun will rise tomorrow. We cannot know that we are awake now and not really dreaming. We cannot even know that 2 + 2 = 4. Skepticism is a very common philosophical position in the contemporary West. However, most Chinese thinkers have been epistemological optimists:

---

3. Some philosophers use the term "realist" in place of "objectivist."

they have confidence that we can have knowledge. (Zhuangzi is a possible exception.) Of course, some people in the contemporary West are also epistemological optimists. If you think that the natural sciences (such as physics and biology) have a method that gives us knowledge about the world, then you are an epistemological optimist. Still other contemporary Westerners are falliblists. By "fallibilism" I mean the position that it is possible for us to have knowledge, but we cannot have absolute certainty. The falliblist says we can know that $E = mc^2$, but we should admit that we might be wrong. Further evidence might show that we were mistaken.

The third common assumption among contemporary Westerners is pluralism as opposed to ethical monism. Pluralism is often confused with relativism, but it is importantly different. Consider the life of a good kindergarten teacher and a good defense attorney. Which is better? A relativist would say that it depends on your opinion. If you think that being a defense attorney is a challenging and important job, while being a kindergarten teacher is a trivial one, then that is true, relative to your viewpoint. (Or so the relativist claims.) In contrast, a pluralist would say that a kindergarten teacher and a defense attorney are *both* very valuable ways of life. If a person thinks that one is not valuable, that is simply due to ignorance or narrow-mindedness. Of course, a pluralist does not say that every way of life is equally valuable. Being an assassin or a thief is not a good way of life, even if someone thinks that it is. Westerners (and here I include myself for once) tend to believe in some version of pluralism while most premodern Chinese thinkers are ethical monists. They think there is one way of life that is best, but they do admit some variety. One traditional Chinese list of the social hierarchy is scholar-farmer-craftsman-merchant. Each class is needed for the proper functioning of society. However, the scholars who run the government are the most important and most exalted, while merchants are the least.[4]

Finally, we generally believe in democracy as opposed to paternalism. Remember Lincoln's famous line in the Gettysburg Address that American democracy is "of the people, by the people, and for the people"? Almost all Chinese thinkers agree that government should be "for the people," in the sense that it is aimed at benefiting them. They also agree that government is "of the people," in the sense that those born into aristocratic backgrounds are not always virtuous and those born in humble circumstances may deserve to rise to the highest levels of government because of their virtue and talents. However, no one in ancient China thought that government should be "by the people," in the sense that representatives should be democratically elected. So the traditional

---

4. This is somewhat ironic in the current day, given the economic success of East Asian nations like the People's Republic of China, Taiwan, South Korea, Japan, and Singapore.

Chinese view was paternalistic (government should be made up *of* the most virtuous people, who will work *for* the benefit of the people), but not democratic (government is not *by* popular vote).

So keep in mind that you live in a culture whose background assumptions (and in some cases even dogmas) are relativism, skepticism, pluralism, and democracy. But you are reading texts that largely assume objectivism about right and wrong, an optimistic epistemology, a monistic conception of the good way of life, and political paternalism.

Let's summarize the main points of this chapter. Read classic texts *intensively:* read them carefully, thoughtfully, and repeatedly. Part of understanding a text is seeing the connections between different claims made in that work. Another part is becoming aware of and questioning your own preconceptions as you read. I invite you to do each of these as you explore Chinese thought.

Review Questions

1. What is hermeneutics?
2. What is the difference between intensive reading and extensive reading?
3. What is the difference between a hermeneutic of suspicion and a hermeneutic of faith?
4. What is the hermeneutic circle inside a text?
5. What is the hermeneutic circle between the text and the reader?
6. According to Plato, what is the purpose of learning?
7. According to Francis Bacon, what is the purpose of learning?
8. According to Kongzi, what is the purpose of learning?
9. According to Kongzi, how does learning affect human nature?
10. What is the definition of "relativism"?
11. What is the definition of "epistemological optimism"? of "skepticism"? of "falliblism"?
12. What is the definition of "pluralism"? of "ethical monism"?
13. To what extent would ancient Chinese thinkers agree that government should be "of the people, by the people, and for the people"?

■ APPENDIX B ■

THE CHINESE LANGUAGE AND WRITING SYSTEM

Shen Nong made knots in rope to order things and regularize activities. . . . Cang Jie, a court official of the Yellow Emperor, looked at the tracks of birds and beasts and noticed that their patterns could be differentiated. It was then that he first created writing.

—Xu Shen

This image shows a sample of Chinese text written in the ancient seal script form of the characters.

Western languages are written in alphabets, systems in which symbols represent individual sounds (consonants and vowels). In contrast, the Chinese language is written in characters. What are characters and how do they convey meaning?

I. The Five Types of Chinese Characters

Almost two thousand years ago, the Chinese lexicographer Xǔ Shèn 許慎 noted that there are five kinds of Chinese characters: pictograms, simple ideograms, compound ideograms, loan characters, and semantic-phonetic compounds.[1] We can illustrate four of these fives types using symbols that are familiar to contemporary English readers who do not know Chinese.

Pictograms were originally drawings of something:

As these examples illustrate, the pictures are usually stylized, sometimes to the point of being purely conventional. The image on the far right actually looks nothing like a real human heart, but children are taught in kindergarten that it is a "picture" of a heart. In addition, the relationship between the picture's meaning and what is depicts has a large element of conventionality. Does the middle symbol mean "smoking permitted here," or does it mean "tobacco sold here," or does it mean "warning: flammable materials present"? Would our culture have made a mistake if it decided to use the middle symbol for one of the latter two meanings? Presumably not. So pictograms are pictures of something, but their meaning is still determined to a great extent by social convention.

Simple ideograms are characters whose structure suggests their meaning, but which were never pictures of anything concrete:

---

1. In Chinese, these are known as *xiàng xíng zì* 象形字 (pictograms), *zhǐ shì zì* 指事字 (simple ideograms), *huì yì zì* 會意字 (compound ideograms), *xíng shēng zì* 形聲字 (semantic-phonetic compounds, which are also referred to as *xié shēng zì* 諧聲字), and *jiǎ jiè zì* 假借字 (loan characters).

The simple ideogram on the far left means "five," but it is not a picture, because the number five is an abstract entity, so there could not be a picture of it. As with pictograms, there is an element of conventionality in the meanings of simple ideograms. The middle symbol is posted on roads and means "U-turn allowed," but we as a society could have decided that it means "watch out for falling balls," and posted it on golf courses or at baseball parks. I stress the conventionality of meaning of Chinese characters so that you will understand that even if you know exactly what the structure of a Chinese character is, you will not necessarily know what it means. To know the meaning of a character, you must know how it is used.

Compound ideograms are characters with one or more meaningful components that when brought into conjunction suggest the meaning of the composite symbol:

Notice that the components of the compound ideogram on the left are themselves ideograms. However, the compound ideogram in the middle has one component that is a pictogram, and one that is an ideogram. And the compound ideogram on the far right has two components that are pictograms. In general, the components of a compound ideogram do *not* have to be ideograms themselves. All that is necessary is that the conjunction of meaningful symbols suggests the meaning of the whole.

In order to understand phonetic loan characters, consider the following "sentence":

It means "I love you," but how does it get this meaning? The symbols are a pictogram of an eye (from the seal on the back of the U.S. dollar bill), a pictogram of a human heart, and a pictogram of a hand pointing at the reader. The eye pictogram does not stand for a human eye here, of course. Instead, it stands for a word that sounds the same as "eye" in English: "I." This is how phonetic loans work: they borrow preexisting symbols that already have a word associated with them and use them to represent *different* words that *sound* the same. The other four types categorize characters according to the way in which they are *created*. Phonetic loans are characters that already exist but that are *recycled* to represent a new meaning.

Most people, if they have any preconceptions about Chinese characters, seem to think that they all work like pictograms or ideograms. In fact, only a small percentage of Chinese characters are either pictograms or ideograms. Almost all Chinese characters (97 percent) are semantic-phonetic compounds. As we have seen, there are examples of pictograms, ideograms, and phonetic loans that will be familiar to English readers. However, semantic-phonetic compounds are a little harder to illustrate. Consider the following sentence:

The first symbol in the above sentence is a pictogram of an eye, being used as a phonetic loan for "I." The third symbol is still a pictogram for "you." But what is the eye pictogram doing in its second occurrence? It means "see." So the sentence means "I see you." Perhaps you guessed this immediately, but if there were lots of pictograms in common use and they were sometimes used as pictograms but other times recycled as phonetic loans, you could easily get confused about what a given pictogram is doing in a sentence. So we might start to distinguish one use of a pictogram from another by providing an additional hint:

The first symbol is now a semantic-phonetic compound. In this semantic-phonetic compound, the eye pictogram is the phonetic component; it tells us what the pronunciation of the symbol is. The man pictogram is the semantic component; it gives us a hint about what the meaning of the symbol is. If we were properly trained in reading this written language, we would immediately read the above sentence as "I see you." Now, consider the following pictogram of a handsaw:

Suppose we combine this symbol with the eye symbol, producing the semantic-phonetic compound in the middle of the sentence below:

This sentence would mean "I saw you." The first two words in the sentence are compounds in which one part gives a hint about the meaning of the word and another part gives a hint about the pronunciation of the symbol. Chinese semantic-phonetic compounds work the same way.

Now that we understand the types of Chinese characters, let's look at some actual examples. Pictograms, once again, are stylized pictures that have a meaning that is conventionally connected to what they depict:

日   月   女   子

Try to guess what these four characters are pictures of, and then look at the footnote for the answers.[2] If you guessed even one of them correctly, you have done as well as any student has ever done in the many years I have been using this example. In all likelihood, you couldn't guess any of them. As I stressed before, pictograms are highly stylized symbols whose meaning is not transparent.

---

2. Believe it or not, these are (from left to right) pictograms of the sun, the moon, a woman, and a child.

Simple ideograms, as we have seen, are characters whose structure suggests their meaning but which are not pictures of anything concrete. Simple ideograms are quite rare in Chinese:

一　二　三　上　下

You might be able to guess the meanings of the first three symbols, especially when you see them written side by side like this. The fourth and the fifth character are harder to guess, though.[3]

Compound ideograms are characters with two parts, each of which has a meaning of its own which suggests the meaning of the whole character when they are brought into conjunction:

明　好

You now know the meanings of the components of each of these two compound ideograms. (Look back under the examples of pictograms if you've forgotten.) Try to guess the meaning of each of them before looking at the footnote.[4] Recognizing the extent to which the meaning of Chinese characters is conventional helps to inoculate us against what has been called "the ideographic myth": the mistaken belief that most Chinese characters somehow directly represent ideas or meanings, without conventions or connections to the spoken language.

Semantic-phonetic compounds have one part that hints at the meaning of the character (the semantic component) and one part that hints at the pronunciation (the phonetic component). The pictogram 門 depicts a gate and is pronounced *mén.* It occurs as the phonetic component in the following semantic-phonetic compounds:

問 *wèn,* "to ask" (the semantic component is 口, "mouth")
聞 *wén,* "to hear" (the semantic component is 耳, "ear")
們 *mén* (pluralizing suffix; the semantic component is 人, "person")
悶 *mèn,* "to be sad" (the semantic component is 心, "heart")

3. From left to right, these are the simple ideograms for the numbers one, two, and three, and for "above" and "below."

4. The compound ideogram on the left means "bright" (suggested by the brightness of the sun, 日, and the moon, 月), while the one on the right means (in Classical Chinese) "to be fond of" (suggested by a woman, 女, holding her child, 子). The original form of 明 may have shown a window and the moon, which would also be a compound ideogram, but with different components. In modern Chinese, the character 好 usually means "good."

Not all phonetic components are as useful as these. The pronunciations of Chinese characters have changed greatly over time, so a phonetic element that was helpful when the character was first created two thousand or more years ago may be almost useless today.

Phonetic loan characters are originally created in one of the four previous ways: as pictograms, simple ideograms, compound ideograms, or semantic-phonetic compounds. But they are recycled to represent *different* words that *sound the same* (or similar to) the words they originally represented. For example, the character 來 was originally a pictogram of wheat. It was borrowed to represent the homophone (i.e., same-sounding word) meaning "to come." Similarly, the character 其, pronounced *qí,* was originally a pictogram of a basket, but it was borrowed to represent the homophone meaning "his," "her," "its," or "their." One way to understand the process of phonetic borrowing is to imagine four steps:

1. The character 來 is created as a pictogram of wheat. The character is pronounced *lái* because the spoken word for "wheat" is pronounced *lái.*[5]

2. There is no character for a different spoken word, also pronounced *lái,* that means "to come."

3. Because it is pronounced the same, the character 來 is borrowed to represent the spoken word that means "to come."

4. The character 來 is so frequently used with the meaning of "to come" that it is no longer used in its old meaning of "wheat."[6]

So almost all Chinese characters (again, about 97 percent) are semantic-phonetic compounds, in which part of the character gives a hint about the meaning, and the other part gives a hint about the pronunciation. In addition, a handful of characters are created as pictograms, simple ideograms, or complex ideograms. Finally, a few characters that are created in one of the four preceding ways are "recycled," and used to represent different words that sound the same as the words they originally represented.

How many characters are there? It is not as easy to answer this question as it might seem, because the answer depends on whether we count variant forms of the same character (some of them extremely obscure) and whether

---

5. This is technically a misrepresentation, because I am using the modern Mandarin pronunciation of this character. When the character was created, it was pronounced differently, because Chinese (like all languages) has changed its pronunciation over time. However, the example is still accurate because 來 *was* originally a pictogram of wheat and the original pronunciations of the Chinese words for "wheat" and "to come" were similar.

6. This fourth step is not required in order for a character to be a phonetic loan, but it often happens.

we count characters that are now completely obsolete.[7] The larger Chinese dictionaries that aim at being comprehensive have between fifty thousand and one hundred thousand entries. But don't despair: the three thousand most common characters include approximately 99 percent of all characters in use in contemporary Chinese documents. In addition, consider the dictionary that I keep on my desk and refer to first if I do not recognize a character: Liang Shih-ch'iu's *Far East Chinese-English Dictionary*. It has 7,331 characters. In decades of reading modern and Classical Chinese, I have seldom been unable to find a character I was looking for in this dictionary.

There have been various proposals for reforming or simplifying the Chinese written language. In the 1950s, the Chinese Communists introduced a series of simplified characters.[8] These characters are largely based on the handwritten "cursive" style of characters that has been used by scholars for centuries when writing informally. So, for example, 習, "to practice," was simplified to 习, and 門, "gate," was simplified to 门. Outside of the People's Republic of China (PRC), the traditional long form characters are still in use. In addition, well-educated people in the PRC also recognize the long form characters. Most contemporary Chinese language programs at U.S. colleges and universities emphasize the simplified forms.

II. Spoken Chinese

Two aspects of spoken Chinese make it especially challenging: dialects and tones. The dialects of Chinese are as different from one another as French, Spanish, and Italian are from one another. Fortunately, everyone in China who has graduated from high school can speak what we call the Mandarin dialect (even though they may have been raised speaking another dialect and use that in their home village). Mandarin is called "common speech" in Mainland China and the "national language" on Taiwan. Cantonese and Shanghainese are other mainland dialects with many speakers.[9] Many people in Taiwan speak Taiwanese (a version of the Hokkien dialect), but as on the mainland, most people do speak Mandarin. We do not know exactly how spoken Chinese

---

7. By way of analogy, does the British spelling "civilisation" count as a different word from "civilization"? Is Shakespeare's "fardels" still an English word?

8. Not all characters have a special simplified form; in those cases, people use the long form. In Chinese, simplified characters is *jiǎn tǐ zì*, and is written (with the short form in parentheses) 簡 體字 (简体字), while long form characters is *fán tǐ zì* 繁體字 (繁体字).

9. Historically, many Chinese immigrants to the United States spoke Cantonese.

sounded in the time of Confucius, so it is standard to pronounce the characters in classical texts in the Mandarin dialect.

Because Chinese is a tonal language, the same set of phonemes (i.e., basic sounds) will be a different word, depending on the tone in which they are read. Mandarin has four tones (or five if you count the absence of a tone as a tone). Nowadays, tones are usually represented with accent marks over the vowels. So (to use an example found in almost every textbook), *ma* can have five meanings, depending on the tone:

mā 媽, "Mom"

má 麻, "hemp"

mǎ 馬, "horse"

mà 罵, "to scold"

ma 嗎 (question-marking grammatical particle)

Notice that 馬, a pictogram of a horse, occurs as the phonetic element in three of the characters.

The best way to learn the tones is by hearing and copying someone who can say them correctly. However, as a first approximation, the first tone is high and level, similar to the way you would say "g" if a music teacher said, "Give me a 'g.'" The second tone rises up, as if you were saying, "Huh?" The third tone dips down slightly, then rises up, like an old teacher answering a knock at the door by saying, "Yeeeeeeees?" The fourth tone goes down, like disciplining a naughty dog, "No!"

III. Radicals and Dictionaries

How does one look up characters in a Chinese dictionary?

Most Chinese dictionaries nowadays follow the famous *Kāng Xī zìdiǎn* 康熙字典 (published 1716 CE) in organizing characters according to 214 "radicals" (*bù shǒu* 部首). In principle, every Chinese character has at least one of these radicals in it (or the character *is* a radical). So if you encounter a character that you do not recognize, you take a guess at what the radical of that character is. Usually the radical is fairly easy to spot, but sometimes there is more than one radical, and other times the radical may be obscure. Next, count the number of "strokes" in the character in addition to the radical. There is a standard way of writing Chinese characters. With practice, you can almost always figure out how many strokes it takes to write a character, where a stroke is usually defined by when you would lift up the pen or brush in order to draw the next line. Finally, go to the part of the dictionary or its index that lists all characters with that radical and that number of additional strokes. There will typically be several characters fitting this description, so you go down the list until you find the character you are looking for.

Dictionaries usually also have indices that allow you to find a character by alternative methods. You can look up a character by its pronunciation (if you happen to know it) or by looking up the total number of strokes in the character. The latter method is very tedious as, for example, there are about two hundred characters with six strokes in even a basic desk dictionary.

The sounds of Chinese words and characters can be written using a romanization system, which is a method of writing a language using the letters of the Roman alphabet. The standard phonetic system for Mandarin Chinese today is Pinyin, which is the one used by the People's Republic of China, the United Nations, U.S. news organizations, and almost all contemporary Chinese language textbooks. Prior to the development of Pinyin, Wade-Giles was the standard romanization system. Many older books, articles, reference works, and library catalogues use Wade-Giles, so if you continue studying the Chinese language, you will eventually have to learn to read Wade-Giles. (You can recognize a Wade-Giles romanization by the frequent use of apostrophes and hyphens. For example, "Kongzi" in Pinyin becomes "K'ung-tzu" in Wade-Giles.)

IV. The Sapir-Whorf Hypothesis

The Sapir-Whorf Hypothesis, which takes its name from linguists Edward Sapir and Benjamin Whorf, is one of the most interesting (and controversial) claims to come out of comparative linguistics. There are both strong and weak versions of the Sapir-Whorf Hypothesis. The strong version of the Sapir-Whorf Hypothesis asserts that the language a person uses *determines* the way she perceives the world. The weak version of the Sapir-Whorf Hypothesis claims that a person's language *influences* the way she perceives the world.

I find the strong version of the Sapir-Whorf Hypothesis much less plausible. If language *determines* the way that we perceive the world, how do people ever discover new things? However, there is very good evidence that the weak version of the Sapir-Whorf Hypothesis is true. For example, it used to be the grammatical convention in English that the masculine form of pronouns was used to refer to an indeterminate person: "If someone wants to become a college professor, he will need a graduate degree." However, most people would now agree that this usage *influences* us to conceptualize the "standard" college professor or graduate student as male. We still haven't come up with an easy way of getting around this problem in English. I tend to alternate using "she" and "he." Others use "they" as if it were a third-person singular pronoun: "As soon as a doctor graduates from medical school, they should get malpractice insurance." The important point here is that even something as subtle as the choice of pronouns can illustrate the weak version of the Sapir-Whorf Hypothesis.

In the West, philosophy first developed in the Greek-speaking world and then flourished in the Latin-speaking world. Greek and Latin are in the Indo-European language family (as is English). Chinese, in contrast, is in the Sino-Tibetan language family.[10] There has been some interesting speculation about whether (as the Sapir-Whorf Hypothesis predicts) the structural differences between the Indo-European and Sino-Tibetan languages *influenced* the different development of philosophy in Europe and China.

One major difference is that all the Indo-European languages have forms of the verb "to be" (for example, *einai* in Greek or *esse* in Latin). This verb expresses existence ("there *are* mice in the basement"), predication ("the mice *are* happy"), identity ("Clark Kent *is* Superman"), membership in a group ("Clark Kent *is* a reporter"), and truth ("Is not!" "Is so!"). There is no one verb or grammatical construction that performs all of these roles in Classical Chinese. There are separate Classical Chinese expressions for "existence" (有/無, "to have"/"to not have") and "truth" (然/不然, "is so"/"is not so"), while predication is handled by full verbs (樂/不樂, "is happy"/"is not happy") and both identity and group membership by a particular grammatical construction (X Y 也/ X 非 Y 也, X is (a) Y/X is not (a) Y).

The fact that Greek and Latin had the verb "to be" while Classical Chinese did not may have led to some of the characteristic differences between Chinese and Western philosophy. Plato is one of the fathers of Western philosophy, and one of his main concerns was the nature of Being. But there is no way to say "Being" in Classical Chinese.[11] Consequently, certain metaphysical issues became central to Western philosophy in a way that they almost couldn't have in Chinese philosophy.

In comparison with many Indo-European languages, some other things seem to be "missing" from Classical Chinese. Nouns have no "number"; therefore, 牛 could be "ox" or "oxen," and 人 could be "person" or "persons." In other words, most Chinese nouns are like the English "deer" or "sheep," which have one form for singular and plural. Classical Chinese verbs do not

---

10. Although both cultures adopted Chinese characters for their writing systems, spoken Japanese and Korean are not linguistically related to Chinese; they are in the Altaic language group.

11. Some translations obscure this fact by translating the Chinese 有 as "Being," but 有 means something more like "to have," and expresses simple existence rather than the rarified notion of Being with a capital "B."

have an intrinsic tense: by itself 學 could mean "to learn," "have learned," "learned," "am learning" or "will learn."

These "missing" elements might seem to imply that Classical Chinese is vague. Classical Chinese can be vague, but so can any other language. Classical Chinese can also have a level of precision limited only by one's own mind. In addition, context disambiguates most expressions to a great extent. By providing context, a careful writer of Classical Chinese can be as precise as she wishes.

V. For Further Reading

- Angus C. Graham, "The Relation of Chinese Thought to the Chinese Language," in his *Disputers of the Tao* (Chicago: Open Court Press, 1989), pp. 389–428. A provocative discussion.

- Daniel Kane, *The Chinese Language: Its History and Current Usage* (North Clarendon, VT: Tuttle Publishing, 2006). An accessible introduction to the Chinese language.

- Xigui Qiu, *Chinese Writing,* trans. Gilbert Mattos and Jerry Norman (Berkeley: Society for the Study of Early China, 2000). A very scholarly but reliable study of the development of Chinese characters, including many etymologies.

- Shou-hsin Teng, ed., *The Far East 3000 Chinese Character Dictionary* (Taibei: Far East Book Company, 2003). Shows the proper way to write the most common Chinese characters.

Review Questions

1. Explain the five types of Chinese characters.
2. Almost all Chinese characters belong to which type?
3. Approximately how many Chinece characters are there in total: 1,000? 10,000? 100,000? or 1,000,000?
4. How many thousands of Chinese characters do you need to know in order to recognize 99 percent of the characters in most contemporary writing?
5. What is the English name of the official and most commonly spoken dialect of Chinese on both the Mainland and in Taiwan? Can you name any other dialects?
6. How are the characters organized in a traditional Chinese dictionary?

7. What is the strong version of the Sapir-Whorf Hypothesis? What is the weak version of the Sapir-Whorf Hypothesis?

8. What is an example of a linguistic difference between the Indo-European languages and Chinese that might be philosophically important?

■ APPENDIX C ■

KONGZI AS SYSTEMATIC PHILOSOPHER

The Master said, "Zigong, do you regard me as simply one who learns much and remembers it?"

Zigong said, "I do. Is that not the case?"

The Master said, "It is not. I string it together by means of one thing."

—Analects 15.3

This famous depiction of Kongzi is by Wu Daozi of the Tang dynasty.

Kongzi was knowledgeable about and discussed many things: the *Odes,* history, ritual, astronomy, and even the most mundane practical activities (9.6). Consequently, it was easy for people to lose sight of the overarching purpose of what Kongzi said and did. However, as Kongzi assured his disciple Zigong (15.3), he ultimately had one goal that bound his teachings together: moving individuals and society closer to the Way.

In this book, I present the Confucian Way as emphasizing the cultivation of Virtue. The result of this cultivation is to produce a genuine "gentleman," who has ethical insight that transcends any rules, procedures, or doctrines. But this is certainly not the only way to understand Kongzi. Even a book could not do justice to the variety of major alternative interpretations that exist. However, there are at least three other understandings of Kongzi that are sufficiently influential that you should be familiar with them. Although they are very different, these interpretations have in common the fact that they interpret Kongzi as having some key, central doctrine that is the basis for his other teachings.

I. The "One Thread" of Analects 4.15

A disciple of Kongzi (who later became a "master" in his own right) offered what has become one major interpretation of the Way of Kongzi:

> The Master said, "Zeng! All that I teach can be strung together on a single thread."
>
> "Yes, sir," Master Zeng responded.
>
> After the Master left, the disciples asked, "What did he mean by that?"
>
> Master Zeng said, "All that the Master teaches amounts to nothing more than dutifulness tempered by sympathetic understanding." (4.15)

In this passage, Kongzi announced that his Way is threaded together by *one* thing. So why did Master Zeng explain it as being made up of two things? Perhaps the "one" is Goodness, but it has two aspects: dutifulness and sympathetic understanding. In Chapter 3, I explained that "dutifulness" is devotion or loyalty, even when that commitment conflicts with one's own self-interest. What about "sympathetic understanding"? Kongzi himself characterized it with the motto, "Do not impose upon others what you yourself do not desire" (15.24). This has reminded many people of the so-called Golden Rule of the Western tradition: "Do unto others as you would have them do unto you."

Dutifulness and sympathetic understanding certainly seem like important values, but how do they together constitute all of the Confucian Way? According to one reading, dutifulness is not merely loyalty to a particular person. Rather, it is devotion to the obligations that go with one's ritually defined role. For example, part of the role of a college professor is to teach students and to grade their work in a timely and fair manner. This requires maintaining high standards, even though it may often be easier to be lax. ("When teaching is not strict, it is due to the laziness of the teacher," an old Chinese saying has it.) Of course, a good teacher is not pointlessly strict. If a student has papers for three separate classes due on one day, each of his professors would be carrying out his or her obligations by enforcing the due date for his or her class. However, most professors will allow an extension in such a situation, as long as the student asks for one in advance. This is an application of sympathetic understanding. The professor imagines (or just reminds herself) what it is like to be a student with multiple deadlines on one day. This allows her to realize that it is appropriate to deviate from what would normally be her obligation to enforce deadlines.

So, "dutifulness" is a commitment to the normal obligations that go with one's role, while "sympathetic understanding" is mentally putting oneself in another's place to understand when it is appropriate to bend or even suspend the rules. Many brilliant interpreters of Confucianism have seen something like the preceding as the key to understanding the Way of Kongzi. There are several considerations in favor of this interpretation:

- The later Confucian tradition regarded Master Zeng as one of the greatest of Kongzi's disciples, and the one who passed on his Way to future generations. Consequently, his interpretation is often taken to be authoritative.

- There are some passages about Goodness that can be seen as implicitly characterizing it in terms of dutifulness and sympathetic understanding.[1]

- Kongzi emphasized the importance of the rules that normally govern the roles a person occupies: ruler, minister, parent, child, teacher, student, etc. This is dutifulness. However, we have also seen that Kongzi was particularistic in his belief that rules are not enough. This is sympathetic understanding.[i]

However, there are also some weaknesses of the Zengzian interpretation:

- Despite the high esteem in which he was later held in the tradition, Zeng was characterized in the *Analects* as "stupid" (11.18*). Not only is there no

---

1. Consider how 12.2, 15.15*, and the comments about Zigong in 5.4 and 5.12 can be interpreted in this light.

passage in the *Analects* in which Kongzi praises Zeng, there is no passage outside of 4.15 in which Zeng is even shown having a conversation with the Master. So the *Analects* does not present Zeng as an important or insightful disciple.

- *Analects* 4.15 is the only passage in that text that *explicitly* links dutifulness and sympathetic understanding. Even in this passage, it is Zeng, not Kongzi, who claims that dutifulness and sympathetic understanding constitute the Way. Note that the Master neither hears nor endorses this interpretation. Furthermore, the passages that might be read as even *implicitly* linking the two are a small percentage of those in the *Analects*.

- Kongzi himself explicitly pairs other virtues (most notably Goodness and wisdom) that could account for his emphasis on rules and exceptions. As we saw in Chapter 3, an important part of Goodness is caring for others, and an important part of wisdom is understanding the particularistic details of complex and changing circumstances.

II. The "Rectification of Names" of Analects 13.3

Other interpreters have found the key to the Confucian Way in the doctrine of rectifying names. Kongzi supposedly articulated this doctrine during his visit to the state of Wei, in response to the complex political situation there.

Nanzi was the consort of the Duke of Wei. She did not hold political office, but she was powerful because of her influence on the duke. It was also an open secret that she was cheating on him. The duke's eldest son, the heir to the dukedom, was outraged by his stepmother's behavior and plotted to have her assassinated. When his plot was discovered, he fled the state. Then, after the duke passed away, the grandson of the duke succeeded to the rulership. However, *his* father (the previous heir, who had attempted to murder his stepmother) returned from exile and attempted to take power from his son (cf 7.15*).

Kongzi visited the state of Wei and even had an audience with Nanzi. Kongzi's disciple Zilu thought that Kongzi's meeting with Nanzi was scandalous, but Kongzi protested that he had done nothing wrong and that it was appropriate to visit her in her capacity as a leading figure in the state (6.28). On another occasion, Zilu asked Kongzi,

> "If the Duke of Wei were to employ you to serve in the government of his state, what would be your first priority?"
> The Master answered, "It would, of course, be the rectification of names."

Zilu said, "Could you, Master, really be so far off the mark? Why worry about rectifying names?"

The Master replied, "How boorish you are, Zilu! When it comes to matters that he does not understand, the gentleman should remain silent. If names are not rectified, speech will not be appropriate; when speech is not appropriate, things will not be successfully accomplished. . . ." (13.3)

What is meant by "rectifying names" (also translated "correcting terms"), and why does Kongzi apparently regard it as so important? Consider 12.11, in which Kongzi is asked about governing well and responds simply, "Let the lord be a lord, the ministers be ministers, the fathers be fathers and the sons be sons." This could be interpreted as an injunction for lords to live up to the implications of the title "lord," ministers to live up to the implications of the title "minister," and so on. For instance, part of what is implied by the title "father" is someone who loves, protects, nurtures, and guides his children. A father who lived up to his name would be fulfilling his obligations. Of course, this is only true if names are used as they would be in an ideal society (like that of the sage-kings). If we call anyone who biologically sires a child a "father," it eliminates the moral content of the term (cf 2.7 on the term "filial"). Similarly, if we are to maintain the deep significance and function of the rituals, we must use only the right ritual implements in appropriate ways, as indicated by their correct names. So, when a particular ceremony called for a ritual cup of the *gu* type, but Kongzi's contemporaries used a different kind, he moaned, "A *gu* that is not a *gu*—is it really a *gu*? Is it really a *gu*?" (6.25) In other words, according to this interpretation, the term "gu" refers to a cup of a particular type, but Kongzi's contemporaries called something else a "gu" and used it in the ceremony instead.

There is some evidence for this interpretation: Kongzi does discuss appropriate and inappropriate uses of words in several passages. For example, in 12.20*, a disciple asks Kongzi "What must a scholar-official be like such that he can be called 'accomplished'?" Kongzi replies, "What do you mean by 'accomplished'?" When the disciple states that he means someone well known in both the state and in his clan, Kongzi explains "This is being well known; it is not being accomplished."[ii2]

However, there are also important objections that one might raise against this reading:

---

2. For other passages where Kongzi discusses words and their proper uses, see 1.11, 1.14*, 2.7, 4.20, 5.15*, 6.22, 6.30, 11.24*, 13.20, 13.28*, and possibly 4.5.

- Many passages that have been assumed to be about rectifying names do not actually refer to names at all. For example, 6.25 does *not* say "A so-called *gu*—is it really a *gu?*" and 12.11 does *not* say "Let those who are called 'lords' be lords, let those who are called 'ministers' be ministers." In passages such as 6.25 and 12.11, Kongzi expresses concern with what people *do,* not with what they *say.* To use the jargon of modern philosophy, these passages use words but they do not mention words.

- The passages in which Kongzi explicitly discusses names or what something is "so-called" are a very small percentage of the *Analects.* Furthermore, every philosopher in every tradition sometimes discusses correct and incorrect uses of names. Kongzi's occasional references do not show that this is a central or distinctive preoccupation of his philosophy.

- In 13.3, Zilu asks Kongzi specifically what he would do if employed by the ruler of Wei, so the passage seems to be a narrow comment about a particular situation rather than an exposition of Kongzi's general, systematic philosophy.

III. The "Broadening of the Way" of Analects 15.29

A third interpretation makes Kongzi sound refreshingly modern in his outlook. Kongzi comments that

> Human beings can broaden the Way—it is not the Way that broadens human beings. (15.29)

It is not obvious what this means, but one interpretation is that humans should *not* think of the Way as something fixed that they should seek to follow. Rather, humans are responsible for creatively transforming the content of the Way. This is a challenging inversion of how Kongzi is normally understood. Instead of seeing Kongzi as someone who called upon people to live up to the highest ideals of a Way that has already been *discovered,* Kongzi challenges us to creatively *invent* a new Way (or at least new aspects of the Way). This is sometimes referred to as a postmodern interpretation of Kongzi.[3]

---

3. "Postmodernism" defies simple definition, but we might say that it is a label for a group of philosophical positions that reject fixed, preexisting standards for truth and rationality in favor of temporary standards that are subject to continual "deconstruction."

There are several strengths of the postmodern interpretation:

- It gives an intriguing reading of Kongzi's puzzling comment about broadening the Way.

- Many people find Kongzi's traditionalism hard to swallow. However, in the alternative interpretation, Kongzi emphasizes individual creativity in a manner that is reminiscent of Nietzsche or Ralph Waldo Emerson.

- Kongzi's particularism also requires creativity, since one must imagine how to respond to new situations without mechanically applying rules. The postmodern interpretation highlights the central importance of creativity in Kongzi's thought.

- The postmodern interpretation offers one way to explain Kongzi's willingness to switch from using linen caps to silk caps in a particular ritual on the grounds that the latter are more "frugal" (9.3).[iii]

However, there are also some strong arguments against this interpretation:

- Chinese commentators have traditionally understood 15.29 as saying the exact opposite of what the postmodern interpretation claims. As one scholar put it, "Human beings can harmonize with the Way—this is why the text reads: 'Human beings are able to broaden the Way.' The Way does not harmonize with humans—this is why the text reads: 'It is not the Way that broadens humans.'" An alternative translation of 15.29 that might better bring out this sense is, "Human beings can glorify the Way; it is not that the Way glorifies humans."[iv] It is possible that the Chinese commentators are wrong. However, they show that we are not compelled to accept the postmodern reading.

- It is not an argument in favor of an interpretation that makes someone from another era and culture sound just like us. In fact, we should be suspicious of any interpretation that renders a foreign worldview too familiar.

- There is a difference between being creative in applying the Way and creatively transforming the Way itself. The fact that Kongzi demands the former does not mean that he encourages the latter.

- When Kongzi agreed to "follow the majority" in switching to ritual caps made of silk, he was not endorsing change, but merely accepting a change that had already become standard. This is the *only* time Kongzi agreed to any change in ritual practice. Indeed, in the very same passage, he rejects another proposed change to the rituals (9.3).

- The biggest problem with the postmodern reading is that it flies in the face of considerable textual evidence in the *Analects*. Kongzi stated proudly: "I transmit rather than innovate. I trust in and love the ancient ways" (7.1). As a rule, Kongzi insisted on maintaining old rituals, even when they had fallen into disuse. For example, when a disciple suggested doing away with a ritual that involves sacrificing a lamb, Kongzi replied, "You regret the loss of the lamb, whereas I regret the loss of the rite" (3.17).[4]

IV. Conclusion

This quick overview only touches upon some of the arguments that can be given in support of the preceding positions. I have not provided a definitive response to the knowledgeable and insightful scholars who favor these alternative interpretations of the *Analects*. However, at least now you are aware of these views and have some notion of what can be said about them, pro and con.

---

4. On Kongzi's unwillingness to deviate from or abandon traditional rituals, see also 3.1, 6.25, 7.18, 15.11, and 17.21.

■ SOURCES FOR FACTS AND MYTHS ■

Chinese word for "crisis": Victor Mair, "danger+opportunity≠crisis," http://www.pinyin.info/chinese/crisis.html, accessed on August 2, 2010.

"A journey of a thousand leagues begins with a single step." See *Laozi* (*Daodejing*), chapter 64.

Chinese characters as "pictographs": John DeFrancis, *The Chinese Language: Fact and Fantasy* (Honolulu: University of Hawaii Press, 1984), p. 84, Table 3.

"May you live in interesting times": Fred R. Shapiro et al., *The Yale Book of Quotations* (New Haven: Yale University Press, 2006), p. 669.

Fortune cookies: Ask anyone who's actually from China whether they eat them.

Gunpowder, magnetic compass, printing with moveable type: Joseph Needham, "Science and China's Influence on the World," in Needham, *The Grand Titration* (London: Allen and Unwin, 1969), pp. 55–122 (especially pp. 62–76).

Influence of the Chinese civil service examination system: Ssu-Yü Teng, "Chinese Influence on the Western Examination System," *Harvard Journal of Asiatic Studies,* 7 (1943), 267–312.

Viewing the Great Wall from space: López-Gil, Norberto, "Is it Really Possible to See the Great Wall of China from Space with a Naked Eye?" *Journal of Optometry* 1 (1), 3–4.

Words for "tea": Östen Dahl. 2008. "Tea," in Martin Haspelmath, Matthew S. Dryer, David Gil, and Bernard Comrie, eds., *The World Atlas of Language Structures Online* (Munich: Max Planck Digital Library, 2008), chapter 138. Available online at http://wals.info/feature/138, accessed on August 2, 2010.

"Gung ho": Albert F. Moe, "Gung Ho," *American Speech* 42 (February 1967): 19–30.

Chinese word for "contradiction": See *Readings in Classical Chinese Philosophy,* p. 330.

■ ILLUSTRATION CREDITS ■

Chapter 1. Fu Xi and Nuwa, mid-eighth century, painting on silk.

Chapter 2. Image of Kongzi on a Chinese postage stamp.

Chapter 3. Star trails, by permission of the photographer, Joshua Bury.

Chapter 4. Xi Shu determining the solstice, from the *Qinding Shujing Tushuo*.

Chapter 5. Photograph of Dwarf Japanese Juniper bonsai. This image is protected by a Creative Commons Attribution-Share Alike 3.0 Unported license (Creative Commons BY-SA 3.0) (http://creativecommons.org/licenses/by-sa/3.0/deed.en). Sage Ross http://en.wikipedia.org/wiki/File:Dwarf_Japanese_Juniper,_1975-2007.jpg

Chapter 6. Image of Mengzi on a Chinese postage stamp.

Chapter 7. Horse and Groom, after Li Gonglin, Zhao Yong (1291–1361), China, Yuan dynasty, 1347, hand scroll, ink on paper.

Chapter 8. Laozi riding an ox, middle Ming dynasty, hanging scroll.

Chapter 9. The Hai Riyo, from Charles Gould, *Mythical Monsters*, London, Allen and Co., 1886.

Chapter 10. Image of Xunzi on a Chinese postage stamp.

Chapter 11. Bronze battle axe, Shang dynasty, excavated at Yidu, Shandong Province. This image is protected by a Creative Commons Attribution-Share Alike 2.5 Generic license (Creative Commons BY-SA 2.5) (http://creativecommons.org/licenses/by-sa/2.5/deed.en). Editor at Large http://commons.wikimedia.org/wiki/File:CMOC_Treasures_of_Ancient_China_exhibit_-_bronze_battle_axe.jpg

Chapter 12. Great Wall of China, Herbert Ponting, 1907.

Appendix A. The first page of Confucius, *Analects*, with commentary of Zhu Xi.

Appendix B. The Xunzi in seal script, Deng Shiru, 1743–1805, hanging scroll, ink on paper.

Appendix C. Kongzi, woodblock reproduction of image by Wu Daozi, Tang dynasty.

■ ENDNOTES ■

Chapter 1. The Historical Context

i. For a brilliant inquiry into Chinese myths about the early sages, see Michael J. Puett, *The Ambivalence of Creation* (Stanford: Stanford University Press, 2001).

ii. Ssu-ma Ch'ien, *The Grand Scribe's Records,* vol. 1, William H. Nienhauser, Jr., ed. (Bloomington: Indiana University Press, 1994), p. 50 (3:105).

iii. *History,* "Shao gao"; cf James Legge, *The Shoo King,* vol. 3 of *The Chinese Classics,* reprint (Taibei: SMC Publishing, 1991), pp. 420–33.

iv. *History,* "Shao gao."

v. *History,* "Kang gao"; cf Legge, *The Shoo King,* pp. 381–98.

vi. *History,* "Kang gao."

vii. *History,* "Shao gao."

Chapter 2. Kongzi and Confucianism

i. *Zuo zhuan,* Duke Zhao, year 13.

ii. Sunzi, *Bingfa* 1, from Sun Tzu, *Art of War,* trans. Ralph D. Sawyer (Boulder, CO: Westview Press, 1994), p. 167.

iii. Simone Weil, "Draft for a Statement of Human Obligations," in Weil, *Two Moral Essays,* ed. Ronald Hathaway (Wallingford, PA: Pendle Hill Publications, 1981), p. 5.

iv. Martin Luther King, Jr., "I Have a Dream," in James W. Washington, ed., *The Essential Writings and Speeches of Martin Luther King, Jr.* (New York: HarperCollins, 1991), pp. 217–20. See also King's "Letter from Birmingham City Jail" (ibid., pp. 289–302) for his revivalistic use of Christianity.

v. Philip J. Ivanhoe explores the historical dialectic of thinking and learning in his *Confucian Moral Self Cultivation,* 2nd ed. (Indianapolis: Hackett Publishing, 2000).

vi. Arthur Waley, trans., *The Book of Songs* (New York: Grove Press, 1960), p. 309, Mao no. 113.

vii. Iris Murdoch, *The Sovereignty of Good* (New York: Routledge & Kegan Paul, 1970), p. 84. Emphasis in original.

Chapter 3. Kongzi and Virtue Ethics

i. See "Lu's Questions," *Mozi* 49; translated in Yi-pao Mei, *The Ethical and Political Works of Motse,* reprint (Westport, CT: Hyperion Press, 1973), p. 253.

ii. G. E. M. Anscombe, "Mr. Truman's Degree" in Anscombe, *The Collected Philosophical Papers of G. E. M. Anscombe,* vol. 3 (Minneapolis: University of Minnesota Press, 1981), pp. 62–71.

iii. "Anti-Confucianism," *Mozi* 39; translation modified from Mei, pp. 203–4.

Chapter 4. Mohist Consequentialism

i. "Against Confucianism," *Mozi* 39. Translation modified from Mei, pp. 202–3. Cf Burton Watson, *Mo Tzu: Basic Writings* (New York: Columbia University Press, 1962), p. 127.

ii. "Gong Shu," *Mozi* 50. See Mei, pp. 257–59.

iii. *Mythbusters,* "Chinese Invasion Alarm," season 3, episode 2 (first broadcast 19 October 2005 by The Discovery Channel).

iv. For more on the development of anthropological ideas, see Donald E. Brown, *Human Universals* (New York: McGraw-Hill, 1991), Bryan W. Van Norden, *Virtue Ethics and Consequentialism in Early Chinese Philosophy* (New York: Cambridge University Press, 2007), pp. 348–49, and Steven Pinker, *The Blank Slate: The Modern Denial of Human Nature* (New York: Penguin, 2002).

v. "Against Fatalism," *Mozi* 35. Translation modified from Mei, p. 183. Cf Watson, p. 119.

vi. "Against Fatalism," *Mozi* 35. See Mei, p. 187, and Watson, pp. 122–23.

vii. "Against Fatalism," *Mozi* 36. Translation modified from Mei, pp. 189–90.

viii. "Against Fatalism," *Mozi* 35. Translation modified from Mei, pp. 186–87. Cf Watson, p. 122.

ix. "Against Confucians," *Mozi* 39. See Watson, pp. 126–27.

x. *Mozi* 31, "On Ghosts." Cf Watson, p. 107.

xi. For a more technical discussion of this issue, see Van Norden, *Virtue Ethics and Consequentialism in Early Chinese Philosophy,* pp. 151–61 and 361–77.

Chapter 5. Yang Zhu and Egoism

i. *South Park,* "Toilet Paper," episode no. 703 (first broadcast 2 April 2003 by Comedy Central). (The dialogue was edited slightly for readability.)

ii. *Zhongyong* 1. See Daniel K. Gardner, trans., *The Four Books* (Indianapolis: Hackett Publishing, 2007), p. 110.

iii. *Lüshi chunqiu, Jibu* 1.2, "The Root of Life."

iv. "Geng Zhu," *Mozi* 46. Translation modified from Mei, pp. 219–20.

v. *Liezi,* "Yang Zhu." Translation modified from Angus C. Graham, *Disputers of the Tao* (Chicago: Open Court Press, 1989), pp. 60–61.

Chapter 6. Mengzi and Human Nature

i. Cheng Yi (eleventh century CE), cited in Zhu Xi, *Mengzi jizhu,* commentary on *Mengzi* 1A1.

ii. Arthur Waley, *The Analects of Confucius,* reprint (New York: Vintage Books, 1989), p. 45.

iii. For a more detailed discussion of the School of the Way, see Van Norden, *Virtue Ethics and Consequentialism in Early Chinese Philosophy,* pp. 23–29, and Bryan W. Van Norden, *Mengzi: With Selections from Traditional Commentaries* (Indianapolis: Hackett Publishing, 2008), pp. xxxix–xliv.

Chapter 7. Language and Paradox in the "School of Names"

i. *Lüshi chunqiu* 18.4. Translation by John Knoblock and Jeffrey Riegel, *The Annals of Lü Buwei* (Stanford: Stanford University Press, 2000), p. 454.

ii. *Zhuangzi* 33 (not in *Readings*).

iii. See Graham, *Disputers of the Tao,* p. 79; Christoph Harbsmeier, *Language and Logic,* vol. VII, part I of Joseph Needham, ed., *Science and Civilisation in China* (New York: Cambridge University Press, 1998), p. 298.

iv. This is a combination of *Mozi* A73, A74, and B35. Cf Graham, *Disputers of the Tao,* pp. 167–68; Harbsmeier, pp. 330–31. (No selections from the Later Mohist writings are included in *Readings*.)

v. *Mozi* B79. Cf Graham, *Disputers of the Tao,* pp. 185–86; Harbsmeier, pp. 344–45.

vi. *Mozi* B71. Cf Graham, *Disputers of the Tao,* pp. 185–86; Harbsmeier, p. 345.

vii. *Mozi* A61. Translation and suggested interpretation from Graham, *Disputers of the Tao,* pp. 160–61.

viii. *Mozi* B68. Cf Harbsmeier, p. 343.

ix. *Mozi* B67. Cf Graham, *Disputers of the Tao,* pp. 84–85. The relevance of this passage to "On the White Horse" was noted at least as early as Fung Yu-lan's *A History of Chinese Philosophy,* Derk Bodde, trans., vol. 1 (Princeton: Princeton University Press, 1952), pp. 268–69. (Fung's Platonistic interpretation of "On the White Horse" itself has been universally rejected, though.)

x. Translation by Graham, *Disputers of the Tao,* p. 157; "Expounding the Canons" 8, *Mozi.*

xi. "Expounding the Canons" 2, *Mozi.* (This text assumes this definition of "sage," but does not identify it as a definition.)

xii. *Mozi* A80, A58, and A93. Translation of the latter two modified from Graham, *Diputers of the Tao,* p. 144.

xiii. "Names and Objects" 14–15 in *Mozi,* 44–45.

xiv. Translation by Graham, *Disputers of the Tao,* p. 153; "Names and Objects" 12, *Mozi.*

xv. *Lushi chunqiu* 18.5. Translation modified from Knoblock and Riegel, *The Annals of Lu Buwei,* pp. 457–58.

xvi. Bertrand Russell, *The Philosophy of Logical Atomism,* reprint (Chicago: Open Court Press, 1985), p. 53.

Chapter 8. The *Daodejing* and Mysticism

i. The episode of *The Simpsons* was "Dead Putting Society," episode 7F08 (first broadcast 15 November 1990 by Fox). Peckinpah's title comes from *Daodejing* 5. Ronald W. Reagan cited the opening line of *Daodejing* 60 in his State of the Union Address (January 25, 1988). For Wright's interest in the *Daodejing*, see the reference in Graham, *Disputers of the Tao*, p. 234. On Heidegger's interest in the *Daodejing*, see Paul Shih-yi Hsiao, "Heidegger and Our Translation of the *Tao Te Ching*," in Graham Parkes, ed., *Heidegger and Asian Thought* (Honolulu: University of Hawaii Press, 1990).

ii. For a discussion of this phenomenon, see Paul R. Goldin, "Those Who Don't Know Speak: Translations of *Laozi* by People Who Do Not Know Chinese," in Goldin, *After Confucius* (Honolulu: University of Hawaii Press, 2005), pp. 119–33.

iii. Ssu-ma Ch'ien, *The Grand Scribe's Records*, volume VII, p. 23 (*Shiji* 63:2142).

iv. Ssu-ma Ch'ien, pp. 21–22 (*Shiji* 63:2140).

v. Richard John Lynn, trans., *The Classic of the Way and Virtue: A New Translation of the Tao-te ching of Laozi as Interpreted by Wang Bi* (New York: Columbia University Press, 1999), p. 34.

vi. Wang Bi, quoted in He Shao's biography of him, preserved in the *Sanguozhi;* translation from Lynn, *The Classic of the Way and Virtue*, p. 12 (emphasis mine).

vii. Wang Bi, "Outline Introduction to the *Laozi*" (*Laozi zhilue*), translated in Lynn, *The Classic of the Way and Virtue*, p. 30.

viii. My definition is only one possible characterization. The first and second traits I identify are what William James identifies as the two most important characteristics of mysticism in *The Varieties of Religious Experience*, Lectures 16–17 in *Writings 1902–1910* (New York: Library of America, 1987), pp. 343–44.

ix. See selection 6.3 in Mark Csikszentmihalyi, trans., *Readings in Han Chinese Thought* (Indianapolis: Hackett Publishing, 2006), p. 114.

x. Jigoro Kano, *Kodokan Judō* (New York: Kodansha International, 1986), pp. 16–17.

xi. See He Shao's biography of Wang Bi, preserved in the *Sanguozhi;* translated in Lynn, *The Classic of the Way and Virtue*, p. 12.

Chapter 9. Zhuangzi's Therapeutic Skepticism and Relativism

i. For a different and extremely thoughtful perspective on relativism that uses insights from both Western and Chinese philosophy, see David Wong's *Natural Moralities* (New York: Oxford University Press, 2009).

ii. Ludwig Wittgenstein, *Tractatus Logico-Philosophicus*, C. K. Ogden, trans. (London: Routledge & Kegan Paul, 1922), 6.54.

iii. Cited in Huang Jinhong, *Zhuangzi Duben* (Taibei: Sanmin shuju, 1974), p. 70n100.

iv. T'ao Ch'ien, "Poems after Drinking Wine (No. 5)," trans. James Robert Hightower, cited in Victor Mair, ed., *The Columbia Anthology of Traditional Chinese Literature* (New York: Columbia University Press, 1994), pp. 180–81.

v. For an outstanding study of this topic, see Peipei Qiu, *Bashō and the Dao: Zhuangzi and the Transformation of Haikai* (Honolulu: University of Hawaii Press, 2005).

vi. Cao Xueqin and Gao E, *Story of the Stone: Also Known as the Dream of the Red Chamber,* vol. 4, trans. John Minford (New York: Penguin Books, 1982), p. 152 (Chapter 86).

vii. Cao, *Story of the Stone,* p. 154 (Chapter 86).

Chapter 10. Xunzi's Confucian Naturalism

i. For an excellent translation of some of Zhang's writings, see Philip J. Ivanhoe, trans., *Ethics and History: Essays and Letters of Zhang Xuecheng* (Stanford: Stanford University Press, 2009).

Chapter 11. Han Feizi

i. Translation modified from Ssu-ma Ch'ien, *The Grand Scribe's Records,* vol. VII, p. 25 (*Shiji* 63:2146).

ii. Translation mine; *Han Feizi* 46: Liu Fan.

iii. Burton Watson, trans., *Han Fei Tzu: Basic Writings* (New York: Columbia University Press, 1964), p. 97.

iv. Watson, *Han Fei Tzu,* p. 97.

v. Sun Tzu [Sunzi], *Art of War,* Ralph D. Sawyer, trans. (Boulder: Westview Press, 1994), pp. 187–88 (*Bingfa* 5).

vi. Sun Tzu, *Art of War,* pp. 183–84 (*Bingfa* 4).

vii. W. K. Liao, trans., *Han Fei Tzu,* vol. II (London: Arthur Probsthain, 1959), p. 326.

viii. For a thoughtful defense of an alternative reading of Han Feizi, see Eirik L. Harris, "Han Fei on the Role of Morality in Political Philosophy," in Paul R. Goldin, ed., *Dao Companion to the Philosophy of Han Fei* (New York: Springer, forthcoming).

ix. Watson, *Han Fei Tzu,* p. 14.

Chapter 12. Later Chinese History

i. For an excellent illustration, see selection 5.1 in Csikszentmihalyi, *Readings in Han Chinese Thought,* pp. 84–88.

ii. Benjamin Schwartz, *The World of Thought in Ancient China* (Cambridge, MA: Belknap/ Harvard University Press, 1985), p. 381.

iii. Benjamin E. Wallacker, "Han Confucianism and Confucius in the Han," in *Ancient China: Studies in Early Civilization,* David T. Roy and Tsuen-hsuin Tsien, eds. (Hong Kong: Chinese University of Hong Kong Press, 1978), p. 227.

iv. N. K. G. Mendis, ed., *The Questions of King Milinda* (Kandy, Sri Lanka: Buddhist Publication Society, 1993), pp. 29–32.

v. Graham, *Disputers of the Tao,* p. 101.

vi. Schwartz, *The World of Thought in Ancient China,* p. 183.

vii. Central Committee of the Chinese Communist Party, "Decision concerning the Great Proletarian Cultural Revolution" (August 1966), reprinted in Winberg Chai, ed., *Essential Works of Chinese Communism,* revised ed. (New York: Bantam Books, 1972), p. 409.

viii. Liu Shaoqi, "Self-Criticism" (October 1966), reprinted in Chai, *Essential Works of Chinese Communism,* p. 428. (Brackets in Chai.)

ix. Carson Chang, Hsieh Yu-wei, Hsu Foo-kwan, Mou Chung-san, and Tang Chun-i [*sic*], "A Manifesto on the Reappraisal of Chinese Culture," reprinted in T'ang Chun-i, *Essays on Chinese Philosophy and Culture* (Taibei: Student Book Company, 1988), p. 504.

x. "Manifesto," p. 515.

xi. "Manifesto," p. 522. Solecisms in the translation *sic*.

xii. "Manifesto," pp. 526–27.

xiii. Yu Dan, *Lunyu xinde* (Taibei: Linking Books, 2007).

Appendix A: Hermeneutics, or How to Read a Text

i. Francis Bacon, "Of Studies" in *Essays,* in *The Works of Francis Bacon,* vol. XII, ed. James Spedding et al. (Boston: Houghton, Mifflin and Company, n.d.), pp. 252–53.

ii. Francis Bacon, *Novum Organum,* Part I, Aphorism 3 in *The Works of Francis Bacon,* vol. VIII (Boston: Taggard & Thompson, 1863), p. 67–68.

Appendix C: Kongzi as Systematic Philosopher

i. For a defense of the Zengzian interpretation of the *Analects,* see Philip J. Ivanhoe, "The 'Golden Rule' in the *Analects,*" in David Jones, ed., *Confucius Now: Contemporary Encounters with the* Analects (Chicago: Open Court Press, 2008), pp. 81–108.

ii. For a defense of this general line of interpretation, see Hui-chieh Loy, "*Analects* 13.3 and the Doctrine of 'Correcting Names,'" in Jones, *Confucius Now,* pp. 223–42.

iii. For a defense of the postmodern interpretation of Kongzi, see Roger T. Ames, "Paronomasia: A Confucian Way of Making Meaning," in Jones, *Confucius Now,* pp. 37–48. See also David L. Hall and Roger T. Ames, *Thinking through Confucius* (Albany: State University of New York Press, 1987).

iv. The Chinese commentary quoted is by Cai Mo (Jin dynasty), cited in *Readings in Classical Chinese Philosophy,* p. 46n136. See also the more extensive selection of traditional commentaries on this passage in Edward Slingerland, trans., *Analects: With Selections from Traditional Commentaries* (Indianapolis: Hackett Publishing, 2003), pp. 185–86. For an example in which *hong* ("broaden") clearly means "glorify," see "Kang Gao" from the *Documents of Zhou* in the *History* (James Legge, *The Shoo King,* p. 387).

■ INDEX ■

A

a posteriori, 115
a priori, 115–16
afterlife. *See* spirits
Ames, Roger T., 264n3 (of Appendix C)
Analects (Lúnyǔ 論語), composition and influence of the text, 21, 40, 129, 157, 204, 210, 211, 222; illustration of, 223
Anaximander, 209
Anscombe, Elizabeth, 35–36
argumentation, 53–55, 118–19, 143; Mohist theories of, 62, 64, 66–67, 111–18. *See also* state-of-nature argument
Aristotle, 23, 36, 41–42, 42–43, 116, 179–80
Art of War. See Sūnzǐ
astronomy, 3–4, 9, 33; gnomons used in, 49, 62
Augustine, 30, 66, 174

B

bà 霸 (Hegemon), 12–13, 18
Bacon, Francis, 29n3, 224, 229–30
Being, 245
benevolence. *See rén* (Goodness, humaneness, benevolence)
Bentham, Jeremy, 34, 36–37, 52
Bǐ Gān 比干, 6, 77
bonsai trees, 76; illustration of, 69
Brown, Donald E., 260n4 (of Chapter 4)
Buddhism (Fójiào 佛教) 21, 45, 99, 133, 134, 135–36, 160, 181, 206–10, 221. *See also* Neo-Confucianism

C

Cāng Jié 倉頡, 3, 235
Cat in the Hat, The, 153–54
Changes (Yìjīng 易經), 2, 181, 204, 218
characters, Chinese, 3, 5, 6, 40, 42, 75, 197n3, 203, 206, 208, 223, 235–44; 245n10

chariot, social and military significance of, 6, 123; Buddhist simile of the, 207
Chéng, King, 成, 9
Chéng Yí 程頤, 260n1 (of Chapter 6)
Communist Party, Chinese (Zhōngguó gòngchǎn dǎng 中國共產黨), 216–21 passim, 242
Confucianism (Rújiā 儒家), xi, 8, 9, 12, 13, 37, 60, 67, 68, 75, 83, 84, 85, 86, 88, 91, 99–100, 102, 118, 124, 125, 126, 142, 164, 170, 178, 181–82, 198, 202, 204–6, 212, 215, 216, 218, 221, 222, 251; criticisms of, 44–45, 50–58, 64, 70, 76–77, 126, 129, 130, 134–35, 153, 155, 157, 180, 187–89; etymology of name, 20; five themes of, 21–31; similarities to Daoism, 124–26, 129, 157; two aspects of emphasis on family in, 24; two aspects of ethical cultivation in, 29; as virtue ethics, 38–46. *See also* Kǒngzǐ; Mèngzǐ; Neo-Confucianism; New Confucianism; Xúnzǐ
Confucius. *See* Kǒngzǐ
consequentialism, 41, 46, 51–52, 63–64, 66, 67, 114–15; defined, 34–37; rule- vs. act-, 34
conservatism. *See* revivalism; traditionalism
courage. *See yǒng*
Csikszentmihalyi, Mark, 262n9 (of Chapter 8), 263n1 (of Chapter 12)
cultivation, ethical, 29–31, 36, 37, 43–44, 86, 92–97, 98, 99, 100, 125, 126, 134–35, 152, 160, 171–78 passim, 178–80, 181, 208, 218, 250, 259n5 (of Chapter 2). *See also* mysticism
cyclic view of history (dynasties), 5, 7–8, 18, 201 (epigraph)

D

dào 道 (Way), 18, 20, 24, 30, 44, 46, 51, 64, 66, 70, 75, 76–77, 85, 86, 88, 96, 98, 99, 121, 124–30 passim, 136, 139,

dào 道 (Way) (*continued*)
142, 143, 145, 147,151–60 passim,
164–81 passim, 187, 188, 189, 195–98,
208n2, 209, 215, 220, 227, 250–51, 252,
254–56; defined, 11, 75; as metaphysical
entity, 131–33, 135, 154, 155
Dàodéjīng 道德經 (*Classic of the Way and
Virtue*), 11, 20, 119, 121–39, 142, 150,
157, 180, 195–96, 218; composition of,
123–24, 204; metaphor of unhewn wood,
128, 129–30, 135; mysticism in, 125,
133–35, 136; on dangers of names,
130–31; *via negativa* in, 132. *See also
wú wéi*; knowing how vs. knowing that
Daoism (Dàojiā 道家), 122, 134, 136, 160,
206, 221. *See also Dàodéjīng*; *Lǎozǐ*
dé 德 (Virtue), 7, 8, 9, 13, 18, 19, 20, 29,
33, 46, 124, 126, 128–29, 135, 147, 157,
165, 188, 191, 195, 196, 250; defined, 8.
See also virtues
democracy, 4, 23,45, 60, 180, 215, 220,
221, 232–33
Dèng Xī 鄧析, 102, 112, 118
deontology, 34, 35–36, 37, 45, 91–92, 95;
rule- vs. act-, 36
Descartes, René, 98, 144
differentiated caring (*ài yǒu chā děng* 愛有差
等 or *bié ài* 別愛), 24–25, 37, 44, 53,
55–56, 58, 86, 106–7, 143, 147–48, 153,
210. *See also xiào*
Documents. See History
Dǒng Zhòngshū 董仲舒, 205
Dream of the Red Chamber (Hóng lóu mèng
紅樓夢), 2, 160
Durkheim, Emile, 25
dutifulness. *See zhōng*

E

egoism, distinction between psychological
and ethical, 70; ethical, 74; paradox of, 73;
psychological, 70–74. *See also Yáng Zhū*
Enter the Dragon, 137
epistemological optimism, 231–32
epistemology, defined, 144

F

facts vs. myths, *See* myth vs. fact (text boxes)
falliblism, 232

false dichotomy, 55–56
fatalism, 62–64. *See also mìng* (fate)
family. *See* differentiated caring
filial piety. *See xiào*
Five Classics (Wǔjīng 五經), 181, 204–5, 211
Foucault, Michel, 198, 225
Four Books (Sìshū 四書), 211
Freud, Sigmund, 2, 225
Fù Hǎo 婦好, 6
Fú Xī 伏羲, 2–3, 44; illustration, 1
functionalism. *See lǐ* (ritual, rites)
Fung, Yu-lan (Féng Yǒulán 馮友蘭), 261n9
(of Chapter 7)

G

Gadamer, Hans-Georg, 230
Gandhi, Mahatma, 8, 99
generalism. *See* particularism
gentleman. *See jūnzǐ*
Gettysburg Address, 232–33
ghosts. *See* spirits
gnomon, illustration of, 49. *See also*
astronomy
Goldin, Paul R., 262n2 (of Chapter 8),
263n8 (of Chapter 11)
Gōngsūn Lóng 公孫龍, 101, 102, 103,
108–11, 118
Goodness. *See rén* (Goodness, humaneness,
benevolence)
graded love. *See* differentiated caring
Graham, Angus C., 9–10, 12, 14, 209, 246,
261nn3–7
Great Wall (Cháng chéng 長城), 123, 202,
203; illustration of, 201
Greater Learning (Dà xué 大學), 205, 209,
211
Guǎn Zhòng 管仲, 13

H

Hàn dynasty 漢朝, 122, 124, 181, 203–6,
209
Hán Fēizǐ 韓非子, 136, 182, 185–99, 203,
263n8 (of Chapter 11); emptiness and
stillness in, 195; life of, 186; name and
form in, 192; nonaction in, 195–96;
opposition to traditionalism, 188–89;
similarities to Western philosophers, 198;
similarities to Xunzi, 187–88; story of

farmer "watch[ing] a stump awaiting a rabbit," 189

Hán Yù 韓愈, 99, 208–9

Harbsmeier, Christoph, 161nn3–7

Harris, Eirik L., 263n8 (of Chapter 11)

Heaven. *See tiān*

Hegemon. *See bà*

Heidegger, Martin, 122, 133

hermeneutics, 2–3, 8–9, 124, 223–30; diagram of, 231

Hero, 221–22

History (Shūjīng 書經 or Shàngshū 尚書), 49, 179, 181, 204, 264n4 (of Appendix C); quoted, 7–9

Hoff, Benjamin, 122n1

hóng 弘 (broaden, glorify), 264n4 (to Appendix C)

Hong Kong, 212, 219

Huán, Duke of Qí, 齊桓公, 12–13

Huáng Dì 黃帝, 3, 44, 77, 235

Huì Shī 惠施, 101–8, 111, 112–13, 114, 118, 146, 149, 154–57

humility, 39, 41

I

I Ching. *See Changes*

inaction. *See wú wéi*

Indra's Net, 207, 210

Ivanhoe, Philip J., 259n5 (of Chapter 2), 263n1 (of Chapter 10), 264n1 (of Appendix C)

J

James, William, 262n8 (of Chapter 8)

Japan, 35, 136, 160, 208, 211, 213–15, 216, 232n4, 245n10

Jì family of Lǔ 魯季氏, 19

Jié, Tyrant, 桀, 5, 63, 164, 194, 195, 210

judgmental, as a vice, 40–41

judō, 136–37

jūnzǐ 君子 (gentleman), 24, 26, 30, 31, 33 (epigraph), 42, 44, 46, 51, 64, 84, 85, 94, 96, 97, 123, 134, 160, 165, 176, 179, 227, 250, 253; two senses of, 19–20

K

kanji. *See* characters, Chinese

Kanō Jigorō, 136–37

Kant, Immanuel, 28, 128

King, Martin Luther, Jr., 8, 23, 99, 259n4 (of Chapter 2)

knowing how vs. knowing that, 127–28, 142, 153

Kǒngzǐ 孔子, historical influence and later interpretations of, 11n2, 17 (caption), 50, 76–77, 83 (caption), 99, 123, 129, 135, 143, 147, 151–52, 157–58, 164, 180, 181, 188, 204, 205, 209, 211, 215, 216, 220, 222, 223; illustrations of, 17, 249; life of, 18–20, 25, 43, 50, 161; thought of, 3–4, 18–32, 33, 38–47, 51, 53, 64, 85, 86, 91, 95, 134, 191, 204, 227–30, 249 (epigraph), 250–56

Korea, 208, 211, 214, 217, 232n4, 245n10

kung fu (gōngfu 功夫), 137

L

Lǎozǐ 老子, illustration of, 121; stories about, 122–23, 129, 135. *See also Dàodéjīng*

Later Mohism. *See* Mohism

learning. *See xué*

Lee, Bruce, 137–138

lǐ 禮 (ritual, rites), 2, 5, 6, 18, 22, 43, 44, 45, 46, 64, 65, 66, 84, 85, 86, 91, 95, 99, 122, 123, 128–29,164–71, 174, 175, 177–81, 188, 205, 210, 222, 250, 251, 253, 255, 256; defined, 25; functionalist interpretation of, 25–28, 165–66; regarding burials and mourning, 25, 27–28, 50, 52–53, 57, 85, 87, 157, 165–66, 177–78; term used for Mengzian virtue of propriety, 92

lǐ 理 (Pattern), 151, 153, 164, 170–71, 173, 178, 209–10, 211, 220, 235

Lǐ Sī 李斯, 186, 199, 203

Líu Shǎoqí 劉少奇, 218–19

logic, formal, 116–18. *See also* argumentation

Loy, Hui Chieh, 264n2 (to Appendix C)

loyalty. *See zhōng*

Lǔ Xùn 魯迅, 216

M

mandate. *See mìng*

Máo Zédōng 毛澤東 (Mao Tse-tung), 138, 216–19, 221–22

Marx, Karl, 218, 221, 225
May Fourth Movement (Wǔsì yùndong 五四運動), 215–16, 220
Mean (Zhōngyōng 中庸), 75, 205, 209, 211
Mencius. *See* Mèngzǐ
Mèngzǐ 孟子, 24n1, 30, 44, 64n3, 68, 69, 84–100, 128–29, 134–35, 142, 155, 160–61, 165, 204, 205; cardinal virtues of, 91–92; debate with Yi Zhi, 87–88; definition of benevolent government, 85–86; extension in, 95–97; historical influence and later interpretations of, 43, 99–100, 164, 172, 174–78, 181, 209, 211, 220; illustration of, 83; life of, 84–85, 98–99, 103n1; metaphor of "climbing a tree in search of a fish," 86; mother of, 85; objection to directly aiming at profit or benefit, 84–85, 87; on cultivating one's *qi*, 97–98; on Heaven, 88, 97, 99, 165, 178; on human nature, 86, 87–91, 97, 99, 160, 161, 164, 165, 174–78, 181, 211, 220; reflection in, 93–95; regarded as the Second Sage, 83, 99; story of child about to fall into a well, 88–89; story of farmer from Song, 96–97; story of King Xuan sparing an ox, 93–94; story of Ox Mountain, 90–91
metaphysics, defined, 164
Mill, John Stuart, 34, 35
Millay, Edna St. Vincent, 229
míng 命 (mandate), 7–9, 18, 75, 97; (fate), 97, 157. *See also* fatalism
Mohism (Mòjiā 墨家), 1, 8, 12, 24, 27, 34, 37, 41, 44, 49–68, 70, 75, 77–79, 86, 87–88, 97, 102, 122, 123, 124, 125, 126, 129, 130, 142, 145–46, 153, 164, 166, 168, 188, 189, 191, 206, 208; Later Mohism, 104, 111–18
monism, ethical, 45, 80, 232; metaphysical, 210
Mòzǐ 墨子, 77–78, 83, 86, 188; life of, 50. *See also* Mohism
Murdoch, Iris, 30, 229n2
music, 25, 45, 53, 57, 81, 168, 181
mysticism, 125, 133–35, 136, 154–55, 208, 262n8 (of Chapter 8)
myth vs. fact (text boxes), 5, 20, 42, 53, 73, 90, 107, 123, 150, 172, 190
Mythbusters, 51

N

Nationalist Party (Guómíndǎng 國民黨), 216–17, 220
naturalism, defined, 164
nature. *See* xìng
Neo-Confucianism (Dàoxué 道學), 99, 100, 181, 208–11, 219, 220
New Confucianism (Xīnrújiā 新儒家), 219–20, 221
New Culture Movement. *See* May Fourth Movement
Nietzsche, Friedrich, 225–26, 255
nonaction. *See* wú wéi
normative ethical theories. *See* consequentialism; deontology; virtue ethics
Nǚwā 女媧, 2–3; illustration of, 1

O

Ockham, William of, 61
Odes (Shījīng 詩經), 29–30, 41, 179, 181, 204, 250
opaque contexts, 117–18
Opium Wars (Yāpiàn zhànzhēng 鴉片戰爭), 212, 213, 214
oracle bones (jiǎgǔ 甲骨), 5–6, 25, 149
otherworldliness, as an ethical value, 21–22, 125

P

Parmenides, 118
particularism, 37, 45–46, 51, 95, 252, 255; defined, 36
Peckinpah, Sam, 122
People's Republic of China (Zhōnghuá rénmín gònghé guó 中華人民共和國), 8, 13, 215n5, 217–19, 221–22, 232n4, 242, 244
petty person. *See* xiǎo rén
philosophy of history. *See* cyclic view of history
Pinker, Steven, 260n4 (of Chapter 4)
Plato, 21–22, 29n3, 42–43, 61, 108, 112n4, 116, 118, 133, 225–26, 229–30, 245, 261n9 (of Chapter 7)
pluralism, 45, 80, 232, 233
propriety. *See* lǐ (ritual, rites)
Protagoras, 102, 112n4
Puett, Michael J., 259n1 (of Chapter 1)

Q

qì 氣 (psychophysical stuff), 97–98, 134–35, 152, 156, 160–61, 176, 177, 209–10, 211

Qín 秦, state and dynasty, 13, 87, 92, 103, 164, 182, 186, 202–4, 221–22

Qiu, Peipei, 262n5 (of Chapter 9)

R

Ramayana, 30

reading, intensively or extensively, 224

Reagan, Ronald Wilson, 122

Record of Rites. See Rites

reflection. *See sī* (reflecting, thinking, concentrating)

relativism, 95–96, 112n4, 142, 144–46, 152–53, 155, 230–31, 232, 233, 262n1 (of Chapter 9)

rén 仁 (Goodness, humaneness), (as Goodness), 17 (epigraph), 24, 28, 40, 41–46 passim, 85, 250, 251, 252; Goodness defined, 39–40; (as benevolence), 29, 37, 51, 60, 71–72, 74, 80, 89, 90, 91, 93, 94, 95, 96, 126, 128, 158, 160, 161, 170, 178, 188; benevolence defined, 91, 115; benevolence in governing, 19, 20, 59, 63, 84–87, 93–94, 180, 189

Republic of China (Zhōnghuá mínguó 中華民國), 215, 216, 220–21

revivalism, 23–24, 38, 44, 259n4 (of Chapter 2). *See also* traditionalism

righteousness. *See yì*

rites. *See lǐ* (ritual, rites)

Rites (Lǐjì 禮記), 181, 205, 209

rituals (li). *See lǐ* (ritual, rites)

"Robber Zhi" (Dào Zhí 盜跖). *See* Yáng Zhū

Romance of the Three Kingdoms (Sānguó yǎnyì 三國演義), 201

romanization system, 6, 244

Russell, Bertrand, 118–19

S

Sapir-Whorf Hypothesis, 244–46

"School of Names" (míng jiā 名家), 101–19, 131, 206; origin of name, 102

Schwartz, Benjamin, 209

Shāng dynasty 商朝, 5–9, 18

Shén Nóng 神農, 3, 44, 77, 235

Shùn, Emperor, 舜, 4, 30, 45, 63, 96, 129, 161, 188, 189, 191, 194, 195, 215

sī 私 (private, selfish), 187, 189, 193, 197, 210

sī 思 (reflecting, thinking, concentrating), as technique of ethical cultivation, 22–23, 29–31, 43–44, 91, 94–95, 130, 137, 151, 178, 208, 218, 228, 259n5 (of Chapter 2); defined, 93

Sīmǎ Qiān 司馬遷, 6, 186, 205–6

Simpsons, The, 122

Singer, Peter, 34

skepticism, 142, 143–44, 146, 152–53, 155, 159, 170, 188, 231

small person. *See xiǎo rén*

Socrates, 21, 61, 116, 128

Son of Heaven (Tiānzǐ 天子), 58–59, 60, 61; defined, 8

South Park, 73–74

spirits (*shén* 神 or *guǐ* 鬼), 5, 6, 7, 8, 21–22, 25, 26, 64–67, 151, 154, 156, 159, 165, 202, 224–25; spiritual autobiography of Kongzi, 43; Spiritual Farmer, *See* Shén Nóng

Spring and Autumn Annals (Chūnqiū 春秋), 11, 11n2, 204

Spring and Autumn Period (Chūnqiū shídài 春秋時代), 11–13, 18, 102, 123

state-of-nature argument, 58–59, 76–77, 164, 166–67, 169

Stoicism, 28

Straw Dogs, 122

study. *See xué*

Sūnzǐ 孫子, thought of, 19, 190, 192; fundamental difference from Kongzi, 18

T

Taiping Rebellion (Tàipíng pànluàn 太平叛亂), 213, 214

Táiwān 臺灣, 212, 213, 214, 217, 219, 220–21, 232n4, 242

Tāng, King, 湯, 5, 7, 77, 189

Tao of Pooh, The, 122n1

Táo Qián 陶潛, 159–160

Teresa, Mother, 57, 96

thinking. *See sī* (reflecting, thinking, concentrating)

thought experiment, 54–56, 88–89; defined, 54

Three Dynasties (Sān dài 三代), of Xia, Shang, and Zhou, 4–13
Three Families of Lu (Sān huán 三桓), 19. *See also* Jì family
tiān 天, 7, 8, 9, 204, 205, 220; defined, 8. *See also* astronomy
traditionalism, 22–24, 31, 38, 44–45, 86, 188–89, 213, 216, 218–19, 222, 255–56
transparent contexts, 117
Tyrant Zhou. *See* Zhòu, Tyrant

U

utilitarianism. *See* consequentialism

V

via negativa. See Dàodéjīng
Vietnam, 206, 217n9
Virtue. *See dé*
virtue ethics, four questions of, 36; moderate vs. radical, 37–38, 45–46. *See also* Confucianism
virtues, 4, 8, 21–22, 29, 36–37, 39–47, 64, 85, 90, 91–92, 93, 96, 98, 99, 100, 126, 128, 133, 165, 175–77, 179–80, 181, 187–88, 189, 205, 220, 227, 228, 232–33, 252; discussed by Kongzi, 39–43

W

Waley, Arthur, 93
Wallacker, Benjamin E., 263n3 (of Chapter 12)
Wáng Bì 王弼, 124, 129, 132, 139
Wáng Yángmíng 王陽明, 99
Warring States Period (Zhànguó shídài 戰國時代), 11, 13, 68, 118, 122, 123, 125, 143, 164, 197, 198, 204, 209, 222
Way. *See dào*
Weil, Simone, 21–22
Wén, Duke of Jìn, 晉文公, 13
Wén, King, 文, 7, 9
white horse paradox, 101, 108–11, 113–14, 131, 261n9 (of Chapter 7)
wisdom. *See zhì*
Wittgenstein, Ludwig, 133, 154–55
Wong, David, 262n1
Wright, Frank Lloyd, 122
Wǔ, Emperor of the Hàn, 漢武帝, 205–6

Wǔ, King of the Zhōu, 周武王, 9, 63, 77, 189
wú wéi 無為 (nonaction), 124, 126–30, 133, 135, 137–38, 150–52, 157, 160, 195–96

X

Xià dynasty 夏朝, 4, 5, 6, 7
xiào 孝 (filial piety), 4, 24, 76, 147, 210. *See also* differentiated caring
xiǎo rén 小人 (petty person, small person), 19, 31, 42, 44, 46, 179, 191; two senses of, 20
xīn 心 (heart, mind), 6, 7, 8, 30, 43, 65, 77, 78, 85–98 passim, 129, 134–35, 136, 138, 142, 147, 152, 155, 157, 160–61, 167, 172–73, 179, 180, 187, 193, 195, 209, 220, 240
xìn 信 (trustworthiness, faithfulness), 22, 256; defined, 42
xìng 性 (nature), 29, 36–37, 43–44, 56–57, 59, 70, 77, 79–80, 86, 87–91, 97, 99, 160, 163, 164, 165, 167–68, 169, 171–78, 181–82, 187, 211, 220, 227–28, 260n4 (of Chapter 4); defined, 75–76
Xǔ Shèn 許慎, 235, 236
xué 學 (learning), as technique of ethical cultivation, 23, 24, 29–31, 41, 43–44, 46, 85, 88, 95, 123, 127, 151, 153–54, 157, 164, 170, 171–78 passim, 178–80, 181, 188, 218, 219, 227–30, 249, 259n5 (of Chapter 2)
Xúnzǐ 荀子, 26, 31, 43, 44, 68, 97, 99, 161, 163–82, 186, 187–88, 198, 205, 209, 210; artificiality in, 164, 170, 174, 176, 180; craftsperson metaphor in, 164, 168–71, 180–81; difference from Augustine on human nature, 174; difference from Mengzi on human nature, 164, 165, 172, 174, 175–78, 181–82; distinction between desire and approval in, 172–73; distinction between humans and other animals in, 173–74, 176–77; functionalist understanding of ritual, 164–68; illustration of, 163; ladder of souls in, 176–77; naturalism of, 164–65; state-of-nature argument in, 164, 166–68,

169, 174; view of Heaven, 164–65, 170–71, 175, 178; wood metaphor of, 175–76

Y

Yáng Zhū 楊朱, 37, 44, 67–79, 83, 86, 88–89, 142, 147, 150, 164, 170, 191; and "Robber Zhi" dialogue, 76–77; basic criticism of Confucians and Mohists, 70; criticized by Mohists, 77–79; state-of-nature argument by, 77

Yáo, Emperor, 堯, 3–4, 49, 188, 189, 191, 194, 195

Yellow Emperor. *See* Huáng Dì

yì 義 (righteousness, rightness, integrity), 9, 50, 74, 84, 86–93 passim, 95, 96, 115, 126, 128, 147, 158, 160, 161, 188, 210; defined, 42; standards of, 166–70 passim, 172, 175, 176–77, 180

Yí Zhī 夷之, 87–88

Yijing. See Changes

yīn and yáng 陰陽, 165, 204, 206, 218; defined, 176

Yīn 殷, capital of Shang dynasty, 5, 6. *See also* Shāng dynasty

yŏng 勇 (courage), 39, 42–43

Yōu, King, 幽, 10

Yŭ, King, 禹, 4, 5, 7, 161, 189, 191

Yú Dān 于丹, 222

Z

Zhāng Xuéchéng 張學誠, 181

Zhāng Yìmóu 張藝謀, 221–22

zhì 智 (wisdom), 8, 9, 20, 37–38, 45, 46, 91, 95, 124, 126, 136, 178, 252; defined, 40–41, 92

zhōng 忠 (dutifulness, loyalty), 6, 9, 23, 42, 45, 77, 126, 147, 250–52; defined, 42

Zhōu, Duke of, 周公, 9, 23

Zhōu dynasty 周朝, 6–13, 18, 27, 65, 123, 191, 202; divided into Western Zhou and Eastern Zhou, 10; Eastern Zhou divided into Spring and Autumn and Warring States periods, 11; government structure of, 10, 25, 202

Zhòu, Tyrant, 紂, 6–9, 63, 77, 194, 195

Zhuāngzǐ 莊子, 112, 141–61, 164, 170, 208n2, 209–10, 231, 232, 262n5 (to Chapter 9); appropriation of the figure of Kongzi, 142–43, 147, 151–52, 157–58; arguments for relativism of, 145–46; arguments for skepticism of, 143–44, 159; compared to the *Daodejing*, 142, 147, 150, 154, 157; detachment in, 144, 147–50, 156–58, 161; story of the bird Breeze, 141, 159; story of the butcher carving an ox, 142, 151, 153, 160, 164, 170, 180, 208n2, 209–10; story of the butterfly dream, 158–59; story of "three in the morning, four at night," 146, 147, 153, 157; vision of the wistful Daoist, 157–59

Zhū Xī 朱熹, 99, 181, 210–11, 220; quoted, 223

Zuŏ zhuàn 左傳 (Zuo's Commentary on the *Spring and Autumn Annals*), 11–12, 18